Five-a-Day Fruit & Vegetable Cookbook

Five-a-Day Fruit & Vegetable Cookbook

**Over 200 recipes to ensure you achieve the
health experts' recommended five-portion
daily minimum for you and your family**

KATE WHITEMAN • MAGGIE MAYHEW • CHRISTINE INGRAM

HH
HERMES
HOUSE

This edition is published by Hermes House

Hermes House is an imprint of Anness Publishing Ltd
Hermes House, 88–89 Blackfriars Road, London SE1 8HA
tel. 020 7401 2077; fax 020 7633 9499

www.hermeshouse.com; www.annesspublishing.com

If you like the images in this book and would like to investigate
using them for publishing, promotions or advertising, please visit
our website www.practicalpictures.com for more information.

A CIP catalogue record for this book is available from the
British Library.

Publisher: Joanna Lorenz
Project Editor: Linda Fraser
Designers: Nigel Partridge and Patrick McLeavey
Photography and styling: William Lingwood (fruit recipes),
Don Last (fruit reference) and Patrick McLeavey (vegetable
reference and recipes)
Food for photography: Bridget Sargeson (fruit recipes),
Christine France (fruits) and Jane Stevenson (vegetables)
Indexer: Hiliary Bird
Production Controller: Pedro Nelson

10 9 8 7 6 5 4 3 2 1

NOTES

For all recipes, quantities are given in both metric and imperial
measures and, where appropriate, measures are also given in
standard cups and spoons. Follow one set of measures, but
not a mixture, because they are not interchangeable.

Standard spoon and cup measures are level.
1 tsp = 5ml, 1 tbsp = 15ml, 1 cup = 250ml/8fl oz

Australian standard tablespoons are 20ml. Australian readers
should use 3 tsp in place of 1 tbsp for measuring small
quantities of gelatine, cornflour, salt, etc.

American pints are 16fl oz/2 cups. American readers should
use 20fl oz/2.5 cups in place of 1 pint when measuring liquids.

Electric oven temperatures in this book are for conventional
ovens. When using a fan oven, the temperature will probably
need to be reduced by about 10–20°C/20–40°F. Since ovens
vary, you should check with your manufacturer's instruction
book for guidance.

Medium eggs are used unless otherwise stated.

The diets and information in this book are not intended to
replace advice from a qualified medical practitioner, doctor
or dietician. Always consult your health practitioner before
adopting any of the suggestions in this book. Neither the
author nor the publishers can accept any liability for failure
to follow this advice.

CONTENTS

MAKE IT FIVE

Research has shown that eating a balanced diet with at least five portions of fruit and vegetables a day can significantly reduce the risk of many chronic diseases such as heart disease, cancer and stroke as well as offering many other health benefits. Eating more of them can also help you to increase fibre intake, reduce fat intake and maintain a healthy weight.

Frozen fruit and vegetables are just as good as fresh, and are sometimes even better because they are frozen so soon after picking. Canned fruit and vegetables make a good substitute, but try to buy ones canned in water or fruit juice rather than brine or sugar syrup.

Balance and Variety

Eating a healthy diet doesn't have to mean giving up all your favourite foods. It's all about balance and making sure you eat the right proportions of the right foods. Balance, moderation and variety are the key words.

There are five main food groups: starchy foods such as potatoes, pasta and bread; fruit and vegetables; dairy foods such as milk, yogurt and cheese; protein foods such as meat, chicken, fish and tofu; and foods high in fat and sugar such as cakes and cookies.

Starchy foods and fruit and vegetables should make up the largest part of each meal. Protein foods and

dairy products are important, but should be eaten in moderation. Fatty and sugary foods should be enjoyed only as an occasional treat.

As with all foods, different types of fruit and vegetables contain different combinations of fibre and nutrients. To ensure you obtain the maximum benefit, make sure you eat a variety.

How Big is a Portion?

The size of a portion, and how many times you can count it in a single day, varies depending on the type of fruit or vegetable. Use the table below to check whether you're eating enough.

ONE PORTION	HOW MUCH IS THAT?	HOW DOES IT COUNT?
Fruit (fresh, frozen or canned)	• 1 medium-size piece of fruit such as an apple or banana • 2 smaller pieces of fruit such as satsumas or figs • a handful of small fruits such as grapes or strawberries • 3 heaped tablespoons of fruit salad • half a larger piece of fruit such as a grapefruit • 5cm/2in slice of very large fruit such as melon	Every portion of fruit you eat counts towards your daily five.
Dried fruit	• 3 small fruits such as apricots • 15ml/1 tbsp very small dried fruits such as raisins	Dried fruit counts as only one portion a day, no matter how much of it you eat.
100% pure fruit or vegetable juice	• one glass	Juices count as only one portion a day, no matter how many glasses of juice you drink.
Vegetables	• 3 heaped tablespoons cooked vegetables such as carrots or peas	Every portion of vegetables you eat counts towards your daily five. **But remember** – potatoes are counted as a starchy food, not a vegetable, so they can't be included in your daily five portions.
Salad	• 1 cereal bowl	Every portion of salad you eat counts towards your daily five.
Beans and lentils	• 45ml/3 tbsp cooked beans or lentils such as kidney beans or chickpeas	Beans and lentils count as only one portion a day, no matter how many portions you eat.

Easy Ways to Five

If you don't usually eat five portions of fruit and vegetables a day, achieving this target can sometimes seem like an unmanageable task. The good news is that it doesn't need but be a struggle. There are so many delicious ways to prepare fruit and vegetables, and clever ways to "sneak" them into your diet that you'll find it a pure pleasure achieving your daily target. Listed below are some simple ways to work more fruits and vegetables into your diet.

• Enjoy a fresh fruit smoothie at any time of day. Simply blend soft fruits such as raspberries or mangoes with milk to make a rich, creamy drink that is packed with nutrients. Unlike fruit juices, smoothies still contain all the fibre of the original fruit.
• Add a chopped banana, or a handful of strawberries or raisins to a bowl of cereal in the morning. It will taste like a special breakfast but it's actually helping you on your way to five-a-day.
• When you feel like a sweet treat, eat a few dried apricots or figs instead of reaching for the cookie tin. They taste just as sweet, but they're healthier and can count as one of your portions.

Above: Snacking on raw vegetables is an easy way to eat more fruit and veg. They taste great and are low in fat too.

• Instead of spreading jam on toast, use a mashed banana instead. It tastes great and is so much healthier than a sugar-packed spread.
• Desserts and cakes don't need to be all bad. Although they are high in fat and sugar so should be eaten in moderation, choosing a slice of cake packed with dried fruit, or a dessert

Above: Drink your way to five portions a day with a delicious, healthy blend of ripe strawberries, yogurt and milk.

containing lots of fruit will contribute to your five daily portions – rather than just offering empty calories.
• When making sandwiches, add plenty of extra salad. They will look more appealing and taste much nicer.
• Chopped raw vegetables such as carrots, cucumber and peppers make a great snack at any time of day and are so much healthier than a packet of potato chips or a cookie.
• Add a few extra chopped vegetables to non-vegetable dishes such as meat stews, or stir baby spinach into mashed potatoes just before serving.

About this Book

The recipes in this book have been specially designed to make the most of the delicious fruits and vegetables that are available in the supermarket, helping you to enjoy a tastier, healthier diet. There is a huge choice of recipes for every occasion – from healthy salads and low-fat desserts, to rich and creamy risottos, spicy curries, golden pies and pizzas and indulgent cakes. No matter what your mood, you are sure to find the perfect recipe to help you on your way to five-a-day.

Left: Eating a variety of different fruits and vegetables every day is essential to good health.

FRUIT

DISCOVERING FRUIT

FRUITS ARE NATURE'S most bountiful and versatile creation. No other foods offer such a variety of colours, textures, scents and flavours. Almost all fruits are pleasing to the senses of sight, smell and taste. Just think of the crispness of an apple, the velvety skin of a peach, the jewel-like colours of redcurrants, the juicy tartness of citrus fruits. There is nothing like the sight of a glorious display of fruit in a market to lift the spirits and whet the appetite. Without colourful, health-giving fruits, our diet would be infinitely more dull.

Fruit is not only good for the soul; it is a supremely healthy food, bursting with natural energy-giving sugars, minerals and vitamins. When energy levels are low, a few grapes, a banana or an apple will revitalize us in moments. Fruit provides the perfect guilt-free snack, since most varieties are completely fat free and contain very few calories. Nearly all fruits have a high proportion of water – between 75 and 90 per cent – which makes them wonderfully thirst quenching in hot weather. Picture the pleasure of eating a large wedge of chilled watermelon or a

Below: The vibrant seeds from ripe pomegranates can be eaten raw as they are or added to both sweet and savoury dishes.

Below: When ripe, bananas are bursting with energy-giving nutrients.

refreshing bowl of fresh fruit salad when the temperature is soaring.

Most fruit can be eaten raw, just as it is (be sure to wash it first), although some varieties may need peeling. Nothing beats a simple dessert of perfectly ripe juicy fruit, perhaps served with a scoop or two of vanilla ice cream or a dollop of cream, or with some good cheese – try crisp apples with a wedge of farmhouse Cheddar or Lancashire cheese, juicy, ripe pears with either blue Stilton or Gorgonzola, or raspberries and sliced peaches with mascarpone cheese.

All fruits can be served on their own, or used to create sweet and savoury dishes of infinite variety, from pies to puddings, cakes, muffins, ice creams, mousses, soufflés and featherlight fruit-topped pavlovas.

You could easily base an entire meal on fresh fruit without repeating any colours, textures or flavours. The meal might begin with the classic combination of melon with Parma ham, or a refreshing fruit soup, followed by Normandy pheasant with apples and cider, then a platter of cheese, fresh and dried fruit and nuts and finally a tropical fruit salad, a bowl of bright red berries or a lemon tart.

Fruit is enormously rewarding to cook with and is very versatile. Almost all fruits complement each other, so you can create all manner of interesting combinations. Although the recipes in this book concentrate on the use of fruits in sweet dishes, they have an important role to play in savouries too. Tart fruits like gooseberries, rhubarb and cranberries cut the richness of fatty fish like mackerel, and can also enhance the sometimes insipid flavour of poultry. Dried fruits are used extensively in North African and Middle Eastern cooking – the combination of meat and sweet, sticky dates, prunes or dried apricots is superb. Most fruits also marry well with exotic spices, such as cinnamon, ginger and vanilla, and even those fruits that are relatively bland can be lifted by the addition of a squeeze of lemon or lime juice.

The hundreds of different kinds of fruit can be divided into four main categories: soft fruits, such as raspberries, strawberries, blueberries and red-, black- and whitecurrants; stone fruits, including peaches, apricots, cherries and plums; "pome" fruits of the apple and pear families; and citrus fruits. In addition there are the "one-offs" that do not fit into any other category. These include figs, grapes, melons and rhubarb (which is actually a vegetable, but is always treated as an honorary fruit).

Fruits are no longer the seasonal produce they once were. Nowadays, thanks to sophisticated transportation methods, all types of fruit from every country are available almost all year round. Travellers who have enjoyed exotic produce abroad now find it

Above: Orleans Reinette apples – one of the "pome" fruits.

Left: Watermelons, like other melon varieties, are in a category of their own.

gracing the shelves of their local greengrocer or supermarket, giving less fortunate stay-at-homes a taste of the Tropics. The disadvantage of this is that we no longer wait with eager anticipation for a particular fruit to come into season; somewhere in the world it will be grown year-round. So strawberries, raspberries and peaches have ceased to be exclusively summer treats, but can be bought in almost any season, although they will never taste as good as when freshly picked, and are still always at their best and cheapest in the summer.

There are many other ways of savouring fruits throughout the year. They can be frozen, bottled or preserved in other ways – as juices or liqueurs or macerated in alcohol; canned, dried or candied; or made into jams, jellies, curds, chutneys and relishes. There is no time of year when fruit is not readily available in one form or another, so you need never go without nature's most precious bounty.

EQUIPMENT

Although most fruits can be prepared with the aid of a good sharp knife, a wide variety of special implements is available to make the task easier, safer and more efficient. The following items are very useful – provided you have space for them in your kitchen.

Peeling and Coring

Paring knife The most useful item in any kitchen. Choose a really sharp knife with a short blade and a handle that is comfortable to hold. Always use a stainless steel knife for preparing fruit, as the acids may damage other metals.

Apple corer This utensil removes apple and pear cores in one easy movement. Place over the core at the stem end and push down firmly right through the fruit, then twist slightly and pull out the core and pips.

Apple segmenter Use this handy device to core and slice an apple into twelve even-size segments in one simple operation.

Apple processor Perfect for people with a huge glut of home-grown apples, this hand-cranked implement peels, cores and neatly slices the fruit into rings in seconds. The processor is expensive to buy, but worth it if you have apple trees that bear fruit in abundance.

Above right: Apple corer
Below left: Paring knife
Below right: Apple segmenter

Above: Fixed- and swivel-blade vegetable peelers

Pineapple easy slicer Cores and slices a pineapple in one easy corkscrew-like action. This simple-to-operate utensil is useful for keeping the pineapple shell intact for use as a serving container, but only works with smaller pineapples.

Swivel-blade vegetable peeler Use this tool to pare off the thinnest possible layer of peel or skin so that no nutrients are lost.

Fixed-blade vegetable peeler This type of peeler takes a thicker strip of peel or skin than the swivel-blade version.

Grating and Zesting

Box grater Choose a stainless steel grater with four different grating

Right: Box grater
Below: Canelle knife and citrus zester

Left: Pineapple easy slicer

surfaces and make sure it will stand firmly on a chopping board or in a bowl. Most include a flat blade suitable for slicing lemons or limes.

Citrus zester The row of holes at the top of the zester shaves off thin shreds of zest, leaving behind the bitter pith.

Canelle knife This tool has a tooth-like blade that pares off the zest in ribbons or julienne strips. Combined zesters/canelle knives are available.

Juicing

Lemon squeezer Hand-operated squeezers catch the juice in the base. Basic models can also be used for limes and small oranges. Some have interchangeable heads to accommodate citrus fruits of various sizes.

Left: Citrus press
Below: Reamer

Citrus press These hand-operated chrome juicers have a geared mechanism to enable as much juice as possible to be extracted. When the handle is pulled forward, the juice is squeezed into a container.

Electric juice extractor These machines will extract juice from other fruits besides citrus. They take up a lot of space, but are invaluable for lovers of fresh fruit juice.

Stoning and Preparing

Cherry stoner The bowl of this implement has a hole through which the cherry stone is ejected when the fruit is pressed. Useful for large quantities.

Grapefruit knife A curved knife serrated on both sides. Run it between the membranes and flesh to release the segments.

Left: Cherry stoner

Below: Grapefruit knife

Grapefruit segmenter This curved implement has a V-shaped blade. Position with the point against the inside of the rind and push down, round and inwards to cut out the segments.

Melon baller Insert this small round scoop into the melon flesh and twist to remove neat balls of fruit. It comes in various sizes and can also be used for other fruits. Tiny ones sometimes double as a cherry stoner.

Preserving

Funnel Essential for pouring hot jams and jellies into jars. Stainless steel funnels will withstand heat better than plastic ones.

Jelly bag A heavy muslin filter bag for straining jellies and juices. Suspend it from the legs of a chair placed upside down or, far better, buy one on a stand.

Preserving pan Especially designed for preserving, this is a thick-bottomed double-handled pan. The heavy base prevents the fruit preserve from burning and sticking.

Sugar thermometer Use this for checking the temperature of a syrup or to determine whether the setting point of a jam and jelly has been reached.

Above: Sugar thermometer
Below: Funnel with strainer

Reamer This wooden device enables you to squeeze the fruit directly into a bowl or pan. Insert into the cut fruit and twist.

Lemon tap A simple gadget that turns citrus fruit into a "juice jug". If only a small amount of juice is required, leave the tap inserted in the fruit to keep the juice fresh between squeezings.

Below: Lemon squeezer

Above: Melon baller

PURCHASING, PREPARING AND COOKING

BUYING FRUIT

Obviously, the best time to buy fruit is when it is fully ripe and at its peak. The exceptions are fruits, such as bananas and pears, that ripen quickly and should therefore be bought at different stages of maturity so that they are not all ready at the same time. You are most likely to find top quality fruits in markets and shops that have a quick turnover of fresh produce, preferably with a daily delivery. Although most fruits are now available almost year round, they are best and cheapest when in season in the country of origin. Only buy as much fruit as you need at one time so that it remains fresh and appetizing.

PREPARING FRUIT

For some fruits, the only preparation needed is washing or wiping with a damp cloth; others must be peeled or skinned, cored, stoned or seeded. Wash fruit only just before using. If necessary, cut away any bruised or damaged parts.

Firm Fruit

Peeling

Some firm fruits, such as eating apples and pears, can be eaten raw without peeling. For cooking, peeling is often necessary. Pare off the skin as thinly as possible to avoid losing the valuable nutrients under the skin.

1 Wash the fruit and pat dry using kitchen paper. Use a small, sharp paring knife or a vegetable peeler to pare off the skin in long, thin vertical strips. Pears are best peeled by this method.

2 Alternatively, for apples, thinly peel all round the fruit in a spiral.

Coring

1 To core whole apples and pears, place the sharp edge of a corer over the stem end of the fruit.

2 Press down firmly, then twist slightly; the core, complete with pips, will come away in the centre of the corer. Pull out the core from the handle end.

Storing
Storage methods depend on the type of fruit, but there are some basic guidelines:
• Do not wash fruit before storing, but only when ready to use.
• Store fruit at the bottom of the fridge or in the salad crisper.
• Do not refrigerate unripe fruit; keep it at room temperature or in a cool, dark place, depending on the variety (see individual fruits).
• Fragile fruits, such as berries, are easily squashed, so spread them out in a single layer on a tray lined with kitchen paper.

Segmenting

1 Halve the fruit lengthways, then cut into quarters or segments.

2 Cut out the central core and pips with a small sharp knife.

Preventing discoloration
Some fruits, such as apples, pears and bananas, quickly oxidize and turn brown when exposed to the air. To prevent discoloration, brush cut fruits with lemon juice. Alternatively, acidulate a bowl of cold water by stirring in the juice of half a lemon. Drop the cut fruits into the bowl immediately after preparing.

Citrus Fruit

Peeling

It is very important to remove all of the bitter white pith that lies just beneath the rind of citrus fruits.

1 To peel firm-skinned fruits, hold the fruit over a bowl to catch the juice and use a sharp knife to cut off the rind.

2 For loose-skinned fruit, such as tangerines, pierce the skin with your thumb at the stalk end and peel off the rind. Finally, pull off all the white shreds adhering to the fruit.

Segmenting

Use a small serrated knife to cut down between the membranes enclosing the segments; carefully ease out the flesh.

Grating

Citrus zest adds a wonderful flavour to many dishes. If it is to be eaten raw, grate it finely, using the fine face of a grater. Remove only the coloured zest, if you grate too deeply into the peel, you will be in danger of including the bitter white pith. For cooking, pare off long, thin strips of zest using a zester.

Garnishing and decorating

To make thick julienne strips of zest, cut lengthways, using a canelle knife.

To make twists, slice the fruits thinly, cut to the centre, then twist the ends in opposite directions to make an S-shape.

Soft Fruit

Peeling

Fruits such as peaches, nectarines and apricots can be peeled with a sharp paring knife, but this may waste some of the delicious flesh. It is better to loosen the skins by dipping them *briefly* in boiling water.

1 Make a tiny nick in the skin.

2 Cover with boiling water and leave for 15–30 seconds, depending on the ripeness of the fruit. Remove the fruit with a slotted spoon and peel off the skin, which should come away easily.

Removing stones and pips

To stone peaches, apricots etc, cut all around the fruit through the seam. Twist the halves in opposite directions, then lever out the stone with a knife.

To stone cherries, put the fruit in a cherry stoner and push the bar into the fruit. The stone will be ejected.

To remove grape pips, cut the grapes in half, then pick out the pips with the tip of a small sharp knife.

COOKING FRUIT

Most fruits can be cooked and in a great variety of ways.

Poaching

Apples and pears, stone fruits, figs, rhubarb and even grapes can be poached, either whole, halved or in segments. The classic poaching liquid is syrup and usually consists of 1 part sugar boiled with 2 parts water for about 2 minutes or until clear. The syrup can be flavoured with lemon, orange or spices, such as cinnamon or vanilla. Red or white wine can also be used for poaching, usually with added sugar. Alternatively, use fruit juice.

Bring the poaching liquid to the boil. Lower the heat and add the fruit. Simmer gently until the fruit is just tender.

Stewing

This method is suitable for all fruits that can be poached.

Cut up the fruit. Put in a saucepan with just enough water, wine or fruit juice to cover. Add sugar to taste. Simmer gently until tender. Only stir if you want the fruit to become a pulp.

Grilling

Any firm fruits can be grilled, with or without sugar. Tropical fruits, such as pineapple and bananas, are particularly good for grilling. For desserts, they can be cut into 2.5cm/1in wedges or chunks and threaded on to skewers to make kebabs. Brush the fruit with clear honey before grilling.

For savoury dishes, halve the fruit or cut into pieces, removing the core if necessary. Brush with melted butter and grill under a medium heat, turning occasionally until tender and browned on all sides.

Baking

Apples and pears; stone fruits, such as peaches, nectarines, apricots and plums; figs and rhubarb can be baked whole or in halves, wedges or slices according to type.

1 Put the fruit in a shallow ovenproof dish, add a little water, and sprinkle with sugar to taste.

2 Top the fruit with small pieces of butter. Bake in a preheated oven at 180°C/350°F/Gas 4 until tender.

Microwave Cooking

All fruits which can be conventionally cooked can be microwaved, with excellent results, although the skins on some fruits, such as plums, may not soften sufficiently in the short cooking time. Whole fruits, such as apples should be scored, or they may burst. Place the fruit in a suitable dish, cover and cook on High for the time recommended, or until tender.

Sautéeing

Slice or dice the fruit (peel it or not, as you wish) and toss quickly in hot butter until lightly browned all over. Add sugar and flavourings to taste.

Deep Frying

For fruit fritters, such as pineapple, apple or banana, peel the fruit and cut into chunks.

Heat oil for deep frying to 185°C/360°F or until a cube of dried bread sizzles when it is added to the pan. Coat the pieces of fruit in batter and deep fry until the fritters rise to the surface of the hot oil and are golden brown. Drain the fritters on kitchen paper and sprinkle with sugar.

Puréeing

Fruit can be puréed for sauces, fools, ice creams and sorbets. Some types must be cooked first; others, like berries, can be puréed raw.

For berries, wash briefly and push through a fine nylon sieve, using the back of a large spoon or ladle. If you prefer, purée the berries in a food processor, then sieve the purée to remove any pips.

For cooked, peeled fruit, mash with a potato masher for a coarse purée. For a finer purée, whizz cooked, peeled fruit in a food processor or push through a food mill.

Caramelizing

Fruits look pretty when caramelized. Small fruits like cherries can be used whole; larger fruits should be cubed.

1 Combine 200g/7oz/scant 1 cup granulated sugar and 60ml/4 tbsp water in a small heavy-based saucepan. Stir over a low heat until the sugar has dissolved. When the mixture boils, add 5ml/1 tsp lemon juice and boil until the syrup turns a deep golden brown.

2 Carefully add 15ml/1 tbsp hot water (protecting your hand with an oven glove as the mixture will "spit") and shake the pan to mix.
3 Spear a piece of fruit on a fork and dip it into the caramel to coat. Leave on an oiled baking sheet until the caramel cools and hardens.

Candying

Also known as crystallized or glacé fruits, candied fruits make a delicious end to a meal. Suitable fruits include citrus (slices and peel), cherries and other stone fruits, physalis and pineapple. For professional results, the candying process is a lengthy one, but this simplified method works well for candied citrus zest or for fruit that is to be eaten within a few days.

1 Cut the fruit into slices or chunks. Make a syrup, using 225g/8oz/1 cup granulated sugar and 150ml/¼ pint/ ⅔ cup water; follow the instructions under Caramelizing. Immerse the pieces of fruit in the syrup. Leave in a cool, dry place to soak for 2 weeks. Drain.

2 Place the fruit on a rack over a baking sheet. Dry for 3–6 hours in a very low oven (maximum of 50°C/122°F/Gas low). Cool, then store in an airtight container.

Frosting

Try this technique with grapes, red– and blackcurrants and cranberries. Eat on the day they are prepared.

Leave the fruit on the stalk. Dip in lightly beaten egg white, then roll in caster sugar until frosted all over. Leave to dry before serving.

Drying

Suitable fruits include apples, pears, stone fruits, figs, grapes and bananas. Commercial dehydrators are available, but you can dry the fruit in a low oven.

Prepare the fruit: peel, core and slice apples; peel, core and halve pears; halve and stone peaches or similar fruits. Leave smaller fruits whole. Lay the fruit on clean wooden slatted trays, cut-side up. Dry in an oven preheated to the lowest possible temperature. Cool completely before storing.

Preserving in Alcohol

All fruits can be preserved in alcohol. In the eighteenth century, seafarers discovered that their cargoes of exotic fruits could be preserved in barrels of rum. Dark rum is still the classic preserving spirit, but brandy and other spirits can also be used.

The ideal container is a purpose-made *rumtopf*, but a wide-mouthed preserving jar will do. Start with summer fruits, then add other fruits as they come into season.

1 Wash and dry the fruit. Place in a bowl and cover with an equal weight of sugar. Leave for 1 hour.

2 Tip the fruit mixture into a *rumtopf* or preserving jar. Pour in just enough rum to cover the fruit completely. Cover the jar with clear film and store in a cool, dark place.
3 Continue to fill the jar with fruits as they come into season, using only half as much sugar by weight as fruit; cover the fruit with rum each time. When the jar is full, leave for at least two months before using the fruit.

APPLES, PEARS, QUINCES AND MEDLARS

A bowlful of apples, polished to shiny perfection, is one of life's

pleasures — beautiful to behold, delicious and healthy to eat.

Pears are almost as popular, with juicy flesh whose scent is

almost as tempting as their taste. Quinces are even more

aromatic, while medlars are intriguing — not least because they

can only be eaten when they are on the verge of rotting. They

are all "pome" fruits, with an indentation in the stalk end, the

coarse brown remains of a flower at the other and a tough

central core containing a number of brown pips.

APPLES

Ever since Adam bit into the fruit of the Tree of Knowledge, apples have been the stuff of myth and legend. The Ancient Greeks and Romans believed them to be aphrodisiacs, and for the Celts crab apples were a symbol of fertility. In the Middle Ages, the cult of the apple continued in such customs as apple-bobbing at Hallowe'en and wassailing at Christmas.

The most popular of all fruits, apples are also convenient, perfect for eating raw as a nutritious snack and ideal for making into a multitude of hot and cold puddings and desserts. There are thousands of named varieties worldwide, but the choice of those available to buy is, sadly, decreasing year by year. However, because apples are now grown in every temperate country in the world, some varieties can be found in the shops all year round. Delicious as they may be, no shop-bought apples can ever beat the flavour and crisp texture of home-grown apples that have been freshly picked.

Apples come in many shapes and sizes, from tiny cherry-size crab apples to huge cooking varieties like Howgate Wonder, Reverend W. Wilkes and the unbelievably warty Knobby Russet, which looks remarkably like a huge toad. They can be round, oval, or "cornered", with four distinct corners around the calyx, like the Catshead, which is shaped like the face of a Siamese cat.

Left: Granny Smith apples – first cultivated in Australia in the nineteenth century.

Colours range from bright, shiny red through vivid greens, yellows and pale creamy-white to golden russet, while the skins may be ultra-thin or unpalatably thick. As for taste and texture, there is an almost infinite variety – something to suit every palate, from crisp and sour to soft and sweet.

History

Apples have been eaten since prehistoric times, when only wild crab apples existed. The Romans adored apples and were the first people to cultivate the fruit; by the first century AD they were growing at least a dozen varieties throughout the Roman Empire.

The most famous of all apple-growers was the nineteenth-century English nurseryman, Thomas Laxton. With his sons, he hybridized hundreds of varieties of apples, many of which still exist today and bear his name.

The Pilgrim Fathers introduced apples to the New World, planting pips that they had taken with them from England. They proved so popular that in the eighteenth century John Chapman (popularly known as "Johnny Appleseed") planted apple orchards across about 10,000 square miles of North America, using discarded apple pips from cider-making plants. A century later, apple-growing in Australia took off when Mrs Maria Smith cultivated the first Granny Smith apple in her garden in Sydney.

Above: Laxton's Fortune

Below: Braeburn – crisp, juicy apples, which make excellent eating.

Varieties

With over 7,000 named varieties of apples it would be impossible to list more than a tiny fraction. In any case, only about a dozen varieties are readily available in the shops, although nurseries can supply many more to people who wish to grow apples in their gardens.

Growing your own apples will allow you to enjoy exotically flavoured fruit, like the pineapple-flavoured Pine Golden Pippin or Ananas Reinette, or the Winter Banana, which develops a creamy texture and a banana flavour when laid down. D'Arcy Spice is a small golden apple with the flavours of cinnamon and allspice, while Anisa is one of several aniseed-flavoured apples. Other apples are redolent of melon, strawberries, raspberries, peaches, lemons and even fennel.

Uniquely in Britain, apples are categorized as eating (or dessert) fruit or cooking apples. Other countries regard all apples as suitable for both eating and cooking. Of course, there are cider apples as well; many are disagreeably sour, but some are very pleasant to eat.

Below: Beauty of Bath

EATING APPLES

Ashmead's Kernel These late variety apples were first cultivated in Gloucestershire in the seventeenth century. Their flesh has a good acid/sugar balance and develops a strong, spicy, aniseed flavour in some seasons.

Beauty of Bath A beautiful small flattish green apple extensively flushed with red, with sharp, sweet, juicy flesh. Beauty of Bath apples should be eaten straight from the tree, as they rot almost as soon as they are picked. Consequently, you are unlikely to find this apple in the shops.

Blenheim Orange This apple was discovered growing out of a wall in Blenheim Palace in England in the nineteenth century and was named by permission of the Duke of Marlborough, but it also has 67 synonyms! It is a dual-purpose apple, good for both cooking and eating, with a pleasantly nutty flavour. It is suitable for cooking in dishes, such as apple charlotte and apple crumble, and for serving as a dessert fruit.

Braeburn This crisp, juicy apple with a smooth pale green skin, heavily flushed with red, makes excellent eating. Braeburn apples are grown only in the southern hemisphere, as they need plenty of daylight.

Above: Empire

Above left: Egremont Russet – this sweet crisp apple is delicious served at the end of a meal with a wedge of strong-tasting cheese, such as farmhouse Cheddar or Lancashire.

Cox's Orange Pippin A greenish-yellow apple of medium size, with some orange-red russetting. The firm, crisp, juicy flesh of this sweet fruit, with its overtones of acidity, make it one of the world's best and most popular apples. Cox's Orange Pippins are excellent for cooking as well as eating raw.

Crispin Large, pale yellowish-green apples with firm and juicy creamy-white flesh and a pleasant mild flavour.

Discovery Bred from the Worcester Pearmain, Discovery was the first apple to be commercially grown in Britain. It is particularly attractive for its highly coloured bright red skin and contrasting hard, crisp white flesh. It is best eaten straight from the tree.

Egremont Russet Russet apples have rough, porous skins which allow the water to evaporate out, giving a denser flesh and intensifying the nutty flavour. Egremont Russet is the most readily available. It is golden russet in colour, sometimes with a bright orange flush, and has a crisp texture and very sweet taste. It can be used for eating or cooking and goes superbly with cheese.

Elstar This sweet, crisp and juicy apple is a cross between Ingrid Marie and Golden Delicious. Originally bred in Holland, it is now grown extensively throughout Europe. Picked in mid-autumn, Elstar apples will keep for 3–4 months.

Empire A dark red American apple with a shiny skin, best for eating raw, but suitable for cooking. It has crisp green, juicy flesh and a slightly tart flavour.

Above: Cox's Orange Pippin

Left: Jonagold – these dual-purpose apples have a superb flavour.

Fuji This sweet apple has greenish-yellow skin with a rosy blush and crisp, juicy white flesh. It is also suitable for cooking.

Gala This colourful eating apple from New Zealand has a yellow ground colour flushed with bright orange and red. The yellow flesh is very sweet, juicy and crisp. It is at its best when absolutely fresh. Good for either cooking or eating. **Royal Gala** is similar, but red all over.

Golden Delicious Originally grown from a chance seedling in the USA, this conical, freckled, golden apple has become ubiquitous. At its peak, the cream flesh is juicy and crisp with a mild flavour; unfortunately most commercially grown Golden Delicious are sold when they are under- or over-ripe and are consequently tasteless and mealy in texture. Golden Delicious are suitable for cooking or eating.

Granny Smith First grown in Australia by the eponymous "Granny" Smith, this largish

Right: Golden Delicious

all-purpose apple is bright green, becoming yellow as it ripens. Usually sold under-ripe, it has firm, crunchy flesh and á tart flavour.

Greensleeves This James Grieve/Golden Delicious cross has more flavour than a James Grieve and better acidity. It is an early fruiting variety, which should be eaten immediately after picking.

Ida Red By far the favourite North American apple for making apple sauce. American-grown fruits have a good acid flavour, which is often lacking in the European-grown apples.

James Grieve A Scottish apple raised in Edinburgh in the late nineteenth century, with tart, juicy flesh that bruises easily when handled. James Grieve is good for cooking and eating, but, like most early varieties, it does not store well and should be kept for no more than 2–3 weeks after picking.

Jonagold A hybrid of Jonathan and Golden Delicious, this large round green-tinged yellow apple has creamy

Above: Gala are best eaten very fresh, when the flesh is crisp and juicy.

Left: Katy

Right: Orleans Reinette

white flesh and a superb flavour. It can be used for cooking or eating.

Jonathan This smallish, round, orange-red North American apple has white, juicy flesh and a fragrant, slightly acidic flavour. It can be used for cooking.

Katy A highly coloured early apple bred in Sweden from the Worcester Pearmain. Their flesh is crisp, sweet and juicy and they are best eaten immediately after picking.

Kidd's Orange Red A New Zealand apple bred from Cox's Orange Pippin. This deliciously crisp apple is highly aromatic, but needs many hours of sunshine to develop its full flavour and colour, so it cannot be successfully grown in Northern Europe.

Laxton's Fortune A cross between Cox's Orange Pippin and Wealthy, these apples have yellowish skin heavily tinged with red, and sweet, juicy, lightly aromatic flesh. You are most likely to find them in farm shops.

Laxton's Superb Greenish-yellow and partially covered with red, this all-purpose apple has crisp, very juicy flesh. It is sweet with some acidity.

McIntosh A Canadian apple that is popular throughout North America. It is wonderfully decorative, with deep red waxy skin, which can be polished to a

superb sheen, but the skin is quite tough. The pale flesh is melting (and sometimes mushy) with a hint of fresh strawberry flavour.

Orleans Reinette One of the best apples of all, this large orange-flecked russet has a rough skin, but juicy, sweet, aromatic flesh. Orleans Reinette is ideal for cooking and eating.

Pink Lady A pretty Australian cross between Golden Delicious and Lady Williams, this large all-purpose apple has a mild flavour, and is becoming increasing available in supermarkets and greengrocers.

Pomme d'Api Also known as Lady apple, this very attractive fruit has a yellow skin suffused with a bright red blush. Pomme d'Api is a late apple with good keeping qualities.

Red Delicious This North American apple was first grown in the nineteenth century. It has an exceptionally sweet flavour,

Above:
Pink Lady

Above: Spartan – a Canadian apple with a tough skin, but delicious, floral-scented flesh.

Left: Grown mostly in the United States, colourful Red Delicious is another apple with a tough skin that hides juicy, sweet flesh.

but tough skin. Red Delicious apples can be grown in Europe, but not always successfully.

Spartan Another Canadian apple raised in 1926 from McIntosh and Newton's Pippin. It inherits a tough skin from McIntosh, but tastes highly aromatic with a floral perfume.

Worcester Pearmain A conical yellow apple flushed with bright red. The juicy white flesh has a hint of strawberry flavour. Worcester Pearmain are best eaten straight from the tree, but can also be used for cooking.

Above: Worcester Pearmain

Above: Greensleeves

Below left: With their shiny, bright red skin and crisp cream flesh, Washington Red apples are worth looking out for at farmer's markets.

Above: Lord Lambourne

Above: Originally bred in Holland, Elstar apples are now grown throughout Europe.

Other eating varieties of note
Less well-known apple varieties worth looking out for include Lord Derby, Lord Lambourne, Red Pippin, Rome Beauty, Starking, Sturmer Pippin, Tydeman's Late Orange, Washington Red, Winesap and Winston.

Below left: Royal Gala – sweet, juicy and crisp, this apple is good for either cooking or eating.

Below right: Red Pippin – a tasty Cox's Orange Pippin cross.

Above: Bramley's Seedling

Below: Howgate Wonder

COOKING APPLES

Bramley's Seedling The *nonpareil* of cookers, this large, flattish green apple (sometimes faintly flushed with red) has coarse, white, juicy, acid flesh, which cooks into a frothy purée. Bramleys are perfect for baking or as the basis of apple sauce.

Grenadier An irregularly shaped conical apple with yellow skin. The acid flesh is faintly green, firm and juicy. It breaks down during cooking. Grenadiers do not keep well.

Howgate Wonder This apple can grow to an enormous size – in 1997, the world record was achieved with a specimen

weighing 1.6kg/3lb 14oz! The juicy white flesh breaks up during cooking and has an uninspiring flavour, so this variety is grown mainly for exhibition.

Reverend W. Wilkes Very large conical apple with pale greenish-white skin. The fine, very white flesh is crisp, juicy and acidic. The apple can be eaten raw, but it is best as a cooker. It keeps well.

Nutrition

Apples were once believed to be the most nutritious of fruits, giving rise to the saying that "an apple a day keeps the doctor away". In fact, they have fewer vitamins than many other fruits (although they contain some vitamins C and A), but are high in pectin and are a good source of dietary fibre. They provide 52 kilocalories per 100g/3¾oz.

Buying and Storing

Choose apples with undamaged skins and never buy bruised fruits. If possible, smell the fruits to determine their fragrance (not easy when they are pre-bagged) and squeeze gently to ensure they are firm. Do not be too seduced by the skin colour of an apple; those gorgeous-looking specimens with thick, vivid red, waxy skins often have woolly, tasteless flesh.

Apples continue to ripen after they have been picked, so their colour and texture may change during storage. For short-term storage, they can be kept in a ventilated polythene bag in the fridge. To store pick-your-own apples, wrap each one in newspaper and place folded-side down in a single layer in wooden or fibre trays. Keep in a cool, dry, dark place and check occasionally to make sure none has gone rotten. A bad fruit will taint all the others, so remove it immediately.

Dried Apples These have a sweet, concentrated flavour and are an extremely useful storecupboard ingredient. Eat them straight from the

Below: Dried apple rings

Drying apples at home

1 Peel the apples, remove the cores and slice the fruit into rings. Soak in salted water for a few minutes to prevent discoloration.

2 Thread the apple rings on to string. Hang them from the ceiling or suspend across the room until they are completely dry.

3 Alternatively, arrange the rings in a single layer on a wire rack on a baking sheet, making sure that they are not touching. Place in an oven set to 70°C/150°F/Gas Low for several hours until dried.

packet as a nutritious snack, add them to home-made muesli or soak them in water, then cook them in sweet and savoury dishes like fruit compotes, apple sauce or casseroles. Dried apples are available commercially, but it is easy to dry your own when there is a glut, and you can choose your favourite varieties. Russets are particularly delicious when dried.

Preparing

Most apples can be eaten with the skin on. To peel, use a vegetable peeler or small, sharp knife, either in a spiral following the circumference of the apple, or peeling downwards in strips from stem to calyx. Peeled apples go brown very quickly; brush them with lemon juice or drop them into water acidulated with lemon juice or cider vinegar immediately.

Cooking

Some apples are only suitable for eating raw, but most can be cooked in such classic sweet dishes as apple pies, crumbles and tarts, baked apples and strudel. Sweet apples combine well with other fruits, like blackberries, quinces and lemon, and dried fruits like raisins or cranberries. Aromatic spices like cinnamon, nutmeg and cloves highlight their flavour. Their high pectin content will help other fruit jellies and jams to set, or they can be made into crab apple jelly, apple cheese and chutney.

Tart apples make excellent accompaniments for game birds, black pudding and sausages, and rich meats like pork, duck and goose. They go well with red cabbage and are a vital ingredient in Waldorf salad.

To bake apples, core them with an apple corer and score around the circumference to prevent the skin from bursting. Stuff with dried fruit, nuts, butter and sugar and bake in a preheated oven at 180°C/350°F/Gas 4 until soft.

To cook sliced apples and rings, sauté in butter and sugar to help them keep their shape. To stew, cook in the minimum amount of water, or with butter and seasonings.

Making apple purée

1 Peel, core and thickly slice the apples, immediately dropping the pieces into a bowl of cold water acidulated with lemon juice or cider vinegar.

2 Barely cover the base of a saucepan with cold water. Add the apple pieces and cook to a purée, adding sugar to taste towards the end.

3 If you are using firmer eating apples, which will not disintegrate to a purée, cook until very tender, then rub through a coarse sieve.

CRAB APPLES AND CIDER APPLES

Crab apples have grown wild in hedgerows for thousands of years and were eaten in prehistoric times. The fruits are smaller and often more colourful than cultivated varieties. Nowadays crab apples are often grown for their ornamental qualities. The fruits can be vivid yellow, green, orange or bright red.

Crab apples are seldom worth eating raw (and may be completely inedible), although some are perfectly palatable for those without too sweet a tooth. You may find larger self-seeded crab apples, which have grown from the pips of cultivated apples that have become wild; these can be eaten.

Thanks to their high pectin content, all crab apples make wonderful jellies, either on their own or mixed with other wild fruits, such as haw berries.

Cider apples are closer to eating apples than crab apples, but usually have a bitter or sour flavour due to their

Below: Crab apples are almost always too sour to eat raw.

high tannin content. There are hundreds of different varieties with wonderful names like Strawberry Norma and Foxwhelp, and each local grower will insist that his is the best. Some, like Tom Putt, are sweet enough to eat; these are used to make sweet cider.

Apple Drinks

Apple juice, cider and apple brandies, such as Calvados, are the main drinks made from apples. Apple juice is made by crushing eating apples; the best is pressed from a single variety, such as Cox's Orange Pippin or Russet, but most commercial apple juices are made from a mixture of varieties or, worse, from concentrate. Apple juice may be fizzy or still.

Cider may have been brought to Britain by the Phoenicians or the Celts; it has certainly been around for thousands of years. It is a fermented drink made from the juice of cider apples and, depending on the variety of fruit and

Left: Cider – the best is still made by artisan producers.

Right and far right: Calvados and applejack are both types of apple brandy.

pressing technique, can range from sweet and gassy to cloudy and flat. The best ciders are still made by small producers using artisan methods; some of these ciders can be lethally strong. The strongest and crudest cider is scrumpy. It is made from the apples of the poorest quality, but can certainly pack a punch!

Apple brandy is made from fermented and distilled apple juice. The best of all is Calvados, the famous apple brandy from Normandy, which is double distilled and aged in oak. Calvados may only be produced within a defined area; other apple brandies must be labelled *eau-de-vie de cidre* or simply "apple brandy" ("applejack" in North America).

Fermented apple juice can also be made into cider vinegar, which has a strong apple taste and is excellent for making fruit chutneys or adding extra flavour to casseroles containing apples.

PEARS

There are almost as many varieties of pears as there are apples, but only a dozen or so are available in the shops. Pears are related to apples, but are more fragile and are more often eaten raw than cooked. They have fine white granular flesh and a central core containing the pips. Most pears have the familiar shape, wider at the bottom than the top, but some are apple-shaped, while "calabash" pears have an elongated neck, like a gourd. Pears are less vividly coloured than apples, generally varying from bronze to gold, green or yellow, but there are some beautiful red varieties, too.

Right: Anjou pears are sweet, juicy and aromatic.

History

Wild pears are native to Europe and Asia, where they have grown since prehistoric times. They were cultivated by the ancient Phoenicians and the Romans, and they became a royal delicacy for the ancient Persian kings. Their popularity spread so fast that in medieval Italy over 200 varieties of

Below: Beurré Bosc

pear were cultivated. By the seventeenth century, the French were growing 300 different varieties, inspired by Louis XIV's passion for the fruit. There are now said to be more than 5,000 named varieties growing throughout the world.

Varieties

Cooking pears (which cannot be eaten raw) do exist, but almost all the pears available in the shops are eating fruit, which can also be cooked. Pears are seasonal, so only a few varieties are available at any one time.

Anjou These large pears have greenish-yellow skin with brown speckles or russetting. The flesh is juicy and sweet. Suitable for eating and cooking.

Beth This modern pear variety resembles Williams Bon Chrétien in flavour and texture, but has the added advantage of being longer keeping.

Beurré Bosc and **Beurré Hardi** These elongated pears have an uneven green-gold skin, which becomes yellow and completely russetted as the fruit ripens. The creamy white flesh is firm and juicy with a buttery texture (hence the name, which means "buttered"), and the flavour is deliciously sweet and aromatic with some acidity. Both varieties are excellent for eating and cooking.

Beurré Superfin These medium-to-large pears are round and conical in shape. Their uneven, almost knobbly skin is pale greenish-yellow, which changes to yellow with bronze russetting as they ripen. The creamy white flesh is firm, buttery and extremely juicy, with a sweet flavour having a hint of acidity. A truly delicious pear.

Conference First cultivated in Berkshire in 1770, these long, conical pears have remained a favourite in Britain, largely because they keep so well. The yellowish-green skin with extensive russetting turns yellower when the pears are mature. The granular flesh is tender, sweet and juicy. Excellent for eating and cooking.

Doyenné du Comice (also known as **Comice**) This large, roundish pear is one of the finest of all, with creamy white, melting, very juicy flesh and a sweet, aromatic flavour. The thick, yellowish-green skin is covered with speckles and patches of russetting. Doyenné du Comice are best eaten raw, and are delicious with Brie or Camembert.

Forelle A beautiful golden pear with a dark red flush on one side. The grainy flesh is crisp, with a fresh flavour that goes well with cheese, but is at its best when cooked.

Josephine de Malines A French pear, first raised in 1830. The medium-size fruits are round conical in shape, with

Below: Conference are one of the best-loved English pears.

yellowish-green skin flushed with red and some russetting, The tender flesh can be white or pinkish and is very juicy, with an aromatic flavour. It keeps well.

Merton Pride An exceptionally sweet and juicy pear with a superb flavour. The conical fruits have yellow skin wih brown freckles.

Onward A cross between Laxton's Superb and Doyenné du Comice, these roundish pears are best peeled before eating as they have ribbed skin. The yellowish-green skin is flushed with red and mottled with pale russetting. The creamy white flesh is exceptionally good – soft, melting, juicy and very sweet.

Packham's Triumph The first successful Australian pear was produced by Charles Packham in 1896 and remains a favourite. A largish eating pear, it has a smooth green, lightly russetted skin, which changes to yellow as it ripens. The soft white flesh is succulent and sweet, with a touch of acidity.

Passacrena Very plump, roundish pears with russetted greenish-yellow skin. The flesh can sometimes be rather gritty, but is very juicy and sweet.

Above: Doyenné du Comice, also known simply as Comice, are very juicy and aromatic.

Right: Forelle are ideal pears to use for cooking.

Red Williams These pears have shiny, speckled skins, at first green with a red blush, turning to yellow flushed with red. The flesh is sweet and juicy.

Rocha A Portuguese pear with greenish-yellow skin with russet spotting and brown markings at the stem end. The firm white flesh has a sugary flavour and, unlike many other pears which pass their prime almost as soon as they reach it, the fruit remains in excellent condition for several days.

Williams Bon Chrétien Known as "Barlett" in the United States, these irregularly shaped pears are generally swollen on one side of the stalk. The speckled skin is golden yellow with russet patches and sometimes a red tinge. The delicious tender flesh is creamy white and very juicy, and the flavour is sweet and slightly musky. Unfortunately, these superb pears do not keep well. Williams Bon Chrétien are suitable for cooking and eating.

Winter Nelis This roundish medium-size pear has thick but tender greenish-yellow skin with cinnamon brown russetting and sometimes a pink flush. The creamy white flesh is soft and very juicy, and the flavour is sweet. These pears can be cooked or eaten raw.

Left: Packham's Triumph

Nutrition

Pears contain a small amount of vitamins A and C and some potassium and riboflavin. They provide around 60 kilocalories per 100g/3¾oz.

Pears should always be bought when they are in perfect condition, as they deteriorate quickly. Once past their best, they become woolly or squashy and unpleasant. Test for ripeness by pressing the stem end between your forefinger and thumb; it should give a little, but the pear should still be quite firm. Once ripe, pears should be eaten within a couple of days, or they will "go over". Keep ripe fruit in the bottom of the fridge.

Above: Suitable for both eating and cooking, Williams Bon Chrétien have delicious creamy white flesh. They don't keep very well, so use them as soon as they have ripened

Above: The firm-fleshed Rocha will remain in good condition for several days in your fruit bowl.

Below: Juicy, with a red blush, Red Williams make excellent eating.

Dried pears Although dried pears are most often used in winter fruit compotes and savoury casseroles, they have a delicate flavour and are delicious eaten raw. They are readily available in the shops, but it is easy to prepare your own.

Canned pears Pears are among the most successful of all canned fruit and may be used to make almost any dessert that calls for cooked pears. They are often canned in heavy syrup, but are now available in the healthier alternative of apple juice. Purée drained canned pears, flavour them with pear liqueur, lemon or preserved ginger syrup and freeze for a quick and easy sorbet.

Right: Dried pears

Preparing and Cooking

Most pears are eaten raw, by themselves or with a robust cheese, such as Gorgonzola, Parmesan, Stilton or Roquefort. They also make a good addition to winter salads. Whether or not to peel pears before eating raw is a matter of preference, but they should always be peeled before cooking. Pears discolour quickly once they are peeled, so rub the cut surface with a little lemon juice immediately or place them a bowl of acidulated water. For whole poached pears, simply peel, leaving on the stalk. Use an apple corer to core the pears if you want to stuff them with nuts or dried fruit. Poach in port or red wine spiced with cinnamon, cloves and thinly pared lemon rind, or in a vanilla-flavoured syrup. For sautéed or grilled pears, peel and quarter or halve the fruit and scoop out the cores with a melon baller.

Eating or cooking pears can also be cooked in compotes, tarts, terrines, trifles and the famous Poires Belle Hélène (poached pears with vanilla ice cream and hot chocolate sauce). They make marvellous fritters and go very well with ingredients such as nuts and spices, port and marsala. Cooked pears are also excellent in savoury dishes; for example they can either be made into chutney, or casseroled with game birds or venison. They can be preserved with sugar and vinegar, or pickled with mustard seeds and horseradish. If you are cooking eating pears, use them while they are still slightly underripe.

Pears may also be dried, canned, crystallized and distilled into spirits like *eau-de-vie de poires* and Poire William. The bottle in which this liqueur is sold sometimes contains a whole pear, an apparent illusion as the neck is too narrow to allow the pear to pass. The effect is achieved by placing the bottle necks over the infant fruits on the tree so that each pear grows inside a bottle. When it has ripened, the bottle is topped up with the pear-flavoured liqueur.

Left: Canned pears

> **Drying pears**
> **1** Peel the pears and cut them in half lengthways.
>
> **2** Scoop out the cores with a small melon baller, removing all the fibrous part of the fruit.
>
> **3** Brush them with lemon juice to prevent discoloration. Spread out in a single layer on a rack over a baking sheet and dry in an oven set to 70°C/150°F/Gas Low for several hours until dried.

ASIAN OR NASHI PEARS

There are many varieties of Asian pear, but their characteristics are very similar. Round rather than pear-shaped, the fruits have a golden-brown russet skin and very crisp, white, juicy flesh. The crunchy texture resembles that of an apple but is more granular. It would be a shame to spoil the crisp texture by cooking. Asian pears are best eaten straight from the fridge, to be enjoyed as a "drink on a stalk". They also make excellent additions to fruit salads or savoury winter salads.

HOSUI PEARS

These pears have much the same crunch and juiciness of Tientsin pears, but look more like apples, with greeny-brown mottled flesh, which tastes like a cross between an apple and an unripe pear.

PERRY PEARS

With the demise of the most famous of the sparkling alcoholic pear drinks, perry pears have largely fallen into disfavour. A few small producers still press perry pears into juice, wine or "champagne" perry, but although there

Left: Tientsin pears are best eaten chilled.

are still about 300 known varieties, you will never find these fruit in the shops. Perry pears are smaller than their eating pear counterparts. Although they look delicious, they contain large quantities of tannin and taste bitter and astringent, whether they are eaten raw or cooked.

TIENTSIN PEARS

These pears from China and Korea are very similar to Asian or Nashi pears in taste and texture. They are available when Asian or Nashipears are out of season. They look rather like elongated apples, tapering gently at both ends. The skin is pale yellow, slightly speckled with light brown. The pure white flesh is exceptionally juicy and crunchy – perfect for a hot day. Tientsin pears are best eaten chilled to appreciate their refreshing quality, and make the perfect healthy alternative to ice lollies.

Left: Asian pears are round rather than pear-shaped and their crunchy texture resembles that of apples, too.

QUINCES

These highly aromatic fruits are known as "apple" or "pear" quinces, according to their shape. Unripe fruits have a downy skin, while ripe quinces have the smooth texture of a pear. Raw quinces are inedible, but they make excellent natural air fresheners – a quince kept in the glove compartment will shrivel but not rot, and will fill your car with the most delicious aroma for up to six months.

History

Quinces originate from Turkestan and Persia, but are grown all over Europe. It is said that they were the mythical golden apples of the Hesperides and that the golden apple Paris gave to Aphrodite, the goddess of Love, was in

Above: Quinces may have been the mythical golden apples of Hesperides.

fact a quince. To the Ancient Greeks and Romans, quinces were a symbol of happiness, love and fruitfulness. The fruits were widely grown in Britain from the sixteenth to the eighteenth century, but their popularity has declined. In Spain, however, they are still highly prized and are used to make a thick fruit paste called *membrillo*.

Choosing and Storing

Quinces are not readily available in the shops, but you may find them growing in gardens. The skin of ripe quinces should be uniformly golden yellow; unripe fruit may still have patches of down, which can be rubbed off. Quinces keep well – the best way to store them is in a bowl in your kitchen or living room. They will fill the room with their delicious scent.

Preparing and Cooking

Quinces are always cooked. They are prepared in much the same way as pears. For jellies and fruit pastes, the skin is left on as it contributes valuable pectin, as do the pips (the word "marmalade" comes from the Portuguese word for quince, *marmelo*). Quince jelly can be spread on bread or served with pork and game. Quinces can be baked whole like apples or pears, stuffed with a rich mixture of butter, sugar and cream. One or two quinces also make a good addition to an apple pie. Peel and slice the quinces

---

Quince jelly
Makes about 2kg/4¹/₂lb

1 Roughly chop 1kg/2¹/₄lb quinces. Put in a large, heavy-based pan with 2 litres/3¹/₂ pints/8 cups water.

2 Bring to the boil, then simmer until the quinces are very tender.

3 Pour into a jelly bag set over a bowl; let the juice run through, but do not squeeze the bag or the finished jelly will be cloudy.

4 Measure the strained juice and pour into a large, heavy-based pan. Add 500g/1¹/₄lb/2¹/₂ cups preserving sugar for each 600ml/1 pint/2¹/₂ cups of the juice. Bring to the boil, stirring until the sugar has dissolved completely. Boil rapidly until setting point is reached.

5 Skim the jelly and pour into sterilized jars. Cover the jars while the jelly is still hot, then label once the jars are cool enough to handle.

(this will be easier to achieve if you parboil them for 10 minutes), then toss them with the apple slices, sugar and cinnamon before layering them in the pie.

In Spain, quince pulp is boiled with sugar to make the fruit paste, *membrillo*, which is then cooled, cut into squares and served with soft cheeses or as a sweet. The French equivalent is known as *cotignac*, while quince cheese is similar, but softer and more spreadable.

Quinces marry well with almost all meats, from poultry to beef and game, and also make a wonderful scented addition to spirits such as vodka, grappa or *eau-de-vie*.

Japonica Quince

As the name suggests, this cultivated quince came originally from Japan. The hard yellowish fruits are virtually inedible raw, but can be cooked and used like quinces. Their perfume is less intense, but they are still sufficiently aromatic to make an excellent addition to pies and tarts. They can also be made into both quince jelly and quince cheese.

Above: Japonica quinces are not edible raw, but they make a wonderful jelly.

MEDLARS

Medlar trees resemble pear trees, but the fruits are quite different. They look rather like large golden brown rosehips with a russetted skin and a distinctive open five-point calyx end, for which the French have an indelicate term (*cul de chien*). They are eaten when overripe, almost rotten. The process is known as "bletting" and is traditionally achieved by spreading out unripe fruit on straw and leaving it to decay for several weeks, by which time the flesh can be spooned out. To speed up the bletting process, whole unripe medlars can be frozen to break up the cell structure, then left to decay at room temperature. The flesh has a dry, sticky texture. It tastes a little like the flesh of dried dates, but is more tart. Medlars are not to everyone's taste; the nineteenth-century horticulturalist George Bunyard described several different varieties of medlar as "all of equal unpleasantness".

Above: Medlars are nowadays seldom sold in shops, nor eaten much either.

History

Medlars were first discovered in the Transcaucasus, but are found growing wild in Asia Minor and southern Europe. They were cultivated by the Assyrians, who then introduced them to Ancient Greece. In Victorian times in England, they were often enjoyed at the end of a meal with the port, but they are seldom eaten nowadays.

Choosing and Storing

Medlars are seldom sold in shops, but are sometimes cultivated or found growing wild. They are extremely hard and, if left on the tree, are unlikely to ripen sufficiently to be eaten. They are therefore picked in their unripe state and left to "blet". A bletted medlar will be soft and yielding to the touch.

Preparing and Cooking

To eat bletted medlars raw, peel back the skin from the five points of the calyx and suck out the flesh, leaving the five pips behind, or scrape it out with a spoon. Unripe medlars can be used with bletted fruits to make medlar jelly, or baked to make a thick sauce that goes well with rich meats. Medlar jelly is made in the same way as quince jelly.

APPLE, PEAR AND QUINCE RECIPES

*Apples, pears and quinces are wonderfully versatile.
Dutch Apple Cake and Chocolate, Pear and Pecan Pie
are just two of the tempting tea-time treats in store,
while Hot Quince Soufflés and Iced Pear Terrine
with Calvados and Chocolate Sauce make
memorable desserts.*

SPICED APPLE CRUMBLE

*ANY FRUIT CAN BE USED IN THIS POPULAR DESSERT, BUT YOU CAN'T BEAT THE FAVOURITES OF
BLACKBERRY AND APPLE. HAZELNUTS AND CARDAMOM SEEDS GIVE THE TOPPING EXTRA FLAVOUR.*

SERVES FOUR TO SIX

INGREDIENTS
butter, for greasing
450g/1lb Bramley apples
115g/4oz/1 cup blackberries
grated rind and juice of 1 orange
50g/2oz/⅓ cup light muscovado sugar
custard, to serve
For the topping
175g/6oz/1½ cups plain flour
75g/3oz/⅓ cup butter
75g/3oz/⅓ cup caster sugar
25g/1oz/¼ cup chopped hazelnuts
2.5ml/½ tsp crushed cardamom seeds

VARIATIONS
This wonderfully good-natured pudding
can be made with all sorts of fruit. Try
plums, apricots, peaches or pears, alone
or in combination with apples. Rhubarb
makes a delectable crumble, especially
when partnered with bananas.

1 Preheat the oven to 200°C/400°F/
Gas 6. Generously butter a 1.2 litre/
2 pint/5 cup baking dish. Peel and
core the apples, then slice them into
the prepared baking dish. Level the
surface, then scatter the blackberries
over. Sprinkle the orange rind and light
muscovado sugar evenly over the top,
then pour over the orange juice. Set the
fruit mixture aside while you make the
crumble topping.

2 Make the topping. Sift the flour into a
bowl and rub in the butter until the
mixture resembles coarse breadcrumbs.
Stir in the caster sugar, hazelnuts and
cardamom seeds. Scatter the topping
over the top of the fruit.

3 Press the topping around the edges
of the dish to seal in the juices. Bake
for 30–35 minutes or until the crumble
is golden. Serve hot, with custard.

BAKED STUFFED APPLES

*THIS TRADITIONAL APPLE DESSERT IS EXCEPTIONALLY SIMPLE AND SPEEDY. BAKE THE APPLES IN THE
OVEN ON THE SHELF UNDER THE SUNDAY ROAST FOR A DELICIOUS END TO THE MEAL.*

SERVES FOUR

INGREDIENTS
4 large Bramley apples
75g/3oz/½ cup light muscovado sugar
75g/3oz/⅓ cup butter, softened
grated rind and juice of ½ orange
1.5ml/¼ tsp ground cinnamon
30ml/2 tbsp crushed ratafia biscuits
50g/2oz/½ cup pecan nuts, chopped
50g/2oz/½ cup luxury mixed glacé
    fruit, chopped

COOK'S TIP
Use a little butter or oil to grease the
baking dish, if you like, or pour a small
amount of water around the stuffed
apples to stop them from sticking to the
dish during baking.

1 Preheat the oven to 180°C/350°F/
Gas 4. Wash and dry the apples.
Remove the cores with an apple corer,
then carefully enlarge each core cavity
to twice its size, by shaving off more
flesh with the corer. Score each apple
around its equator, using a sharp knife.
Stand the apples in a baking dish.

2 Mix the sugar, butter, orange rind
and juice, cinnamon and ratafia crumbs.
Beat well, then stir in the nuts and
glacé fruit. Divide the filling among the
apples, piling it high. Shield the filling in
each apple with a small piece of foil.
Bake for 45–60 minutes until all the
apples are tender.

APPLE CRÊPES WITH BUTTERSCOTCH SAUCE

THESE WONDERFUL DESSERT CRÊPES ARE FLAVOURED WITH SWEET CIDER, FILLED WITH CARAMELIZED APPLES AND DRIZZLED WITH A RICH, SMOOTH BUTTERSCOTCH SAUCE.

3 Make the filling. Core the apples and cut them into thick slices. Heat 15g/ ½ oz/1 tbsp of the butter in a large frying pan. Add the apples to the pan. Cook until golden on both sides, then transfer the slices to a bowl with a slotted spoon and set them aside.

4 Add the rest of the butter to the pan. As soon as it has melted, add the muscovado sugar. When the sugar has dissolved and the mixture is bubbling, stir in the cream. Continue cooking until it forms a smooth sauce.

5 Fold each pancake in half, then fold in half again to form a cone; fill each with some of the fried apples. Place two filled pancakes on each dessert plate, drizzle over some of the butterscotch sauce and serve at once.

VARIATIONS
You could just as easily use plums, pears, strawberries or bananas to fill the crêpes. If you like, add a touch of Grand Marnier to the apples towards the end of cooking.

SERVES FOUR

INGREDIENTS
 115g/4oz/1 cup plain flour
 a pinch of salt
 2 eggs
 175ml/6fl oz/¾ cup creamy milk
 120ml/4fl oz/½ cup sweet cider
 butter, for frying
For the filling and sauce
 4 Braeburn apples
 90g/3½ oz/scant ½ cup butter
 225g/8oz/1⅓ cups light
  muscovado sugar
 150ml/¼ pint/⅔ cup double cream

1 Make the crêpe batter. Sift the flour and salt into a large bowl. Add the eggs and milk and beat until smooth. Stir in the cider; set aside for 30 minutes.

2 Heat a small heavy-based non-stick frying pan. Add a knob of butter and ladle in enough batter to coat the pan thinly. Cook until the crêpe is golden underneath, then flip it over and cook the other side until golden. Slide the crêpe on to a plate. Repeat with the remaining mixture to make seven more.

PEAR AND CINNAMON FRITTERS

IF YOU DON'T LIKE DEEP FRYING AS A RULE, DO MAKE AN EXCEPTION FOR THIS DISH. FRITTERS ARE IRRESISTIBLE, AND A WONDERFUL WAY OF PERSUADING CHILDREN TO EAT MORE FRUIT.

SERVES FOUR

INGREDIENTS

3 ripe, firm pears
30ml/2 tbsp caster sugar
30ml/2 tbsp Kirsch
groundnut oil, for frying
50g/2oz/1 cup amaretti biscuits,
  finely crushed
For the batter
75g/3oz/¾ cup plain flour
1.5ml/¼ tsp salt
1.5ml/¼ tsp ground cinnamon
60ml/4 tbsp milk
2 eggs, separated
45ml/3 tbsp water
To serve
30ml/2 tbsp caster sugar
1.5ml/¼ tsp ground cinnamon
clotted cream

1 Peel the pears, cut them in quarters and remove the cores. Toss the wedges in the caster sugar and Kirsch. Set aside for 15 minutes.

2 Make the batter. Sift the flour, salt and cinnamon into a large bowl. Beat in the milk, egg yolks and water until smooth. Set aside for 10 minutes.

3 Whisk the egg whites in a grease-free bowl until they form stiff peaks; lightly fold them into the batter. Preheat the oven to 150°C/300°F/Gas 2.

4 Pour oil into a deep heavy-based saucepan to a depth of 7.5cm/3in. Heat to 185°C/360°F or until a bread cube, added to the oil, browns in 45 seconds.

5 Toss a pear wedge in the amaretti crumbs, then spear it on a fork and dip it into the batter until evenly coated. Lower it gently into the hot oil and use a knife to push it off the fork. Add more wedges in the same way but do not overcrowd the pan. Cook the fritters for 3–4 minutes or until golden. Drain on kitchen paper. Keep hot in the oven while cooking successive batches.

6 Mix the sugar and cinnamon and sprinkle some over the fritters. Sprinkle a little cinnamon sugar over the clotted cream; serve with the hot fritters.

VARIATIONS
Also try apples, apricots and bananas.

POACHED PEARS IN PORT SYRUP

THE PERFECT CHOICE FOR AUTUMN ENTERTAINING, THIS SIMPLE DESSERT HAS A BEAUTIFUL RICH
COLOUR AND FANTASTIC FLAVOUR THANKS TO THE TASTES OF PORT AND LEMON.

SERVES FOUR

INGREDIENTS
2 ripe, firm pears, such as Williams
  or Comice
pared rind of 1 lemon
175ml/6fl oz/¾ cup ruby port
50g/2oz/¼ cup caster sugar
1 cinnamon stick
60ml/4 tbsp cold water
fresh cream, to serve
To decorate
30ml/2 tbsp sliced hazelnuts, toasted
fresh mint, pear or rose leaves

COOK'S TIP
Choose pears of similar size, with the
stalks intact, for the most attractive
effect when fanned on the plate.

1 Peel the pears, cut them in half and
remove the cores. Place the lemon rind,
port, sugar, cinnamon stick and water in
a shallow pan. Bring to the boil over a
low heat. Add the pears, lower the heat,
cover and poach for 5 minutes. Let the
pears cool in the syrup.

2 When the pears are cold, transfer
them to a bowl with a slotted spoon.
Return the syrup to the heat. Boil
rapidly until it has reduced to form a
syrup that will coat the back of a spoon
lightly. Remove the cinnamon stick and
lemon rind and leave the syrup to cool.

3 To serve, place each pear in turn on
a board, cut side down. Keeping it
intact at the stalk end, slice it
lengthways, then using a palette knife,
carefully lift it off and place on a dessert
plate. Press gently so that the pear fans
out. When all the pears have been
fanned, spoon over the port syrup. Top
each portion with a few hazelnuts and
decorate with fresh mint, pear or rose
leaves. Serve with cream.

APPLE CHARLOTTES

THESE TEMPTING LITTLE FRUIT CHARLOTTES ARE A WONDERFUL WAY TO USE WINDFALLS.

SERVES FOUR

INGREDIENTS

175g/6oz/¾ cup butter
450g/1lb Bramley apples
225g/8oz Braeburn apples
60ml/4 tbsp water
130g/4½oz/scant ⅔ cup caster sugar
2 egg yolks
a pinch of grated nutmeg
9 thin slices white bread,
  crusts removed
extra-thick double cream or custard,
  to serve

COOK'S TIP

A mixture of cooking and eating apples gives the best flavour, but there's no reason why you can't use only cooking apples; just sweeten the pulp to taste.

1 Preheat the oven to 190°C/375°F/ Gas 5. Put a knob of the butter in a saucepan. Peel and core the apples, dice them finely and put them in the pan with the water. Cover and cook for 10 minutes or until the cooking apples have pulped down. Stir in 115g/4oz/ ½ cup of the caster sugar. Then boil, uncovered, until any liquid has evaporated and what remains is a thick pulp. Remove from the heat, beat in the egg yolks and nutmeg and set aside.

2 Melt the remaining butter in a separate saucepan over a low heat until the white curds start to separate from the clear yellow liquid. Remove from the heat. Leave to stand for a few minutes, then strain the clear clarified butter through a muslin-lined sieve.

3 Brush four 150ml/¼ pint/⅔ cup individual charlotte moulds or pudding tins with a little of the clarified butter; sprinkle with the remaining caster sugar. Cut the bread slices into 2.5cm/1in strips. Dip the strips into the remaining clarified butter; use to line the moulds or tins. Overlap the strips on the base to give the effect of a swirl and let the excess bread overhang the tops of the moulds or tins.

4 Fill each bread case with apple pulp. Fold the excess bread over the top of each mould or tin to make a lid; press down lightly. Bake for 45–50 minutes or until golden. Run a knife between each charlotte and its mould or tin, then turn out on to dessert plates. Serve with extra-thick double cream or custard.

HOT QUINCE SOUFFLÉS

THESE DELICIOUS FRUITS ARE MORE OFTEN PICKED THAN PURCHASED AS THEY ARE SELDOM FOUND IN SHOPS OR MARKETS. YOU CAN USE PEARS INSTEAD, BUT THE FLAVOUR WILL NOT BE AS INTENSE.

SERVES SIX

INGREDIENTS
2 quinces, peeled and cored
60ml/4 tbsp water
115g/4oz/½ cup caster sugar,
  plus extra for sprinkling
5 egg whites
melted butter, for greasing
icing sugar, for dusting
For the pastry cream
  250ml/8fl oz/1 cup milk
  1 vanilla pod
  3 egg yolks
  75g/3oz/⅓ cup caster sugar
  25g/1oz/¼ cup plain flour
  15ml/1 tbsp Poire William liqueur

1 Cut the quinces into cubes. Place in a saucepan with the water. Stir in half the sugar. Bring to the boil, lower the heat, cover and simmer for 10 minutes or until tender. Remove the lid; boil until most of the liquid has evaporated.

2 Cool slightly, then purée the fruit in a blender or food processor. Press through a sieve into a bowl; set aside.

3 Make the pastry cream. Pour the milk into a small saucepan. Add the vanilla pod and bring to the boil over a low heat. Meanwhile, beat the egg yolks, caster sugar and flour in a bowl until smooth.

4 Gradually strain the hot milk on to the yolks, whisking frequently until the mixture is smooth.

5 Discard the vanilla pod. Return the mixture to the clean pan and heat gently, stirring until thickened. Cook for a further 2 minutes, whisking constantly, to ensure that the sauce is smooth and the flour is cooked.

6 Remove the pan from the heat and stir in the quince purée and liqueur. Cover the surface of the pastry cream with clear film to prevent it from forming a skin. Allow to cool slightly, while you prepare the ramekins.

7 Preheat the oven to 220°C/425°F/ Gas 7. Place a baking sheet in the oven to heat up. Butter six 150ml/¼ pint/ ⅔ cup ramekins and sprinkle the inside of each with caster sugar. In a grease-free bowl, whisk the egg whites to stiff peaks. Gradually whisk in the remaining caster sugar, then fold the egg whites into the pastry cream.

8 Divide the mixture among the prepared ramekins and level the surface of each. Carefully run a sharp knife between the side of each ramekin and the mixture, then place the ramekins on the hot baking sheet and bake for 8–10 minutes until the tops of the soufflés are well risen and golden. Generously dust the tops with icing sugar and serve the soufflés at once.

COOK'S TIP
Poire William is a clear, colourless pear eau-de-vie, which sometimes is sold with a ripe pear in the bottle. Kirsch, made from cherries, also works well in this recipe to complement the flavour of the quinces.

DUTCH APPLE CAKE

THE APPLE TOPPING MAKES THIS CAKE REALLY MOIST. IT IS EQUALLY AS GOOD HOT OR COLD.

MAKES EIGHT TO TEN SLICES

INGREDIENTS
    250g/9oz/2¼ cups self-raising flour
    10ml/2 tsp baking powder
    5ml/1 tsp ground cinnamon
    130g/4½oz/generous ½ cup
      caster sugar
    50g/2oz/¼ cup butter, melted
    2 eggs, beaten
    150ml/¼ pint/⅔ cup milk
For the topping
    2 Cox's Orange Pippin apples
    15g/½oz/1 tbsp butter, melted
    60ml/4 tbsp demerara sugar
    1.5ml/¼ tsp ground cinnamon

VARIATION
Add a few sultanas or raisins to the
apples if you like.

1 Preheat the oven to 200°C/400°F/
Gas 6. Grease and line a 20cm/8in
round cake tin. Sift the flour, baking
powder and cinnamon into a large
mixing bowl. Stir in the caster sugar.
In a separate bowl, whisk the melted
butter, eggs and milk together, then stir
the mixture into the dry ingredients.

2 Pour the cake mixture into the
prepared tin, smooth the surface, then
make a shallow hollow in a ring around
the edge of the mixture.

3 Make the topping. Peel and core the
apples, slice them into wedges and slice
the wedges thinly. Arrange the slices
around the hollow of the cake mixture.
Brush with the melted butter, then
scatter the demerara sugar and ground
cinnamon over the top.

4 Bake for 45–50 minutes or until the
cake has risen well, is golden and a
skewer inserted into the centre comes
out clean. Serve immediately as a
dessert with cream, or remove from the
tin, peel off the lining paper and cool on
a wire rack before slicing.

PEAR AND POLENTA CAKE

*POLENTA GIVES THE LIGHT SPONGE THAT TOPS SLICED PEARS A NUTTY CORN FLAVOUR THAT
COMPLEMENTS THE FRUIT PERFECTLY. SERVE AS A DESSERT WITH CUSTARD OR CREAM.*

MAKES TEN SLICES

INGREDIENTS
    175g/6oz/¾ cup golden caster sugar
    4 ripe pears
    juice of ½ lemon
    30ml/2 tbsp clear honey
    3 eggs
    seeds from 1 vanilla pod
    120ml/4fl oz/½ cup sunflower oil
    115g/4oz/1 cup self-raising flour
    50g/2oz/⅓ cup instant polenta

1 Preheat the oven to 180°C/350°F/
Gas 4. Generously grease and line a
21cm/8½in round cake tin. Scatter
30ml/2 tbsp of the golden caster sugar
over the base of the prepared tin.

COOK'S TIP
Use the tip of a small, sharp knife to
scrape out the vanilla pod seeds. If you
do not have a vanilla pod, use 5ml/1 tsp
pure vanilla essence instead.

2 Peel and core the pears. Cut them
into chunky slices and toss in the lemon
juice. Arrange them on the base of the
prepared cake tin. Drizzle the honey
over the pears and set aside.

3 Mix together the eggs, seeds from
the vanilla pod and the remaining
golden caster sugar in a bowl.

4 Beat the egg mixture until thick and
creamy, then gradually beat in the oil.
Sift together the flour and polenta and
fold into the egg mixture.

5 Pour the mixture carefully into the tin
over the pears. Bake the cake for about
50 minutes or until a skewer inserted
into the centre comes out clean. Cool in
the tin for 10 minutes, then turn the
cake out on to a plate, peel off the
lining paper, invert and slice.

APPLE AND CIDER SAUCE

THIS SAUCE COULDN'T BE SIMPLER TO MAKE. IT TASTES GREAT WITH ROAST PORK, DUCK OR GOOSE.

MAKES 450G/1LB

INGREDIENTS
    450g/1lb Bramley apples
    150ml/¼ pint/⅔ cup sweet cider
    2.5ml/½ tsp cider vinegar
    25g/1oz/2 tbsp butter
    2 whole cloves
    a few sprigs of fresh thyme
    15ml/1 tbsp clear honey
    10ml/2 tsp Dijon mustard

1 Peel, core and slice the apples. Place them in a saucepan with the cider, cider vinegar, butter, cloves and thyme. Simmer over a low heat for 10 minutes or until the apples are soft and pulpy, stirring occasionally, then raise the heat and cook until most of the liquid has evaporated.

2 Remove the cloves and thyme sprigs and beat in the honey and mustard. Taste and add more honey if necessary, but the sauce is best when slightly tart.

COOK'S TIP
Press the sauce through a sieve if you prefer it to be perfectly smooth.

APPLE AND RED ONION MARMALADE

THIS MARMALADE CHUTNEY IS GOOD ENOUGH TO EAT ON ITS OWN. SERVE IT WITH PORK SAUSAGES FOR THOROUGHLY MODERN HOT DOGS OR IN A HAM SANDWICH INSTEAD OF MUSTARD.

MAKES 450G/1LB

INGREDIENTS
    60ml/4 tbsp extra virgin olive oil
    900g/2lb red onions, thinly sliced
    75g/3oz/½ cup demerara sugar
    2 Cox's Orange Pippin apples
    90ml/6 tbsp cider vinegar

1 Heat the oil in a large, heavy-based saucepan and add the onions.

2 Stir in the sugar and cook, uncovered, over a medium heat for about 40 minutes, stirring occasionally, or until the onions have softened and become a rich golden colour.

3 Peel, core and grate the apples. Add them to the pan with the vinegar and continue to cook for 20 minutes until the chutney is thick and sticky. Spoon into a sterilized jar and cover.

4 When cool, label and store in the fridge for up to 1 month.

STONE FRUITS

One of life's greatest joys is to bite into a perfectly ripe, juicy stone
fruit and savour the wonderful sweetness of the sticky juices.
Stone fruits herald summer — the season starts with cherries,
continues with sun-drenched peaches and apricots, and ends with
plums, from gorgeous greengages to fat, juicy Victorias. Although
stone fruits (or "drupes") may seem very different, they are all
members of the Prunus family and share the characteristics of soft,
juicy flesh and a single stone. Stone fruits are often grown in
greenhouses, but nothing beats the taste of a sun-ripened fruit,
so it is worth waiting until they are in season.

PEACHES

Sometimes known as the "queen of fruits", peaches are certainly among the most beautiful. Their downy, velvety skin is yellow, flushed with red, and they are voluptuously curvaceous – the French call one variety *tétons de Venus* (Venus' breasts).

The most familiar peaches are round or "beaked", with a pointed end, but they can also be flat and disc-shaped. The delicate fine-textured flesh, which can be yellow, white or tinged with red, encloses a heavily ridged stone. In some peaches, the flesh clings firmly to the stone; these are known as "clingstone". In "freestone" fruit, the flesh comes away easily and cleanly from the stone.

Peaches and nectarines originated from the same species and are very similar, except that peaches have fuzzy skin, while nectarines are smooth. So alike are they that peach trees sometimes spontaneously produce nectarines and vice versa.

History

Peaches have been grown in China since the fifth century BC and are regarded as a symbol of longevity and immortality. Even today, some Chinese families place peach trees or branches outside their front doors to ward off evil spirits. Peaches were taken along the old silk routes to Persia where they were discovered by Alexander the Great, who introduced them to the Greeks and Romans; the word "peach" comes from

Above: Mireille, a white-fleshed peach.

the Latin *Persicum malum* (Persian apple). Immensely popular in Europe, peaches were introduced to America by Christopher Columbus and spread so profusely that they were once thought to be indigenous. Nowadays, so many are grown in Georgia that it is known as the "peach state".

Varieties

Peaches are seldom sold by variety, but by the colour of their flesh – yellow or white. Which you choose is a matter of preference; some people believe that white peaches have the finer flavour.

Yellow varieties include Elegant Lady, Royal George and Bellegarde. Mireille is a popular white peach. The finest peaches of all are the *pêches de vigne*, small red-fleshed fruits that are grown in vineyards. They do not look particularly attractive, being covered in greyish down, but the flavour is superb. You are unlikely to find them outside markets in France.

Nutrition

Peaches are a source of vitamins A, B and C and provide about 60 kilo-calories per 100g/3¾oz.

Buying and Storing

Peaches do not ripen successfully after picking, so always buy ripe fruit. The fruits should be handled carefully. Press gently to ensure that they are firm, with some "give". Never buy greenish peaches, except for chutney-making, and avoid fruit with bruised skin. Peaches do not keep well. Firm fruit can be kept at room temperature for a day or two to soften; ripe peaches can be kept in the fridge for not more than two days.

Left: Elegant Lady – a popular yellow variety of peach.

Dried peaches These are not as widely available as dried apricots, but are becoming increasingly popular. Use them in compotes and cakes, or eat them on their own. Peaches are also crystallized or glacéed as a sweetmeat.

Canned peaches Available in syrup or apple juice, canned peaches are fine for cooking, but lack the delicate texture and flavour of the fresh fruit.

Above: Dried peaches

Glacé peaches The fruits are coated in a thick syrup, which hardens to a shiny glaze. Glacé peaches are often included in boxes of assorted glacé fruits. They are very sweet, with a melting texture.

Preparing and Serving

A really ripe peach is delicious eaten on its own or in a fruit salad. Peaches combine well with most other fruits and nuts, particularly raspberries, a marriage that inspired Escoffier to create his famous dessert, Peach Melba, in honour of the great singer

Above: Glacé peaches are coated in a thick sugar syrup and are very sweet.

Stoning a peach or nectarine

1 Slice through the seam line all around the peach.

2 Twist the two halves in opposite directions to separate them.

3 Lever out the stone with a knife.

Left: Canned peaches, available in halves or slices, are fine for cooking but lack the flavour of the fresh fruit.

Dame Nellie Melba. Fresh peaches feature in ice cream sundaes and can be used to make luxurious drinks like Bellini (Champagne, peach liqueur and crushed peach pulp) or Champagne cocktails. They are also made into liqueurs and peach wine and brandy.

The fuzzy skin of a peach is not particularly pleasant to eat, so the fruit is best peeled. Nick the fruit, place it in a heatproof bowl and pour over boiling water. Leave for 15–30 seconds, depending on how ripe the fruits are, then drain and refresh in cold water. The skins will peel off easily.

Cooking and Serving

Peaches can be cooked in a multitude of ways – poached whole in vanilla-flavoured syrup or wine; macerated in alcohol; in compotes, soufflés, pies,

tarts, pancakes, ice creams and sorbets. They make very good jams and jellies, while spiced peaches are delicious with cured or cold meats. Underripe green-tinged peaches can be made into excellent relishes and chutneys.

Peaches are also good, raw or cooked, in salads and are natural partners for gammon and duck. They can be substituted for mangoes in South-east Asian dishes and are particularly good with crab and lobster.

To poach peaches in syrup, put 1 litre/1¾ pints/ 4 cups water in a pan. Add 500g/1¼lb/2 cups granulated sugar, 2 strips of pared lemon rind, a piece of cinnamon and half a split

vanilla pod. Bring to the boil, stirring to dissolve the sugar. Boil for about 5 minutes, then add six to eight peeled peaches (whole or halved) and poach gently until tender, turning occasionally. Leave the fruit to cool in the syrup.

Peaches make a delicious sweet after-dinner liqueur, Crème de Peche, which can be drunk on its own, or combined with Champagne or sparking white wine to make an unusual cocktail. To make a classic Bellini, put some fresh peach pulp in a Champagne glass, add a teaspoon of peach liqueur and top up with Champagne.

Left: Peach liqueur

NECTARINES

The botanical name for nectarines is *Prunus persican*, meaning "Persian plum", although these smooth-skinned fruits are a variant of peaches and natives of China. They taste very similar to peaches, with a touch more acidity. The flesh can be yellow, white or pinkish and is delicate and sweet. Unlike peaches, they

do not require peeling, so some people prefer them as a dessert fruit. They can be prepared and cooked in exactly the same way as peaches. Nectarines are sometimes crossed with peaches, but the fuzzy peach skin is generally dominant, so the hybrids are often actually peaches.

Left: Smooth-skinned white nectarines

Nutrition

Nectarines have a lower calorie count than peaches (containing only about 45 kilocalories per 100g/3¾oz). They are a good source of potassium and phosphorus, dietary fibre and vitamins A and C.

Buying and Storing

Like peaches, nectarines do not continue to mature after picking, so choose ripe fruit. The skins should be bright and smooth, with no blemishes or wrinkles. Nectarines can be kept at room temperature or in the fridge for two or three days.

Left: Yellow nectarines

APRICOTS

These round, yellow-orange fruit have velvety skins flushed with pink. The flesh is firm, sweet and fragrant, and contains little juice. The kernel of the stone is edible and is used to flavour jams, biscuits and Amaretto liqueur.

Left: Ripe apricots are deliciously fragrant.

History

Apricots grew wild in China thousands of years ago and were introduced to Persia and Armenia, from where they got their Latin name *Prunus armeniaca*. Alexander the Great brought apricots to Southern Europe; they were prized by the Romans and Greeks, who called them "golden eggs of the sun". They were first successfully cultivated in Northern Europe in the sixteenth century.

Nutrition

Apricots contain the antioxidant beta-carotene, and are a rich source of minerals and vitamin A. An average 65g/2½oz apricot provides only 20 kilocalories.

Above: Turkish sun-dried apricots

Below: Semi-dried apricots

Buying and Storing

Apricots do not travel well, nor do they continue to ripen after picking, so those that you buy may be disappointing. Look for plump fruit with a rich colour and smooth skin. Do not buy dull-looking or greenish fruit, as their flesh will be woolly. Keep apricots at room temperature for a couple of days, or store in a polythene bag in the fridge for up to five days.

Dried and canned apricots Because apricots are so delicate, they are often preserved by drying or canning. The best dried apricots come from Turkey; they are burnished orange and have a rich flavour. Dried apricots can be substituted for fresh apricots and make excellent jams. Use them just as they are in slow-cooked dishes that contain plenty of liquid, like stews and casseroles, but, unless they are semi-dried, soak them in warm water for a couple of hours before using them in sweet dishes.

Preparing and Cooking

Ripe apricots are delicious raw and can be used in fruit salads and platters. Because

Right: Canned apricots

the flesh is dry, they will not disintegrate during cooking, which makes them ideal for tarts, flans and Danish pastries. Apricots can be poached in syrup or sweet white wine and served with yogurt or spice-flavoured ice cream; they are also very tasty when halved, stuffed with crushed amaretti biscuits and baked, or caramelized and served over *pain perdu*. Apricots make wonderful jams and conserves.

Both fresh and dried apricots make frequent appearances in Middle Eastern and North African recipes, where they go particularly well with lamb, poultry and rice dishes.

later date, plums can be frozen: halve the fruit and remove the stones. Place on trays and open freeze, then pack the fruit into polythene bags and seal.

Preparing and Cooking

Dessert plums are delicious eaten on their own. Dual varieties (suitable for eating and cooking) and cooking plums make excellent pies and tarts, compotes, crumbles, dumplings, sauces, mousses and soufflés. They can be poached, baked or stewed, either whole or in halves or slices. It is not recommended that plums with tough skins are cooked in the microwave, as they will not soften in the short cooking time. Cook plums until just tender; do not let them disintegrate. Plums make tasty ice cream, and the poached fruit goes very well with ice creams flavoured with spices like cardamom, nutmeg and cinnamon.

Plums go extremely well in savoury dishes. The Chinese make them into a thick sweet-sour sauce to serve with Peking duck, lamb or pork. Spiced stewed plums are good with gammon, cured meats, terrines and poultry. Plums add a special flavour to beef or lamb casseroles.

Plums also make superb jams and jellies. They can be preserved in many different

Above: Circiela Queen Rose

Below: Reeves Seedling

Below: Stanley

ways; dried (as prunes), crystallized and candied, bottled or made into wine, liqueurs and plum brandy.

Preserved plums There are many ways of preserving plums, the best-known being by drying them as prunes. In Spain, Elvas plums are partially dried, then rolled in granulated sugar. The Portuguese candy sweet greengages, while Carlsbad plums (named after the spa town, now Karlovy Vary) are a speciality of the Czech Republic. These plums (usually Quetsch) are candied in hot syrup until shrivelled, then halved and stuffed into dried damsons. The process gives them a very intense flavour. Carlsbad plums are considered a great delicacy and are packed into attractive wooden boxes.

Soaking prunes

Sometimes prunes need to be soaked for at least 4 hours before using. Place in a bowl and cover with cold water or tepid weak tea for added flavour. Leave overnight if possible to plump up. For compotes and purées it is not necessary to soak the prunes; cook them directly in wine, water or fruit juice until very tender.

Prunes These wrinkled dried purple or red plums can be prepared in various ways. The plums can be left to dry naturally on the tree, but are more often sun-dried. They can also be desiccated in a low oven. The finest variety of "pruning" plum is the Agen, which is grown in France and California. These prunes are sold complete with stones and must be soaked overnight before being cooked.

Left: Chinese plum sauce has a wonderful sweet-sour flavour and is classically served with Peking duck.

Nowadays, stoned no-soak prunes are also widely available, but they tend to be flabbier than the traditional variety. Apart from their famed laxative qualities, prunes have other healthful properites. They are said to be an excellent cure for hangovers, give a great energy boost, and are purported to be an aphrodisiac.

Culinary Uses

Cooked prunes are traditionally served with custard, but they are equally good with thick cream. They make excellent ice cream, especially when combined with Armagnac. Prunes are often used in savoury dishes, particularly in Middle Eastern cooking, and they go extremely well with pork and chicken. They are an essential ingredient in Scottish cock-a-leekie soup. They go well with citrus flavours and can be made into a compote with red wine and orange or lemon zest.

Below: Californian prunes

Left: Slivovitz – black Madjarka plums are crushed with their stones and slowly fermented to make this eau-de-vie from Croatia.

Puréed prunes can be sweetened, then spiced up with a little ground cinnamon or nutmeg and served as a sauce with vanilla ice cream.

Below: French Agen prunes

GREENGAGES

These small members of the plum family have green skins, sometimes tinged with yellow or rose pink, which turn golden as the fruit ripens. There are many varieties of greengage; all have firm flesh and a delicious honeyed flavour. "Transparent" gages have fine, translucent flesh; if you hold the fruit up to the light, you can clearly see the shadow of the stone. These golden gages have a particularly sweet flavour.

History

Wild greengages from Asia Minor were probably introduced to Britain by the Romans, but disappeared from cultivation until Sir Thomas Gage brought them from France in the eighteenth century (and gave them his name). In France, they are known as *Reine-Claude* after the wife of François I, who adored their sweet flavour.

Preparing and Cooking

The deliciously sweet flavour of greengages makes them ideal for eating raw. They can also be gently poached in syrup, puréed for mousses and fools or made into excellent compotes and jam.

Below: Greengages, named after Sir Thomas Gage, have firm flesh with a deliciously sweet flavour.

DAMSONS

These small plum-like fruits take their name from Damascus, which is probably where they originated. They have deep blue-black skins with an attractive bloom. The flavour is very strong and tart, which makes them more suitable for cooking than eating raw. Damsons grow wild in hedgerows, but are also commercially available.

Preparing and Cooking

Damsons can be stewed and used in pies, tarts, ice creams and fools, but they are most commonly used for bottling or for jams and jellies. Once cooked with sugar, they develop a pleasantly spicy flavour. A traditional old English sweetmeat is damson cheese, very thick fruit pulp boiled with sugar to make a solid jam similar to quince cheese, which can be eaten with bread and butter or biscuits.

The tart flavour of damsons makes them particularly suitable for savoury dishes, such as pork or lamb casseroles. The fruit can also be made into wine or damson gin.

Above: Once cooked, damsons have a pleasantly spicy flavour.

Damson cheese

Damson cheese is a traditional English country dish with a very distinctive flavour, which is an acquired taste. The "cheese" is potted and aged for several months before being eaten. To make 2.5kg/5½lb damson cheese, put 1.5kg/3½lb damsons in a saucepan, barely cover with water and simmer until the flesh is so tender that it falls off the stones. Sieve the pulp, weigh it and return it to the pan with three-quarters of its weight in soft light brown sugar. Boil until the jam is clear, skimming the surface frequently. Pot the jam in oiled straight-sided containers, seal and leave in a cool dark place for at least two months. Serve with bread and butter, and eat with a knife and fork.

BULLACES

The small round plums known as "black bullaces" have bluish-purple skins and mouth-puckeringly acid flesh. So-called "white" bullaces are pale greenish-yellow. They can be found throughout Europe in late autumn growing in thorny hedgerows long after the other wild fruits like sloes and blackberries have finished. Although very bitter and virtually inedible when raw, bullaces can be cooked with sugar to make pies and tarts. They are also good for jams and other preserves.

Right: The pale greenish-yellow fruits, known as "white" bullaces are almost inedible raw, but can be cooked with sugar to make delicious jams and jellies or a filling for pies.

SLOES

Sloes are the fruit of the blackthorn, a thorny shrub, which grows wild throughout Europe (hence its botanical name, *prunus spinosa*, which means spiny plum). These small wild fruits resemble tiny plums. The blue-black skins have a slight bloom. The flesh is highly astringent and cannot be eaten raw. Sloes ripen late and can be picked from the hedgerows in autumn, but they only become edible after the first frosts. They can be made into jams, jellies, sloe wine and liqueurs, but their chief claim to fame is that they are the principal ingredient of the irresistible sloe gin.

Make sloe gin as soon as the fruit is ripe,

and with any luck you'll have a bottle ready in time for Christmas. For each 750ml/1¼ pint bottle of gin, you will need 250g/9oz/2 cups sloes and 130g/4½oz/generous ½ cup caster sugar. Wash the sloes and prick them all over with a darning needle. Pack

them loosely into a perfectly clean flagon or bottle, add the sugar and top up with gin. If you like, add two or three drops of almond essence and shake well. Seal and leave for at least three months before drinking, shaking the bottles three times a week. If pricking the sloes seems too much trouble, freeze them for several hours to crack the skin. Purists however allege that this compromises the flavour of the gin.

Left: Sloes are small wild fruits, which grow in hedgerows throughout Europe. They are best picked in late autumn, after the first frosts.

CHERRIES

Cherry trees in blossom are one of the great delights of spring, followed in summer by clusters of bright shiny fruit hanging in pairs from long, elegant stalks. The skin of these small round stone fruits can vary in colour from pale creamy-yellow to deepest red or almost black. The firm juicy flesh can be sweet or sour, depending on the variety, of which there are hundreds. Cherries are categorized into three main groups: sweet (for eating), sour (for cooking) and hybrids such as the nobly named Dukes and Royals, which are suitable for eating raw or cooking.

Above: Bright red Colney cherries

Left: Napoleons are one of the sweet cherry varieties, with slightly crisp, tart, fragrant flesh.

History

The original wild sweet cherries, known as Mazzards, were found in Asia Minor and were cultivated by the Chinese 3,000 years ago. Mazzards were known to the Ancient Egyptians, Greeks and Romans, and still exist today. Sour cherries were brought to Rome from Greece and all modern varieties derive from these early specimens.

Varieties

Sweet cherries fall into two main groups: **Bigarreaus,** with firm, crisp flesh, and **Geans** or **Guines,** with a softer texture. Today, there are also many hybrids. Sour cherries range from almost sweet to bitter and tart; they are full of flavour and are mainly used for preserving or in the manufacture of liqueurs.

SWEET CHERRIES

BIGARREAUS The best-known of these are the **Napoleons,** large pale yellow cherries tinged with light red. Their crisp fragrant flesh is slightly tart. **Bing** cherries are large, heart-shaped deep red fruit with a superb flavour. They are widely grown in North America.
GEANS/GUINES These fruits have soft, juicy flesh and come in many colours. **Black Tartarian** are deep purplish-black from the skin right through to the stone. **Early Rivers** have dark purple skins and flesh, and very small stones. They are fragrant, sweet and juicy. **Ranier** has golden skin with a pink blush. The famous Swiss black cherry jam is made from intensely dark guines.

Left: Widely grown in North America, sweet Bing cherries have a superb flavour.

SOUR CHERRIES

Most sour cherries are too tart to eat, but are ideal for cooking. The two main types are **Morello** and **Amarelle**. Morellos have dark juice, and amarelles have light, almost colourless juice. The small, dark red morello cherries (known in France as *griottes*) are inedible raw, but are delicious preserved in either brandy or syrup.

Montmorency These are bright red cherries with a sweet-sour flavour. They have given their name to a range of dishes which include the fruit, from duck to gâteaux and ice creams.

English cherries are small, bright orange-red fruit with soft translucent flesh. They are mainly used for preserving in brandy.

Right: Morello cherries, which are often preserved in brandy.

Maraschino cherries

These small wild fruit from Dalmatia are *Damasca* or *Amaresca* cherries. They are distilled into a colourless sweet, sticky Italian liqueur called Maraschino. The familiar bottled Maraschino cherries beloved of barmen were originally Damasca cherries preserved in Maraschino liqueur; nowadays, the vibrant red fruits sold as "maraschino" tend to be ordinary cherries tinted with artificial colouring and steeped in syrup flavoured with bitter almonds. Check the label before buying.

Nutrition

Cherries contain vitamins A and C and some dietary fibre. Their calorie content varies with the type; sweet cherries provide about 77 kilocalories per 100g/3¾oz, while the same quantity of sour fruit provides about 56 kilocalories.

Buying and Storing

Choose plump cherries with shiny, unblemished skins. It is best to buy them still on the stalk. As a rule of thumb, pale cherries are very sweet, while dark cherries tend to be more acidic; if possible, taste before you buy.

Unwashed cherries will keep for a few days in the fridge; wash them just before using. They can also be removed from their stalks and frozen.

Preparing and Cooking

Sweet cherries often need no preparation other than washing and are best eaten on their own or in fruit salads. They make unusual sweets when left on the stalk and dipped into melted dark chocolate. Stoned fresh cherries make a delicious filling for sponge cakes and pavlovas, or an attractive decoration for gâteaux and desserts. There is no reason not to cook with sweet cherries, but they may not have much flavour, due to their low acidity. Although fresh cherries can be served as they are, for cooking they should be stoned.

Cherries can be preserved by drying in the sun or in a low oven, or by placing in sugar or brandy. Candied – or glacé – cherries are a popular ingredient in baking.

Dual-purpose and sour cherries can be cooked in tarts, pies, compotes and sauces. They go well with sweet spices, citrus flavours and chocolate; the classic combination of cherries and chocolate is found in Black Forest Gâteau. In Eastern Europe, they are made into a sweet-sour soup or pickled in spiced vinegar as an accompaniment for rich meats. Cherries go well with all game and are classically served with duck. Amarelle and Morello cherries are used for making jam and preserves, or for crystallizing as glacé cherries.

Above: Dried sour Montmorency and Bing cherries

Left and below: Maraschino cherries may be bottled with their stalks.

Below: Brightly coloured, sweet and sticky glacé cherries are a popular baking ingredient.

STONE FRUIT RECIPES

*Juicy and full of flavour, peaches, plums, apricots,
cherries and nectarines make perfect partners
for crisp pastry. Try the irresistible Baked
Lattice Peaches or Plum and Marzipan Pastries.
For simpler, but equally delicious desserts,
plump for Peach Melba Syllabub or Plum and
Custard Creams.*

PLUM AND CUSTARD CREAMS

IF YOU WERE RELUCTANTLY RAISED ON STEWED PLUMS AND CUSTARD, THIS SOPHISTICATED VERSION, PRETTILY LAYERED IN A GLASS, WILL BRING A SMILE TO YOUR LIPS.

SERVES SIX

INGREDIENTS

675g/1½lb red plums, stoned
  and sliced
grated rind and juice of 1 orange
50g/2oz/¼ cup caster sugar
400g/14oz carton ready-made
  custard
300ml/½ pint/1¼ cups double cream
30ml/2 tbsp water
15ml/1 tbsp powdered gelatine
1 egg white
plum slices and fresh mint sprigs,
  to decorate

COOK'S TIP
Use a long metal skewer or thin metal spoon handle to marble the custard and plum purée mixtures together.

1 Put the plums in a saucepan with the orange rind and juice. Add the caster sugar and heat, stirring constantly, until the sugar has dissolved. Cook the plums for 5 minutes until tender. Cool slightly, then purée in a food processor until smooth. Press through a sieve into a bowl and set aside to cool.

2 Put the custard in a saucepan, add half the cream and heat until boiling. Meanwhile, pour the water into a heatproof bowl and sprinkle the gelatine on top; set aside for 5 minutes until sponged. Whisk the soaked gelatine into the hot custard until it has dissolved. Allow the mixture to cool.

3 Whip the remaining cream to soft peaks, then fold it into the custard mixture. In a grease-free bowl, whisk the egg white to soft peaks; fold it into the custard too. Set aside, stirring occasionally, until just starting to set.

4 Quickly spoon alternate spoonfuls of the custard and plum purée into six tall dessert glasses. Marble the mixtures together. Chill for 2–3 hours or until the custard has set. Decorate each dessert with plum slices and fresh mint sprigs just before serving.

SPICED FRUITS JUBILEE

BASED ON THE CLASSIC CHERRIES JUBILEE, THIS IS A GREAT WAY TO USE A GLUT OF ANY STONE FRUIT.
THE SPICED SYRUP IS A DELICIOUS BONUS. SERVE WITH THE BEST DAIRY VANILLA ICE CREAM.

SERVES SIX

INGREDIENTS

115g/4oz/½ cup caster sugar
thinly pared rind of 1 unwaxed lemon
1 cinnamon stick
4 whole cloves
300ml/½ pint/1¼ cups water
225g/8oz tart red plums, stoned
   and sliced
225g/8oz nectarines, stoned
   and chopped
225g/8oz/1½ cups cherries, stoned
5ml/1 tsp arrowroot
75ml/5 tbsp brandy
vanilla ice cream, to serve

1 Put the sugar, lemon rind, cinnamon stick, cloves and water in a pan. Bring to the boil, stirring. Lower the heat and simmer for 5 minutes, then lift out the spices with a slotted spoon and discard.

2 Add the fruit, cover the pan and simmer for 5 minutes. Drain the fruit and set it aside; return the syrup to the pan. Boil it, uncovered, for 2 minutes or until thick and syrupy.

3 Put the arrowroot in a small bowl and stir in 30ml/2 tbsp of the brandy. Stir the mixture into the syrup. Continue cooking and stirring, until the sauce thickens. Return the fruit to the pan.

4 Place scoops of ice cream in serving bowls and spoon the hot fruit over. Warm the remaining brandy in a small pan, then set it alight. Ladle it over the fruit at the table for maximum effect.

PEACH MELBA SYLLABUB

IF YOU ARE MAKING THESE SOPHISTICATED TEMPTATIONS FOR A DINNER PARTY, COOK THE PEACHES AND RASPBERRIES THE DAY BEFORE TO ALLOW THE FRUIT TO CHILL. WHIP UP THE SYLLABUB AT THE VERY LAST MINUTE TO MAKE A DELICIOUS, LIGHT-AS-A-CLOUD TOPPING.

SERVES SIX

INGREDIENTS
   4 peaches, peeled, stoned and sliced
   300ml/½ pint/1¼ cups blush or red
      grape juice
   115g/4oz/⅔ cup raspberries
   raspberry or mint leaves, to decorate
   ratafias or other dessert biscuits,
      to serve
For the syllabub
   60ml/4 tbsp peach schnapps
   30ml/2 tbsp blush or red grape juice
   300ml/½ pint/1¼ cups double cream

VARIATIONS
Use dessert pears and sliced kiwi fruit
instead of peaches and raspberries.
Instead of the syllabub, top the fruit with
whipped cream flavoured with Advocaat
and finely chopped stem ginger.

1   Place the peach slices in a large saucepan. Add the grape juice. Bring to the boil, then cover, lower the heat and simmer for 5–7 minutes or until tender.

2   Add the raspberries and remove from the heat. Set aside in the fridge until cold. Divide the peach and raspberry mixture among six dessert glasses.

3   For the syllabub, place the peach schnapps and grape juice in a large bowl and whisk in the cream until it forms soft peaks.

4   Spoon the syllabub on top of the fruit and decorate each portion with a fresh raspberry or mint leaf. Serve with ratafias or other dessert biscuits.

NECTARINE AND HAZELNUT MERINGUES

IF IT'S INDULGENCE YOU'RE SEEKING, LOOK NO FURTHER. SWEET NECTARINES AND CREAM SYLLABUB PAIRED WITH CRISP HAZELNUT MERINGUES MAKE A SUPERB SWEET.

SERVES FIVE

INGREDIENTS
   3 egg whites
   175g/6oz/¾ cup caster sugar
   50g/2oz/½ cup chopped
      hazelnuts, toasted
   300ml/½ pint/1¼ cups double cream
   60ml/4 tbsp sweet dessert wine
   2 nectarines, stoned and sliced
   fresh mint sprigs, to decorate

VARIATIONS
Use apricots instead of nectarines if you
prefer, or try this with a raspberry filling.

1   Preheat the oven to 140°C/275°F/ Gas 1. Line two large baking sheets with non-stick baking paper. Whisk or beat the egg whites in a grease-free bowl until they form stiff peaks when the whisk or beaters are lifted. Gradually whisk in the caster sugar a spoonful at a time until the mixture forms a stiff, glossy meringue.

2   Fold in two-thirds of the chopped toasted hazelnuts, then spoon five large ovals on to each lined baking sheet. Scatter the remaining hazelnuts over five of the meringue ovals. Flatten the tops of the remaining five ovals.

3   Bake the meringues for 1–1¼ hours until crisp and dry, then carefully lift them off the baking paper and cool completely on a wire rack.

4   Whip the cream with the dessert wine until the mixture forms soft peaks. Spoon some of the cream syllabub on to each of the plain meringues. Arrange a few nectarine slices on each. Put each meringue on a dessert plate with a hazelnut-topped meringue. Decorate each portion with mint sprigs and serve the meringues immediately.

BLACK CHERRY CLAFOUTIS

THIS FAVOURITE RECIPE HAS BEEN REPRODUCED WITH ALL MANNER OF FRUIT, BUT YOU SIMPLY CAN'T BEAT THE CLASSIC VERSION USING SLIGHTLY TART BLACK CHERRIES.

SERVES SIX

INGREDIENTS

    25g/1oz/2 tbsp butter, for greasing
    450g/1lb/2 cups black
        cherries, stoned
    25g/1oz/¼ cup plain flour
    50g/2oz/½ cup icing sugar, plus extra
        for dusting
    4 eggs, beaten
    250ml/8fl oz/1 cup creamy milk
    30ml/2 tbsp Kirsch

1 Preheat the oven to 180°C/350°F/
Gas 4. Use the butter to thickly grease
a 1.2 litre/2 pint/5 cup gratin dish.
Scatter the cherries over the base.

2 Sift the flour and icing sugar together
into a large mixing bowl and gradually
whisk in the eggs until the mixture is
smooth. Whisk in the milk until
blended, then stir in the Kirsch.

3 Pour the batter carefully over the
cherries, then bake for 35–45 minutes
or until just set and lightly golden.

4 Allow the pudding to cool for about
15 minutes. Dust liberally with icing
sugar just before serving.

VARIATIONS
Try other liqueurs in this dessert.
Almond-flavoured liqueur is delicious
teamed with cherries. Hazelnut,
raspberry or orange liqueur would also
work nicely.

ICED GIN AND DAMSON SOUFFLÉS

FOR AN UNFORGETTABLE TASTE SENSATION, USE SLOE GIN FOR THESE DELICIOUS INDIVIDUAL FROZEN SOUFFLÉS. THEY ARE PERFECT FOR A PARTY AND CAN BE MADE AHEAD.

MAKES SIX

INGREDIENTS
500g/1¼lb damsons
250ml/8fl oz/1 cup water
275g/10oz/1¼ cups caster sugar
30ml/2 tbsp gin or sloe gin
4 large egg whites
300ml/½ pint/1¼ cups double
  cream, whipped
fresh mint leaves, to decorate

1 You will need six 150ml/¼ pint/⅔ cup ramekins. Give each a collar of greased non-stick baking paper that extends about 5cm/2in above the rim.

2 Slice two damsons and set aside for the decoration. Put the rest of the damsons in a pan with half the water and 50g/2oz/¼ cup of the caster sugar. Cover and simmer the mixture for about 7 minutes, or until the damsons are tender. Press the pulp through a sieve placed over a bowl to remove all the stones and skin, then stir in the gin or sloe gin and set aside.

3 Combine the remaining sugar and water in the clean pan and heat gently until the sugar has dissolved. Bring to the boil and cook the syrup until it registers 119°C/238°F on a sugar thermometer, or until a small amount of the mixture dropped into a cup of cold water can be moulded to a soft ball.

4 Meanwhile, whisk the egg whites in a grease-free bowl until they form stiff peaks. Still whisking, slowly pour in the hot syrup until the meringue mixture is stiff and glossy. Fold in the whipped cream and fruit purée until combined.

5 Spoon into the dishes to come 2.5cm/1in above the rim of each. Freeze until firm. Remove from the freezer 10 minutes before serving. Remove the collars, then decorate each with damson slices and mint leaves.

CARAMELIZED APRICOTS WITH PAIN PERDU

PAIN PERDU IS A FRENCH INVENTION THAT LITERALLY TRANSLATES AS "LOST BREAD". AMERICANS CALL IT FRENCH TOAST, WHILE A BRITISH VERSION IS KNOWN AS POOR KNIGHTS OF WINDSOR.

SERVES FOUR

INGREDIENTS
  75g/3oz/6 tbsp unsalted
    butter, clarified
  450g/1lb apricots, stoned and
    thickly sliced
  115g/4oz/½ cup caster sugar
  150ml/¼ pint/⅔ cup double cream
  30ml/2 tbsp apricot brandy or brandy
For the pain perdu
  600ml/1 pint/2½ cups milk
  1 vanilla pod
  50g/2oz/¼ cup caster sugar
  4 large eggs, beaten
  115g/4oz/½ cup unsalted
    butter, clarified
  6 brioche slices, diagonally halved
  2.5ml/½ tsp ground cinnamon

1 Heat a heavy-based frying pan, then melt a quarter of the butter. Add the apricot slices and cook for 2–3 minutes until golden. Using a slotted spoon, transfer them to a bowl. Add the rest of the butter to the pan with the sugar and heat gently, stirring, until golden.

2 Pour in the cream and apricot or brandy and cook gently until the mixture forms a smooth sauce. Boil for 2–3 minutes until thickened, pour the sauce over the apricots and set aside.

3 To make the pain perdu, pour the milk into a saucepan and add the vanilla pod and half the sugar. Heat gently until almost boiling, then set aside to cool.

4 Remove the vanilla pod and pour the flavoured milk into a shallow dish. Whisk in the eggs. Heat a sixth of the butter in the clean frying pan. Dip each slice of brioche in turn into the milk mixture, add it to the pan and fry until golden brown on both sides. Add the remaining butter as needed. As the pain perdu is cooked, remove the slices; keep hot.

5 Warm the apricot sauce and spoon it on to the pain perdu. Mix the remaining sugar with the cinnamon and sprinkle a little of the mixture over each portion.

COOK'S TIP
To clarify the butter, melt it in a small saucepan, then leave it to stand for a few minutes. Carefully pour the clear butter (the clarified butter) on the surface into a small bowl, leaving the milky solids behind in the pan.

FRESH CHERRY AND HAZELNUT STRUDEL

SERVE THIS WONDERFUL OLD-WORLD TREAT AS A WARM DESSERT WITH CUSTARD, OR ALLOW IT TO COOL AND OFFER IT AS A SCRUMPTIOUS CAKE WITH AFTERNOON TEA OR COFFEE.

SERVES SIX TO EIGHT

INGREDIENTS
75g/3oz/6 tbsp butter
90ml/6 tbsp light muscovado sugar
3 egg yolks
grated rind of 1 lemon
1.5ml/¼ tsp grated nutmeg
250g/9oz/generous 1 cup ricotta
  cheese
8 large sheets filo pastry, thawed
  if frozen
75g/3oz ratafias, crushed
450g/1lb/2½ cups cherries, stoned
30ml/2 tbsp chopped hazelnuts
icing sugar, for dusting
crème fraîche, to serve

1 Preheat the oven to 190°C/375°F/ Gas 5. Soften 15g/½oz/1 tbsp of the butter. Place it in a bowl and beat in the sugar and egg yolks until light and fluffy. Beat in the lemon rind, nutmeg and ricotta, then set aside.

2 Melt the remaining butter in a small pan. Working quickly, place a sheet of filo on a clean tea towel and brush it generously with melted butter. Place a second sheet on top and repeat the process. Continue until all the filo has been layered and buttered, reserving some of the melted butter.

3 Scatter the crushed ratafias over the top, leaving a 5cm/2in border around the outside. Spoon the ricotta mixture over the biscuits, spread it lightly to cover, then scatter over the cherries.

4 Fold in the filo pastry border and use the dish towel to carefully roll up the strudel, Swiss-roll style, beginning from one of the long sides of the pastry. Grease a baking sheet with the remaining melted butter.

5 Place the strudel on the baking sheet and scatter the hazelnuts over the surface. Bake for 35–40 minutes or until the strudel is golden and crisp. Dust with icing sugar and serve with a dollop of crème fraîche.

BAKED LATTICE PEACHES

IF YOU WOULD RATHER USE NECTARINES FOR THE RECIPE, THERE'S NO NEED TO PEEL THEM FIRST.

INGREDIENTS
3 peaches
juice of ½ lemon
75g/3oz/scant ½ cup white marzipan
375g/13oz ready-rolled puff pastry,
  thawed if frozen
a large pinch of ground cinnamon
beaten egg, to glaze
caster sugar, for sprinkling
For the caramel sauce
50g/2oz/¼ cup caster sugar
30ml/2 tbsp cold water
150ml/¼ pint/⅔ cup double cream

1 Preheat the oven to 190°C/375°F/
Gas 5. Place the peaches in a large
bowl and pour over boiling water to
cover. Leave for 60 seconds, then drain
the peaches and peel off the skins. Toss
the skinned fruit in the lemon juice to
stop them going brown.

2 Divide the marzipan into six pieces
and shape each to form a small round.
Cut the peaches in half and remove
their stones. Fill the stone cavity in each
with a marzipan round.

3 Unroll the puff pastry and cut it in
half. Set one half aside, then cut out six
rounds from the rest, making each
round slightly larger than a peach half.
Sprinkle a little cinnamon on each
pastry round, then place a peach half,
marzipan side down, on the pastry.

4 Cut the remaining pastry into lattice
pastry, using a special cutter if you have
one. If not, simply cut small slits in rows
all over the pastry, starting each row
slightly lower than the last. Cut the
lattice pastry into six equal squares.

5 Dampen the edges of the pastry
rounds with a little water, then drape a
lattice pastry square over each peach
half. Press around the edge to seal,
then trim off the excess pastry and
decorate with small peach leaves made
from the trimmings. Transfer the peach
pastries to a baking sheet. Brush with
the beaten egg and sprinkle with the
caster sugar. Bake for 20 minutes or
until the pastries are golden.

6 Meanwhile, make the caramel sauce.
Heat the sugar with the water in a small
pan until it dissolves. Bring to the boil
and continue to boil until the syrup
turns a dark golden brown. Stand back
and add the cream. Heat gently, stirring
until smooth. Serve the peach pastries
with the sauce.

COOK'S TIP
Take care when adding the cream to the
hot caramel as the mixture is liable to
spit. Pour it from a jug, protecting your
hand with an oven glove, and use a long-
handled wooden spoon for stirring.

PEACH AND REDCURRANT TARTLETS

TART REDCURRANTS AND SWEET PEACHES MAKE A WINNING COMBINATION IN THESE SIMPLE TARTLETS.

MAKES FOUR

INGREDIENTS
 25g/1oz/2 tbsp butter, melted
 16 × 15cm/6in squares of filo pastry,
  thawed if frozen
 redcurrant sprigs, to decorate
 icing sugar, for dusting
For the filling
 150ml/¼ pint/⅔ cup double cream
 125g/4¼oz carton peach and mango
  fromage frais
 a few drops of pure vanilla essence
 15ml/1 tbsp icing sugar, sifted
For the topping
 2 peaches
 50g/2oz/½ cup redcurrants

COOK'S TIP
To strip redcurrants from their stalks,
pull the stalks through the tines of a fork.

1 Preheat the oven to 190°C/375°F/
Gas 5. Use a little of the butter to grease
four large bun tins or individual tartlet
tins. Brush the pastry squares with
butter, stack them in fours, then place in
the tins to make four pastry cases.

2 Bake for 12–15 minutes until golden.
Cool the filo cases on a wire rack.

3 Make the filling. Whip the cream to
soft peaks, then lightly fold in the
fromage frais, vanilla essence and icing
sugar. Divide among the pastry cases.

4 Slice the peaches and fan them out
on top of the filling, interspersing with
a few redcurrants. Decorate with redcurrant sprigs and dust with icing sugar.

PLUM AND MARZIPAN PASTRIES

THESE DANISH PASTRIES CAN BE MADE WITH ANY STONED FRUIT. TRY APRICOTS, CHERRIES, DAMSONS OR GREENGAGES, ADDING A GLAZE MADE FROM CLEAR HONEY OR A COMPLEMENTARY JAM.

MAKES SIX

INGREDIENTS
375g/13oz ready-rolled puff pastry
90ml/6 tbsp plum jam
115g/4oz/½ cup white
marzipan, coarsely grated
3 red plums, halved and stoned
1 egg, beaten
50g/2oz/½ cup flaked almonds
For the glaze
30ml/2 tbsp plum jam
15ml/1 tbsp water

1 Preheat the oven to 220°C/425°F/
Gas 7. Unroll the pastry, cut it into six
equal squares and place on one or two
dampened baking sheets.

2 Spoon 15ml/1 tbsp jam into the
centre of each pastry square. Divide the
marzipan among them. Place half a
plum, hollow-side down, on top of each
marzipan mound.

3 Brush the edges of the pastry with
beaten egg. Bring up the corners and
press them together lightly, then open
out the pastry corners at the top. Glaze
the pastries with a little beaten egg,
then press a sixth of the flaked almonds
on to each.

4 Bake the pastries for 20–25 minutes
or until they are lightly golden.

5 Meanwhile, make the glaze by
heating the jam and water in a small
pan, stirring until smooth. Press the
mixture through a sieve into a small
bowl, then brush it over the tops of the
pastries while they are still warm. Leave
to cool on a wire rack.

YELLOW PLUM TART

IN THIS TART, GLAZED YELLOW PLUMS SIT ATOP A DELECTABLE ALMOND FILLING IN A CRISP PASTRY SHELL. WHEN THEY ARE IN SEASON, GREENGAGES MAKE AN EXCELLENT ALTERNATIVE TO THE PLUMS.

SERVES EIGHT

INGREDIENTS
  175g/6oz/1½ cups plain flour
  a pinch of salt
  75g/3oz/scant ½ cup butter, chilled
  30ml/2 tbsp caster sugar
  a few drops of pure vanilla essence
  45ml/3 tbsp iced water
  cream or custard, to serve
For the filling
  75g/3oz/⅓ cup caster sugar
  75g/3oz/scant ½ cup butter, softened
  75g/3oz/¾ cup ground almonds
  1 egg, beaten
  30ml/2 tbsp plain flour
  450g/1lb yellow plums or greengages,
    halved and stoned
For the glaze
  45ml/3 tbsp apricot jam, sieved
  15ml/1 tbsp water

1 Sift the flour and salt into a bowl, then rub in the chilled butter until the mixture resembles fine breadcrumbs. Stir in the caster sugar, vanilla essence and enough of the iced water to make a soft dough.

COOK'S TIP
Ceramic baking beans are ideal for baking blind, but any dried beans will do. You can use them over and over again, but make sure you keep them in a special jar, separate from the rest of your dried beans, as you cannot use them for conventional cooking.

2 Knead the dough gently on a lightly floured surface until smooth, then wrap in clear film and chill for 10 minutes.

3 Preheat the oven to 200°C/400°F/ Gas 6. Roll out the pastry and line a 23cm/9in fluted flan tin, allowing excess pastry to overhang the top. Prick the base with a fork and line with non-stick baking paper and baking beans.

4 Bake blind for 10 minutes, remove the paper and beans, then return the pastry case to the oven for 10 minutes. Remove and allow to cool. Trim off any excess pastry with a sharp knife.

5 To make the filling, whisk or beat together all the ingredients except the plums or greengages. Spread on the base of the pastry case. Arrange the plums or greengages on top, cut side down. Make a glaze by heating the jam with the water. Strain through a sieve into a small bowl then brush a little of the jam glaze over the top of the fruit.

6 Bake the tart for 50–60 minutes, until the almond filling is cooked and the plums or greengages are tender. Warm any remaining jam glaze and brush it over the top. Cut into slices and serve with cream or custard.

APRICOT PARCELS

THESE LITTLE FILO PARCELS CONTAIN A SPECIAL APRICOT AND MINCEMEAT FILLING. A GOOD WAY TO USE UP ANY MINCEMEAT AND MARZIPAN THAT HAVE BEEN IN YOUR CUPBOARD SINCE CHRISTMAS!

MAKES EIGHT

INGREDIENTS
  350g/12oz filo pastry, thawed
    if frozen
  50g/2oz/¼ cup butter, melted
  8 apricots, halved and stoned
  60ml/4 tbsp luxury mincemeat
  12 ratafias, crushed
  30ml/2 tbsp grated marzipan
  icing sugar, for dusting

COOK'S TIP
Filo pastry dries out quickly, so keep any squares not currently being used covered under a clean damp dish towel. Also, work as quickly as possible. If the filo should turn dry and brittle, simply brush it with melted butter to moisten.

1 Preheat the oven to 200°C/400°F/ Gas 6. Cut the filo pastry into 32 × 18cm/7in squares. Brush four of the squares with a little melted butter and stack them, giving each layer a quarter turn so that the stack acquires a star shape. Repeat to make eight stars.

2 Place an apricot half, hollow up, in the centre of each pastry star. Mix together the mincemeat, crushed ratafias and marzipan and spoon a little of the mixture into the hollow in each apricot.

3 Top with another apricot half, then bring the corners of each pastry together and squeeze to make a gathered purse.

4 Place the purses on a baking sheet and brush each with a little melted butter. Bake for 15–20 minutes or until the pastry is golden and crisp. Lightly dust with icing sugar to serve. Whipped cream, flavoured with a little brandy, makes an ideal accompaniment.

CRUNCHY-TOPPED FRESH APRICOT CAKE

*ALMONDS ARE PERFECT PARTNERS FOR FRESH APRICOTS, AND THIS IS A GREAT WAY TO USE UP FIRM
FRUITS. SERVE COLD AS A CAKE OR WARM WITH CUSTARD FOR A DESSERT.*

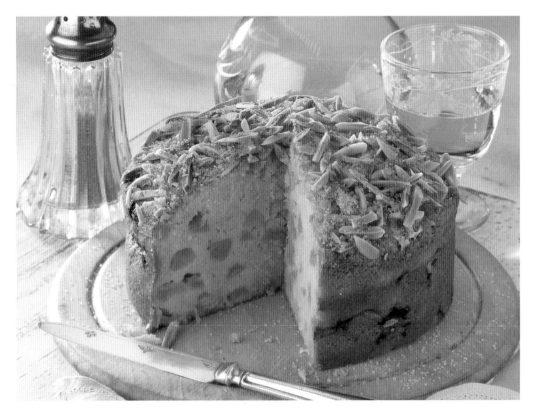

MAKES EIGHT SLICES

INGREDIENTS
 175g/6oz/1½ cups self-raising flour
 175g/6oz/¾ cup butter, softened
 175g/6oz/¾ cup caster sugar
 115g/4oz/1 cup ground almonds
 3 eggs
 5ml/1 tsp almond essence
 2.5ml/½ tsp baking powder
 8 firm apricots, stoned and chopped
For the topping
 30ml/2 tbsp demerara sugar
 50g/2oz/½ cup flaked almonds

1 Preheat the oven to 160°C/325°F/
Gas 3. Grease an 18cm/7in round cake
tin and line with non-stick baking paper.
Put all the cake ingredients, except the
apricots, in a large mixing bowl and
whisk until creamy.

2 Fold the apricots into the cake
mixture, then spoon into the prepared
cake tin. Make a hollow in the centre
with the back of a large spoon, then
scatter 15ml/1 tbsp of the demerara
sugar over for the topping, with the
flaked almonds.

3 Bake for 1½ hours or until a skewer
inserted into the centre comes out
clean. Scatter the remaining demerara
sugar over the top of the cake and
leave to cool for 10 minutes in the tin.
Remove from the tin, peel off the paper
and finish cooling on a wire rack.

PICKLED PEACH AND CHILLI CHUTNEY

THIS IS A REALLY SPICY, RICH CHUTNEY THAT IS GREAT SERVED WITH COLD ROAST MEATS SUCH AS HAM, PORK OR TURKEY. IT IS ALSO GOOD WITH A STRONG FARMHOUSE CHEDDAR CHEESE.

MAKES 450G/1LB

INGREDIENTS
  475ml/16fl oz/2 cups cider vinegar
  275g/10oz/1⅔ cups light
    muscovado sugar
  225g/8oz/1 cup dried dates, stoned
    and finely chopped
  5ml/1 tsp ground allspice
  5ml/1 tsp ground mace
  450g/1lb ripe peaches, stoned and
    cut into small chunks
  3 onions, thinly sliced
  4 fresh red chillies, seeded and
    finely chopped
  4 garlic cloves, crushed
  5cm/2in piece of fresh root ginger,
    finely grated
  5ml/1 tsp salt

1 Place the vinegar, sugar, dates and spices in a large saucepan and bring to the boil, stirring occasionally.

2 Add all the remaining ingredients and return to the boil. Lower the heat and simmer for 40–50 minutes or until thick. Stir often to prevent the mixture from burning on the base of the pan.

3 Spoon into sterilized jars and seal. When cold, store the jars in the fridge and use within 2 months.

COOK'S TIP
To test the consistency of the finished chutney before bottling, spoon a little of the mixture on to a plate: the chutney is ready once it holds its shape.

NECTARINE RELISH

THIS SWEET AND TANGY FRUIT RELISH GOES VERY WELL WITH HOT ROAST MEATS, ESPECIALLY PORK AND GAME BIRDS SUCH AS GUINEA FOWL AND PHEASANT. MAKE WHILE NECTARINES ARE PLENTIFUL AND KEEP TIGHTLY COVERED IN THE FRIDGE TO SERVE AT CHRISTMAS FOR A REALLY SPECIAL TREAT.

MAKES 450G/1LB

INGREDIENTS
  45ml/3 tbsp olive oil
  2 Spanish onions, thinly sliced
  1 fresh green chilli, seeded and
    finely chopped
  5ml/1 tsp finely chopped
    fresh rosemary
  2 bay leaves
  450g/1lb nectarines, stoned and cut
    into chunks
  150g/5oz/1 cup raisins
  10ml/2 tsp crushed coriander seeds
  350g/12oz/2 cups demerara sugar
  200ml/7fl oz/scant 1 cup red
    wine vinegar

1 Heat the oil in a large pan. Add the onions, chilli, rosemary and bay leaves. Cook, stirring often, for 15–20 minutes or until the onions are soft.

COOK'S TIP
Jars of this relish make a welcome gift. Add a colourful tag reminding the recipient to keep it in the fridge.

2 Add all the remaining ingredients and bring to the boil slowly, stirring often. Lower the heat and simmer for 1 hour or until the relish is thick and sticky, stirring occasionally.

3 Spoon into sterilized jars and seal. Cool, then chill. The relish will keep in the fridge for up to 5 months.

BERRIES AND CURRANTS

Small wonders — that sums up the splendour of berries.
The glowing colours and delectable flavours of strawberries and
raspberries, gooseberries, currants, loganberries and blackberries
(to name but a few of the many varieties) give us immense
pleasure. Whether you brave the brambles or pick up a punnet
at your local supermarket, these wonderful treats
are there for the taking.

STRAWBERRIES

For centuries, strawberries have been the most highly prized soft fruit. A sixteenth-century enthusiast, on tasting his first strawberry, summed up their eternal appeal: "Doubtless God could have made a better berry, but doubtless He never did". Nowadays, greenhouse-grown strawberries are available all year round, but these fruits are at their seductive best when grown outdoors.

History

Cultivated strawberries derive from the small wild fraises des bois, tiny fragrant woodland fruits that grow in all temperate countries and which were transplanted into kitchen gardens as early as Roman times. By the fourteenth century, the French had become strawberry enthusiasts, but it was another hundred years before the first bowls of strawberries and cream were served in England, at a banquet given by Cardinal Wolsey in 1509.

The cultivated strawberries we enjoy so much today were developed in the nineteenth century from small scarlet wild strawberries from Virginia. These were crossed with the larger yellow Chilean pine strawberries, which the aptly named French Captain Frézier (the French word for strawberry is *fraise*) had brought to Brittany in 1712. Once the perfect balance of flavour and size had been achieved, enthusiasm for cultivated strawberries blossomed and they remain one of the world's favourite fruits.

Above: These tiny wild woodland fruits, fraises des bois, have a lovely perfumed flavour.

Below: Cultivated strawberries like these are now one of the world's favourite fruits.

Varieties

Strawberries come in many different sizes, colours and shapes, ranging from conical to globular to oval or heart-shaped. New varieties are constantly being developed.

Left: Fraise de Bois liqueur is a wild strawberry version of crème de fraise.

Below: Fragrantly scented and vanilla-flavoured white fraises des bois.

Above: Gorella – conical-shaped and deep red when ripe.

Left: Cambridge Favourite – medium-size strawberries that are popular with both commercial growers and gardeners.

Below: Elsanta have a great flavour.

FRAISES DES BOIS

The smallest wild strawberries are the **Hautbois** varieties, whose tiny red fruits taste wonderfully fragrant. **Alpine** strawberries are generally a little larger and less juicy, with a highly perfumed flavour. Yellow and white varieties look less appealing, but have a delicious flavour of vanilla.

SUMMER STRAWBERRIES

Cambridge Favourite Medium-size berries with an attractive colour and flavour, this variety is indeed a favourite with strawberry-growers large and small.
Elsanta Largish, firm berries with attractive glossy flesh and an excellent sweet flavour.
Elvira These Dutch strawberries were developed in the 1970s. The oval berries are a deep glossy red.
Gorella A deep red conical berry with paler red flesh. This is an extremely consistent variety.
Perpetual and remontant strawberries As their name implies, these late-season strawberries go on to fruit continuously throughout the autumn. Although they are juicier than summer berries, they are not as sweet, so are better for cooking than other varieties. They can be picked while they are still green and made into jams, sauces and compotes.

Preparing strawberries

1 Wipe the strawberries with a piece of damp kitchen paper.

2 Hold the strawberry between your thumb and forefinger and twist off the green frill and stalk. Try to remove the central hull in the same movement.

Below: Chocolate-dipped strawberries make a delectable after-dinner treat, or a delightful decoration for chocolate cakes and desserts.

Nutrition

Strawberries are rich in vitamins B and C and contain considerable amounts of potassium, iron and fibre. 100g/3¾oz strawberries provide less than 30 kilocalories.

Buying and Storing

Size and colour are not necessarily indications of quality. Some smaller, greenish varieties taste succulent and delicious. Try always to buy locally grown fruits and check those at the bottom of the punnet, making sure they are not squashed or mouldy.

Strawberries should ideally be eaten the day they are bought. If this is not possible, keep the berries in the fridge for a day or two, covering them with clear film to prevent them from drying out and from permeating other foods with their scent. Remove from the fridge at least an hour before you serve them.

Frozen strawberries are never as good as fresh, as the texture collapses after freezing, but they are fine for sauces and ice cream. To freeze whole strawberries, sprinkle with a little sugar and pack in a single layer in a plastic box, or open freeze on a tray, then pack in a rigid container. Puréed strawberries can be frozen with or without added sugar.

Preparing and Serving

It is best not to wash strawberries, as they easily become waterlogged. If they are very dirty, wipe them gently.

Really ripe strawberries need no other accompaniment than cream or crème fraîche and perhaps a little sugar. Improbable though this may sound, a grinding of black pepper or sprinkling of balsamic vinegar will bring out the flavour of the fruit. Strawberries are seldom improved by cooking, although they make delicious jam. They are best used in their raw state in such desserts as strawberry tartlets, shortcake and pavlovas. They have an affinity with chocolate and make a fine decoration for chocolate terrines and mousses, or they can be dipped into melted chocolate and served as petits fours.

To "dress up" strawberries, macerate them in red wine, Champagne or orange juice. The classic dish, Strawberries Romanov, simply consists of fresh strawberries macerated in orange juice and orange liqueur. Puréed strawberries can be served as a coulis or made into ice creams and sorbets.

Arbutus (tree strawberry)

The arbutus is a tall shrub, whose bright red fruits look like strawberries, but have a different taste. The sweet spiky berries have a soft, slightly mushy texture and a faint flavour of vanilla. You will not find arbutus berries in shops, but the shrubs can be found growing in Europe, as far north as western Ireland (where they are known as Killarney strawberries), and in the United States and China. The berries are unexciting to eat raw, but are used to make jellies and liqueurs.

RASPBERRIES

Perhaps surprisingly, raspberries are a member of the rose family, as you might guess if you have ever been pricked by a raspberry thorn. Native to hilly areas of Europe and Asia, they grow best in a cool, damp climate and can be found even in Alaska. The deep red (or sometimes yellow) jewel-like fruits have a sweet, intense flavour, and indeed many people prefer them to strawberries.

History

Wild raspberries have been eaten since prehistoric times, but, perhaps because they were so plentiful in the wild, the fruits were not cultivated until the Middle Ages. Nowadays, in colder climates, raspberries are cultivated from native European raspberry varieties, while in North America, they derive from an indigenous species better suited to the drier, hotter conditions that prevail there.

Varieties

Although there are many different varieties of raspberry, and new ones are constantly being developed, those sold in shops and markets are not identified specifically. Gardeners have their own favourites:
Heritage is a late-fruiting variety with outstanding flavour.
Malling Jewel fruits in mid-season, and is a heavy cropper.
Wild raspberries You will often find these tiny, fragrant fruits growing in

Above: Raspberries – deep red fruits, with a wonderfully intense flavour.

Above: Arctic raspberries, grown in the chilly climes of Alaska.

Below: Yellow or golden raspberries are worth seeking out, since they have a delectable flavour.

cool, damp areas of woodland. They are full of pips, but their exquisite flavour makes up for this deficiency.
Yellow and golden raspberries Clear golden berries, not widely available, but worth seeking out for their fine flavour.

Nutrition

Raspberries are a valuable source of vitamin C, potassium, niacin and riboflavin, and dietary fibre. They contain 25 kilocalories per 100g/3¾oz. Raspberry juice is said to be good for the heart, while the leaves have long been renowned for their beneficial effects during childbirth; raspberry leaf tea is said to prevent miscarriages, ease labour and help the uterus to contract after the birth.

Buying and Storing

Raspberries are ripe when they are brightly and evenly coloured. They are always sold hulled, but if you are picking your own, they should slide easily off the hulls. When buying raspberries in a punnet, check the bottom to make sure it is not stained red or leaking – a sure sign that the fruit is soft and past its best.

If possible, always eat raspberries the day they are bought or picked; if necessary, they can be stored for up to two days in the bottom of the fridge, but bring them out at least an hour before serving.

Raspberries freeze very well; whole berries emerge almost as good as before. Open freeze the fruit in a single

Left: Raspberry vinegar makes a sharp, yet refreshingly fruity addition to home-made salad dressing.

layer on a baking sheet, then pack into rigid cartons. Less than perfect raspberries can be puréed and sieved, then sweetened with a little caster sugar or icing sugar before being frozen.

Preparing and Serving

Do not wash raspberries unless this is unavoidable; they are seldom very dirty, and washing will ruin the texture and flavour. All you need do is gently pick off any bits of leaf or stalk.

Good raspberries have such a wonderful flavour that they are best eaten on their own, with a little sugar and cream. They go well with other fruits, like oranges, apples, pears, figs and melon. In the classic dish, Peach Melba, raspberries are used as a coulis to coat a lightly poached peach. They also make delicious fillings for pastries, pavlovas and tartlets, and, because they look so attractive, they are ideal for decoration.

Raspberries can be crushed with a little icing sugar, then pushed through a nylon or stainless steel sieve to make sauces, coulis or bases for ice creams and sorbets. They can be cooked in pies; apple and raspberry is a classic combination. They are rich in pectin, so make excellent jams and jellies. Raspberry vinegar is delicious and makes delectable dressings and sauces.

Preparing a raspberry coulis
1 Put the raspberries in a bowl and crush to a purée with a fork.

2 Tip the purée into a sieve set over a clean bowl. Rub through, using the back of a large spoon.

3 Sweeten to taste with icing or caster sugar and stir well.

CLOUDBERRIES

These deep golden relatives of the raspberry grow on boggy land in the cold northern climates of Scandinavia, Siberia, Canada and even the Arctic Circle. Because they lack warmth, the berries ripen slowly, allowing the flavour

Left: Popular in Scandinavia, cloudberry jam makes a colourful topping for chocolate mousse or soufflé.

to develop to an extraordinary intensity and sweetness, almost like honeyed apples (Canadians call cloudberries "baked apple berries"). These unusual berries are particularly highly prized in Scandinavian countries, where they are made into excellent jams and desserts, and also into wonderful fruit soups.

Cloudberries are also distilled into a nectar-like liqueur, which tastes delicious with bitter chocolate. The berries have a particular affinity with chocolate; try topping a chocolate mousse or soufflé with a spoonful of cloudberry jam.

Above: Brightly coloured cloudberries have an amazingly intense flavour.

BLACKBERRIES AND DEWBERRIES

These two relations of the raspberry and the rose are virtually indistinguishable, the main difference being that blackberries are larger and grow on thorny upright bushes or brambles, while dewberries trail. The shiny purplish-black berries are made up of a number of segments (drupelets), each containing a hard seed. They grow wild almost everywhere in the world, but are also cultivated to give a larger, juicier berry with better keeping properties. Buying cultivated blackberries, however, is not nearly as much fun as picking your own from the hedgerows.

Below: Large, cultivated blackberries

History

Archeological excavations show that man has eaten blackberries since Neolithic times. The Ancient Greeks prized them as much for the medicinal properties of their leaves as for the fruit, and they have remained popular throughout the centuries. Not everyone appreciates the qualities of wild brambles, though; after they had been introduced to Australia by the early settlers, they were declared a noxious weed in some areas!

Nutrition

Blackberries are rich in dietary fibre and vitamin C and are often used to make health drinks. They also contain some calcium, phosphorus and potassium. Blackberries typically contain about 30 kilocalories per 100g/3¾oz.

Choosing and Storing

Whether you pick or buy blackberries, they should be plump and tender, but not wet or mushy. Look for large, shiny fruit, and if you are buying a punnet check that the underside is not stained. Legend has it that blackberries should not be picked after September, or the Devil will be in them and they will taste impossibly sour.

Blackberries do not keep well. If you cannot eat them immediately, store them for no more than one day in the bottom of the fridge.

Preparing and Cooking

If you must wash blackberries, do so just before serving and drain them well on kitchen paper.

Freezing blackberries

Blackberries freeze well. Open freeze perfect specimens in a single layer on a baking sheet, then pack into rigid containers. Damaged berries can be puréed and sieved, then sweetened with sugar or honey.

Above: Wild blackberries – also known as brambles.

Left: Dewberries – a smaller, but very similar fruit to blackberries, which grow on long trailing branches.

Right: Crème de mûre – this richly flavoured blackberry liqueur is seldom drunk on its own. It is more often used as a colourful flavouring for cocktails.

Blackberry Kir Royale

Ripe, juicy blackberries are best eaten just as they are, with sugar and cream. They make a tasty addition to breakfast cereal or a fruit salad. Blackberries can be puréed and sieved to make coulis, ice cream, sorbets and fools. They make delicious jam or bramble jelly and are the classic partner for apples in a pie or crumble. There is no need to cook them before using them in a pie filling or a pudding.

Left: English Bramble liqueur

Above: Dewberry flowers, which appear before the fruits develop.

Blackberries go well with many other fruits besides apples, and can be used in savoury game dishes. Use them to flavour spirits, such as vodka or *eau-de-vie*, or make a cordial to combat a cold. Commercially produced *crème de mûre* (blackberry liqueur) enhances the flavour of any dessert that incorporates fresh uncooked blackberries.

For a delicious variation on the classic Kir Royale, which is usually made with crème de cassis (blackcurrant liqueur), pour a little crème de mûre into a champagne flute and top up with Champagne or sparkling white wine. Alternatively, to make an exceptionally luxurious cocktail, put some blackberries in a champagne flute, add a dash of orange liqueur, such as Cointreau, and top up with Champagne or sparkling white wine.

HYBRID BERRIES

There is a wide variety of raspberry/blackberry crossbreeds. Some of these occurred naturally, like the loganberry; others have been cultivated to produce a more robust or better-flavoured fruit. All these hybrids can be cooked and frozen in the same way as raspberries or blackberries.

Loganberries The first loganberry appeared in 1881 at Santa Cruz in California in the garden of Judge J.H. Logan. It was a natural hybrid, probably derived from a cross between a native dewberry and a raspberry. Since then, loganberries have been

Right: Tayberries were bred in Scotland.

cultivated to produce very large, juicy, dark wine-red berries with the consistency of blackberries, but with an intense raspberry flavour. Loganberries are very tart, so they need to be accompanied by plenty of sugar if they are to be eaten raw.

Youngberries These are a dewberry-loganberry hybrid and resemble a dark red, elongated blackberry, but taste rather like a sweeter loganberry.

Boysenberries An even more elaborate hybrid – a cross between a youngberry and a raspberry, but resembling a large reddish-purple blackberry.

Left: Large, sweet boysenberries are mostly used to make jam.

Boysenberries are sweeter than loganberries and can be eaten raw, although they are more often used to make jam.

Tayberries Tayberries are arguably the finest hybrid of all. Bred in Scotland, they are a cross between the American blackberry Aurora and a tetraploid raspberry. They grow on long, spiny canes. The bright red, elongated berries have a slightly tart, aromatic flavour and although they can be eaten raw, they are better cooked.

Tummelberries are similar to tayberries, but fruit later in the season. Other, similar crossbreeds include **sunberries** and **wineberries.**

Above: Loganberries, which look more like reddish blackberries, have an intense raspberry flavour.

Left: Dark red youngberries are a hybrid of the dewberry and loganberry, but taste rather like a sweeter version of loganberry.

MULBERRIES

Mulberries grow on magnificent dome-headed trees, which can often be very ancient and grow up to 10m/30ft across, so they are rarely found in small modern gardens! Silkworms feed on the leaves, but the berries are left to drop to the ground as they ripen and have a delicious, slightly musky flavour. Luscious black mulberries taste very good but beware – they stain everything with which they come into contact. Legend has it that rubbing a stain created by a ripe mulberry with an unripe mulberry (if you can reach one) will remove it.

Right: Mulberries taste very good, but the juice stains terribly.

dark wine-red berries resemble loganberries.

History

Black mulberries are native to Western Asia. They were known to the Ancient Greeks, but it was the Roman emperor Justinian who deliberately encouraged their propagation as part of an enterprise in silk production.

In the sixteenth century, it was discovered that silkworms preferred to feed on the white mulberry leaves, and many of these trees were planted in Europe in the vain hope of stimulating a silk trade. Some of these white mulberry trees still survive today.

Varieties

White mulberries are actually pinkish or pale red. There is also an American red mulberry, whose leaves turn beautifully yellow in autumn.

Black mulberries are considered finer than the white variety. The elongated,

Preparing and Serving

Ripe mulberries can be eaten just as they are, with or without the addition of cream and are usually sweet enough not to need sugar. They also make a good addition to summer pudding.

Over-ripe fruit is best used for jams, jellies and sauces. Mulberries make excellent ice creams, fools and sorbets. Mulberry sauce goes well with richly flavoured roast meats, such as game, duck and lamb.

HUCKLEBERRIES

These berries, which gave their name to Mark Twain's famous character Huckleberry Finn, are quite similar to blueberries, but have a tougher skin and hard internal seeds. They have a sharper flavour than blueberries, but can be eaten and cooked in exactly the same way.

Another variety of huckleberry is the **tangleberry**, which grows on the coast of North America. These purplish-blue berries are sweeter than huckleberries and have a subtle tang of the sea.

Right: Huckleberries, which are similar to blueberries, have fairly tough skins and a sharp flavour.

BLUEBERRIES AND BILBERRIES

Blueberries and bilberries (also known as blaeberries, whortleberries or whinberries) are both small, round blue-black berries with a silvery bloom. They grow on shrubs on inhospitable, peaty moors and uplands. The flavour is mild and sweet and the texture firm.

American blueberries are generally larger and sweeter than bilberries. Nowadays, they are often cultivated, resulting in large, perfect berries that sometimes lack the distinctive flavour of the wild fruit.

Nutrition

Blueberries and bilberries are a source of vitamin C, iron and dietary fibre. They provide about 60 kilocalories per 100g/3¾oz.

Buying and Storing

The best blueberries and bilberries are those you pick yourself. If you buy them, look for plump berries of uniform size. Reject shrivelled specimens, or those without the characteristic bloom. Unwashed berries will keep for up to a week in the bottom of the fridge.

Blueberries and bilberries can be frozen just as they are, provided they are in a sealed bag. Alternatively, poach them in a little lemon-flavoured syrup and then freeze.

Right: Blueberries – mild and sweet flavoured.

Above: Dried blueberries are available in specialist food shops and greengrocers. They make a tasty addition to home-made fruit cakes and muesli, and are delicious scattered into fresh fruit salads or over breakfast cereal.

Preparing and Cooking

Blueberries and bilberries have soft seeds, so they can be eaten raw. Simply rinse and drain them first. However, they are more usually baked in pies or muffins, or used as a jam-like topping for cheesecake. To cook, make a light sugar syrup and flavour it with lemon, orange and cinnamon or allspice, and poach the berries until tender.

Blueberry Pie is a classic dessert, as is Blueberry Grunt, which consists of blueberries stewed with lemon and spice, baked with a dumpling-like topping. Blueberries can also be made into a sauce to serve with game.

Above: Bilberries are smaller and less sweet than blueberries, but have a distinctive flavour.

GOOSEBERRIES

The gooseberry, a botanical cousin of the blackcurrant, is native to Europe and North America. The fruits, which grow on dauntingly spiny bushes, come in many varieties – hard and sour, succulently soft and sweet, smooth and hairy – and in a range of colours, from vivid green to luscious purple.

History

Gooseberries were popular all over Britain well before Tudor times, when they grew wild in many kitchen gardens. The Tudors served them in savoury sauces and in all manner of sweet dishes. They were first cultivated in the sixteenth century and became so popular that in the nineteenth century competitors formed gooseberry clubs to see who could grow the biggest berry (some are reputed to have been grown to the size of a bantam's egg).

For some reason, their popularity did not spread abroad; even today the French use them only in a sauce to cut the richness of oily fish. There is no specific French word for gooseberry; it shares its name with the redcurrant and is known as *groseille de maquereau* ("redcurrant for mackerel").

Varieties

Gooseberries have a very long season. Early gooseberries are usually bright green and rather hard. They cannot be eaten raw, but taste wonderful cooked. These are followed by the softer, mid-season fruits, which are not generally identified by variety when sold in supermarkets and greengrocers, but which you may find in gardens and farm shops.

Early Sulphur A very early variety with golden, almost transparent berries and a lovely sweet flavour.

Goldendrop As attractive as its name, this small round yellow gooseberry has a fine rich flavour, which makes it ideal for eating

raw as a dessert fruit. Ready to pick in mid-summer.

Langley's Industry A large red hairy berry with a lovely sweet flavour. Ideal for the less green-fingered gardener, it will grow vigorously anywhere and can be picked early for cooking, or left to ripen fully on the bush to eat raw like grapes.

Above: Huge, deep-red London berries are sweet enough to eat raw.

Leveller A mid-season, yellowish-green berry with a sweet flavour.

London This huge mid-season berry is deep red or purple. For thirty-seven years, between 1829 and 1867, it was the unbeaten British champion in major gooseberry competitions! These dessert gooseberries can be eaten raw, just as they are.

Left: Green gooseberries – these early-cropping fruits cannot be eaten raw, but are delicious cooked.

Right: Fully ripe red gooseberries are quite sweet enough to be eaten just as they are.

Nutrition

Gooseberries are high in vitamin C and also contain vitamins A and D, potassium, calcium, phosphorus and niacin. They are rich in dietary fibre and provide only 17 kilocalories per 100g/3¾oz.

Buying and Storing

For cooking, choose slightly unripe green gooseberries. Check that they are not rock hard. Dessert varieties should be yielding and juicy (if possible, taste before you buy). Gooseberries will keep in the fridge for up to a week.

To freeze whole gooseberries, top and tail them and open freeze on baking sheets. Pack the frozen berries into polythene bags. Alternatively, purée and sieve them, sweeten and freeze in rigid containers.

Below: You may find Leveller berries, which have a lovely sweet flavour, in garden centres, pick-your-own farms and farm shops.

Preparing

For recipes using whole gooseberries, wash, then top and tail them (this is not necessary if you are making jam or jelly, or are going to sieve the cooked fruit).

Cooking

Gooseberries are rich in pectin, particularly when they are slightly unripe, which makes them ideal for jams and jellies. Their tartness makes an excellent foil for oily fish and rich poultry or meat.

Cook gooseberries very gently with a little water and sugar to taste until all the fruit has collapsed. If you like, flavour them with cinnamon, lemon or herbs. A few fennel or dill seeds will enhance a gooseberry sauce for fish.

In England, the first gooseberries of the season were traditionally used to make a Whitsun pie. They also make a good filling for suet pudding or crumble.

Worcestershire berries
A North American species of gooseberry that grows on a bush with evil spines. The small purplish-red berries are not much bigger than blackberries, but have the distinctive veining of gooseberries and a gooseberry flavour. Worcestershire berries can be eaten raw or cooked.

Topping and tailing gooseberries
1 Hold the gooseberry between your forefinger and thumb.
2 Snip off the stem and flower end with sharp scissors or trim with a knife.

Puréed, sieved and mixed with whipped cream, they make the perfect fruit fool. Gooseberries have an extraordinary affinity for elderflowers, which come into season at the same time as the early fruit and add a delicious muscat flavour to the berries.

Below: Sweet-tasting Early Sulphur are golden and almost translucent.

CRANBERRIES

These tart, bright red berries grow wild on evergreen shrubs in peaty marshland all over northern Europe and North America. They are closely related to blueberries and bilberries, but are much more sour and are always served cooked. **Cowberries** and **lingonberries** are very similar, but smaller.

Cranberries are sometimes known as "bounceberries", since they were traditionally tested for firmness by being bounced seven times. Any which failed the bounce test were too squashy and were therefore discarded. Because of their waxy skins, cranberries keep for much longer than other berries, which helps to explain their popularity.

Right: Bright red cranberries can be used in sweet and savoury dishes.

History

For centuries before the first settlers arrived in America, the native Americans prized wild cranberries for their nutritional and medicinal value, and used them to make a dye for fabric and for decorative feathers. Although cranberries were already known in Britain, the Pilgrim Fathers found that the American berries were larger and more succulent.

Below: Dried cranberries

Cranberry sauce

1 Thinly pare an orange with a swivel-bladed vegetable peeler, taking care to remove only the zest. Squeeze the juice and put it in a saucepan with the zest.

2 Add 350g/12oz/3 cups cranberries and cook gently for a few minutes until the cranberry skins pop.

3 Stir in caster sugar to taste and simmer for 5 minutes. Stir in 30ml/2 tbsp port (optional). Pour the cranberry sauce into a bowl, then cool and chill before serving.

They called them "craneberries" because the pink blossoms resembled a crane's head, or possibly because the cranes, which lived in the marshlands, were partial to the berries.

Cranberries featured in the first ever Thanksgiving feast in 1620 and have been a traditional part of the celebrations ever since. Commercial cultivation began in the nineteenth century, and nowadays cranberries are available frozen, canned, dried, as juice and in jellies and relishes.

Nutrition

Cranberries contain vitamins C and D, potassium and iron. They were considered to be a good protection against scurvy. They are naturally very low in kilocalories (but need sweetening to make them palatable).

Buying and Storing

Look for plump, firm, bright red berries and make sure that those at the bottom of the pack are neither squashed nor shrivelled. Fresh cranberries will keep in the fridge for four weeks, or they can be frozen in polythene bags and used without being thawed first.

Preparing and Cooking

Cranberries can be used in sweet or savoury dishes. Their most famous incarnation is as cranberry sauce, which is served with turkey or red meat and game. Their distinctive tartness even adds zest to firm-fleshed fish. The berries are high in pectin, so they make excellent jams and jellies. They combine well with orange and apple, and can be mixed with blackberries and raspberries to make an autumnal variation on summer pudding.

Cranberries should be stewed slowly with sugar to taste and a little water or orange juice until the skins pop. Dried cranberries can be used in the same way as raisins. Cranberry juice can be mixed with soda water and white wine or grape juice to make a refreshing drink. It is also good with orange juice and vodka.

Cranberry and chestnut stuffing

The traditional Christmas accompaniments of cranberries and chestnuts can be combined to make the perfect stuffing for turkey or other poultry. To make about 450g/1lb (enough to stuff a 4.5–5.5kg/10–12lb bird), soften 115g/4oz finely chopped onion in 25g/1oz butter in a saucepan. Stir in 175g/6oz unsweetened chestnut purée and 30ml/2 tbsp cooked cranberries or chunky cranberry sauce. Season to taste with salt and pepper and mix thoroughly. Take the pan off the heat and stir in 225g/8oz fresh white breadcrumbs. Coarsely crumble or chop 115g/4oz cooked chestnuts (canned chestnuts are fine) and fold into the stuffing mixture. Leave to cool completely before stuffing the bird.

Below: Cranberry juice and soda makes a refreshing drink.

BLACKCURRANTS, REDCURRANTS AND WHITECURRANTS

These native European berries, with their glowing colours, make a beautiful sight in summer, hanging like tiny bunches of grapes on the bush. Each berry contains a mass of small seeds. Currants can be eaten whole, but because they are highly acidic, this is seldom the preferred option.

History

Currants grow wild all over Europe and even as far north as Siberia. For some inexplicable reason, they were not cultivated by the Romans, but became popular only in the sixteenth century, when they were prized for their health-giving properties.

Nutrition

All currants, particularly blackcurrants, are very rich in vitamin C. Blackcurrants are used in cordials, throat sweets and other remedies designed to ward off colds; in the past, they were used as a cure for quinsy (an inflammation of the throat). They are high in pectin.

Buying and Storing

Choose plump, firm currants with shiny skins. They will keep in the fridge for several days. They can be frozen very successfully: strip the currants from the

Below: Buffalo currants are a type of blackcurrant with larger berries.

Right: Blackcurrants grow wild all over Europe. The fruits have a tart flavour and are usually cooked.

stalks, then rinse and drain them. Freeze in rigid containers. Sweetened or unsweetened blackcurrant purée also freezes well.

Preparing

Strip the currants from the stalks, if this has not already been done. If you wish, you can pick off the calyx tops before cooking the currants by pinching them between the nails of your forefinger and thumb. However, this is a tedious process, and is seldom necessary.

BLACKCURRANTS

Although they are often combined with other currants in cooking (as in summer pudding), blackcurrants are different from other types. They have tougher skins and, unlike other currants, which grow on old wood, they

fruit on new wood. Both the bushes and the currants themselves are highly aromatic and the fruits have a luscious tart flavour.

Cooking

Blackcurrants can be added raw to fruit salads if they are not too tart, but are usually cooked in a little water, with sugar to taste. Simmer until just tender – do not overcook them or they will lose their fresh flavour. Blackcurrants make wonderful jams and jellies and combine well with soft cheeses, rich meats and game. To serve blackcurrants with meat, sauté them lightly in butter, adding a

Stripping currants off the stalk

Hold the bunch of currants by the stem and strip off the berries with the tines of a fork.

Right: Whitecurrants are less tart than other currants and can be eaten raw.

pinch of sugar. They adapt well to other flavourings, such as mint and lemon, and are used to make the liqueur crème de cassis, which is the basis for Kir Royale and similar drinks.

REDCURRANTS

Redcurrants can be eaten raw. Small bunches look very decorative if frosted with egg white and caster sugar. They are an essential ingredient for summer pudding and make a good addition to creamy desserts, such as crème brûlée. For a refreshing summer drink, purée 450g/1lb/4 cups redcurrants with 500ml/18 fl oz/2 cups water and sugar to taste, then press the purée gently through a sieve placed over a jug. Serve with sparkling water or soda water, or add a dash of vodka or gin.

The most familiar use of redcurrants, however, is in the jewel-like redcurrant

jelly that goes so well with lamb and venison. Cumberland sauce (for game, ham and rich meats) is made by heating redcurrant jelly with lemon zest, port and sometimes mustard.

WHITECURRANTS

These beautiful, translucent, silvery-golden currants are an albino strain of redcurrants. They are less tart than other types and can be eaten raw. They look wonderfully decorative frosted with egg white and sugar. **Pink currants** are an even more attractive variety, with a beautiful pink flush.

Above: Redcurrant jelly

Left: Redcurrants are an essential ingredient for summer pudding.

Redcurrant jelly

1 Put the redcurrants (as many as you have) in a preserving pan with just enough water to cover. Simmer for 8–10 minutes or until the currants are very soft.

2 Strain through a jelly bag, then measure the liquid. Pour it back into the pan and add 350g/12oz/1½ cups granulated sugar for every 600ml/1 pint/2½ cups liquid. Stir over a medium heat until the sugar has dissolved.

3 Boil briskly for 10 minutes or until setting point is reached, skimming off any scum as it rises to the surface. Pour the jelly into sterilized jars, seal and label.

Berry and Currant Recipes

For sheer beauty, berries take a lot of beating. Make the most of their tantalizing colours and flavours by serving them simply, as a topping for shortcakes or in a summer pudding. Fresh Blueberry Muffins, Berry Brûlée Tarts, Bramble Jelly — these present the berries at their best.

SUMMER PUDDING

NO FRUIT BOOK WOULD BE COMPLETE WITHOUT THIS WELL-LOVED CLASSIC RECIPE. DON'T RESERVE IT SOLELY FOR SUMMER: IT FREEZES WELL AND PROVIDES A DELICIOUS DESSERT FOR CHRISTMAS DAY, AS A LIGHT AND REFRESHING ALTERNATIVE TO THE TRADITIONAL PUDDING.

SERVES FOUR TO SIX

INGREDIENTS

7-8 × 1cm/½in thick slices of day-old
   white bread, crusts removed
800g/1¾lb/6–7 cups mixed berry
   fruit, such as strawberries,
   raspberries, blackcurrants,
   redcurrants and blueberries
50g/2oz/¼ cup golden caster sugar
lightly whipped double cream or
   crème fraîche, to serve

3 Fold over the excess bread, then cover the fruit with the remaining bread, trimming to fit snugly. Place a small plate or saucer directly on top of the pudding, that fits inside the basin. Weight it with a 900g/2lb weight if you have one, or use a couple of full cans.

4 Leave the pudding in the fridge for at least 8 hours or overnight. To serve, run a knife between the pudding and the basin and turn it out on to a plate. Spoon any reserved juices over the top and serve with whipped cream or crème fraîche.

1 Trim a slice of bread to fit in the base of a 1.2 litre/2 pint/5 cup pudding basin, then trim another 5–6 slices to line the sides of the basin.

2 Place all the fruit in a saucepan with the sugar. Cook gently for 4–5 minutes until the juices begin to run – it will not be necessary to add any water. Allow the mixture to cool slightly before spooning the berries and enough of their juices to moisten the bread lining the pudding basin. Save any leftover juice to serve with the pudding.

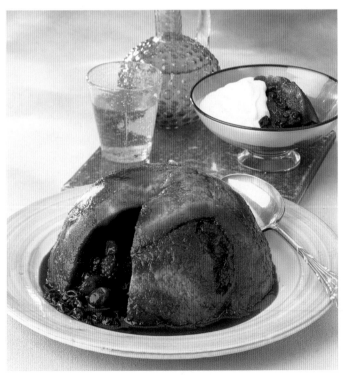

HOT BLACKBERRY AND APPLE SOUFFLÉS

AS THE BLACKBERRY SEASON IS SO SHORT AND THE APPLE SEASON SO LONG, IT'S ALWAYS WORTH FREEZING A BAG OF BLACKBERRIES TO HAVE ON HAND FOR TREATS LIKE THIS ONE.

2 Cook the blackberries and diced apple with the orange rind and juice in a pan for 10 minutes or until the apple has pulped down well. Press through a sieve into a bowl. Stir in 50g/2oz/¼ cup of the caster sugar. Set aside to cool.

3 Put a spoonful of the fruit purée into each prepared dish and smooth the surface. Set the dishes aside.

4 Whisk the egg whites in a large grease-free bowl until they form stiff peaks. Very gradually whisk in the remaining caster sugar to make a stiff, glossy meringue mixture.

5 Fold in the remaining fruit purée and spoon the flavoured meringue into the prepared dishes. Level the tops with a palette knife, and run a table knife around the edge of each dish.

MAKES SIX

INGREDIENTS
  butter, for greasing
  150g/5oz/⅔ cup caster sugar, plus
   extra for dusting
  350g/12oz/3 cups blackberries
  1 large cooking apple, peeled, cored
   and finely diced
  grated rind and juice of 1 orange
  3 egg whites
  icing sugar, for dusting

COOK'S TIP
Running a table knife around the edge of the soufflés before baking helps them to rise evenly without any part sticking to the rim of the dishes.

1 Preheat the oven to 200°C/400°F/ Gas 6. Generously grease six 150ml/ ¼ pint/⅔ cup individual soufflé dishes with butter and dust with caster sugar, shaking out the excess sugar. Put a baking sheet in the oven to heat.

6 Place the dishes on the hot baking sheet and bake for 10–15 minutes until the soufflés have risen well and are lightly browned. Dust the tops with icing sugar and serve immediately.

SUMMER BERRY CRÊPES

THE DELICATE FLAVOUR OF THESE FLUFFY CRÊPES CONTRASTS BEAUTIFULLY WITH TANGY BERRY FRUITS.

SERVES FOUR

INGREDIENTS
115g/4oz/1 cup self-raising flour
1 large egg
300ml/½ pint/1¼ cups milk
a few drops of pure vanilla essence
15g/½oz/1 tbsp butter
15ml/1 tbsp sunflower oil
icing sugar, for dusting
For the fruit
25g/1oz/2 tbsp butter
50g/2oz/¼ cup caster sugar
thinly pared rind of ½ orange
juice of 2 oranges
350g/12oz/3 cups mixed summer
   berries, such as sliced strawberries,
   yellow raspberries, blueberries
   and redcurrants
45ml/3 tbsp Grand Marnier or other
   orange liqueur

1 Preheat the oven to 150°C/300°F/ Gas 2. To make the crêpes, sift the flour into a large bowl and make a well in the centre. Break in the egg and gradually whisk in the milk to make a smooth batter. Stir in the vanilla essence. Set the batter aside in a cool place for up to half an hour.

2 Heat the butter and oil together in an 18cm/7in non-stick frying pan. Swirl to grease the pan, then pour off the excess fat into a small bowl.

3 If the batter has been allowed to stand, whisk it thoroughly until smooth. Pour a little of the batter into the hot pan, swirling to cover the base of the pan evenly. Cook until the mixture comes away from the sides and the crêpe is golden underneath.

4 Flip the crêpe over with a large palette knife and cook the other side briefly until golden.

5 Slide the crêpe on to a heatproof plate. Make seven more crêpes in the same way, greasing the pan with more butter and oil mixture as needed. Cover the crêpes with foil or another plate and keep them hot in the oven.

COOK'S TIP
For safety, when igniting a mixture for flambéing, use a long taper or long wooden match. Stand back as you set the mixture alight.

6 To prepare the fruit, melt the butter in a heavy-based frying pan, stir in the sugar and cook gently until the mixture is golden brown. Add the orange rind and juice and cook until syrupy.

7 Add the fruits and warm through, then add the liqueur and set it alight. Shake the pan to incorporate the liqueur until the flame dies down.

8 Fold the pancakes into quarters and arrange two on each plate. Spoon over some of the fruit mixture and dust liberally with the icing sugar. Serve any remaining fruit mixture separately.

FRESH BERRY PAVLOVA

PAVLOVA IS THE SIMPLEST OF DESSERTS, BUT IT CAN ALSO BE THE MOST STUNNING. FILL WITH A MIX OF BERRY FRUITS IF YOU LIKE — RASPBERRIES AND BLUEBERRIES MAKE A MARVELLOUS COMBINATION.

SERVES SIX TO EIGHT

INGREDIENTS
4 egg whites, at room temperature
225g/8oz/1 cup caster sugar
5ml/1 tsp cornflour
5ml/1 tsp cider vinegar
2.5ml/½ tsp pure vanilla essence
300ml/½ pint/1¼ cups double cream
150ml/¼ pint/⅔ cup crème fraîche
175g/6oz/1 cup raspberries
175g/6oz/1½ cups blueberries
fresh mint sprigs, to decorate
icing sugar, for dusting

COOK'S TIP
To begin, invert a plate on the baking paper and draw round it with a pencil. Turn the paper over and use the circle as a guide for the meringue.

1 Preheat the oven to 140°C/275°F/ Gas 1. Line a baking sheet with non-stick baking paper. Whisk the egg whites in a large grease-free bowl until they form stiff peaks. Gradually whisk in the sugar to make a stiff, glossy meringue. Sift the cornflour over and fold it in with the vinegar and vanilla.

2 Spoon the meringue mixture on to the paper-lined sheet, using the circle drawn on the paper as a guide (see Cook's Tip). Spread into a round, swirling the top, and bake for 1¼ hours or until the meringue is crisp and very lightly golden. Switch off the oven, keeping the door closed, and allow the meringue to cool for 1–2 hours.

3 Carefully peel the paper from the meringue and transfer it to a serving plate. Whip the cream in a large mixing bowl until it forms soft peaks, fold in the crème fraîche, then spoon the mixture into the centre of the meringue case. Top with the raspberries and blueberries and decorate with the fresh mint sprigs. Sift icing sugar over the top and serve at once.

GOOSEBERRY AND ELDERFLOWER FOOL

GOOSEBERRIES AND ELDERFLOWERS ARE A MATCH MADE IN HEAVEN, EACH BRINGING OUT THE FLAVOUR
OF THE OTHER. SERVE WITH AMARETTI OR OTHER DESSERT BISCUITS FOR DIPPING.

SERVES SIX

INGREDIENTS

   450g/1lb/4 cups gooseberries, topped
   and tailed
   30ml/2 tbsp water
   50–75g/2–3oz/¼–⅓ cup caster sugar
   30ml/2 tbsp elderflower cordial
   400g/14oz carton ready-made
   custard
   green food colouring (optional)
   300ml/½ pint/1¼ cups double cream
   crushed amaretti biscuits, to decorate
   amaretti biscuits, to serve

1 Put the gooseberries and water in
a pan. Cover and cook for 5–6 minutes
or until the berries pop open.

2 Add the sugar and elderflower cordial
to the gooseberries, then stir vigorously
or mash until the fruit forms a pulp.
Remove the pan from the heat, spoon
the gooseberry pulp into a bowl and set
aside to cool.

3 Stir the custard into the fruit. Add a
few drops of food colouring, if using.
Whip the cream to soft peaks, then fold
it into the mixture and chill. Serve in
dessert glasses, decorated with crushed
amaretti, and accompanied by amaretti.

FRUITS OF THE FOREST WITH WHITE CHOCOLATE CREAMS

*COLOURFUL FRUITS MACERATED IN A MIXTURE OF WHITE COCONUT RUM AND SUGAR MAKE
A FANTASTIC ACCOMPANIMENT TO A DELIGHTFULLY CREAMY WHITE CHOCOLATE MOUSSE.*

SERVES FOUR

INGREDIENTS
75g/3oz white cooking chocolate,
  in squares
150ml/¼ pint/⅔ cup double cream
30ml/2 tbsp crème fraîche
1 egg, separated
5ml/1 tsp powdered gelatine
30ml/2 tbsp cold water
a few drops of pure vanilla essence
115g/4oz/1 cup small
  strawberries, sliced
75g/3oz/½ cup raspberries
75g/3oz/¾ cup blueberries
45ml/3 tbsp caster sugar
75ml/5 tbsp white coconut rum
strawberry leaves, to decorate
  (optional)

3 Set the bowl in a pan of hot water
until the gelatine has dissolved
completely. Stir the dissolved gelatine
into the chocolate mixture and add the
vanilla essence. Set aside until starting
to thicken and set.

1 Melt the chocolate in a heatproof
bowl set over a pan of hot water. Heat
the cream in a separate pan until
almost boiling, then stir into the
chocolate with the crème fraîche. Cool
slightly, then beat in the egg yolk.

2 Sprinkle the gelatine over the cold
water in another heatproof bowl and set
aside for a few minutes to swell.

COOK'S TIP
For a dramatic effect, decorate each
white chocolate cream with dark
chocolate leaves, made by coating the
veined side of unsprayed rose leaves with
melted chocolate. Let it dry before gently
pulling off the leaves.

4 Brush four dariole moulds or individual
soufflé dishes with oil; line the base of
each with non-stick baking paper.

5 In a grease-free bowl, whisk the egg
white to soft peaks, then fold into the
chocolate mixture.

6 Spoon the mixture into the prepared
dariole moulds or soufflé dishes, then
level the surface of each and chill for
2–3 hours or until firm.

7 Meanwhile, place the fruits in a bowl.
Add the caster sugar and coconut rum
and stir gently to mix. Cover and chill
until required.

8 Ease the chocolate cream away from
the rims of the moulds or dishes and
turn out on to dessert plates. Spoon the
fruits around the outside. Decorate with
the strawberry leaves, if using, then
serve at once.

RASPBERRY AND ROSE PETAL SHORTCAKES

ROSEWATER-SCENTED CREAM AND FRESH RASPBERRIES FORM THE FILLING FOR THIS DELECTABLE DESSERT. THOUGH THEY LOOK IMPRESSIVE, THESE SHORTCAKES ARE EASY TO MAKE.

MAKES SIX

INGREDIENTS
115g/4oz/½ cup unsalted
  butter, softened
50g/2oz/¼ cup caster sugar
½ vanilla pod, split, seeds reserved
115g/4oz/1 cup plain flour, plus
  extra for dusting
50g/2oz/⅓ cup semolina
icing sugar, for dusting
For the filling
300ml/½ pint/1¼ cups double cream
15ml/1 tbsp icing sugar
2.5ml/½ tsp rosewater
450g/1lb/4 cups raspberries
For the decoration
12 miniature roses, unsprayed
6 mint sprigs
1 egg white, beaten
icing sugar, for dusting

1 Cream the butter, caster sugar and vanilla seeds in a bowl until pale and fluffy. Sift the flour and semolina together, then gradually work the dry ingredients into the creamed mixture to make a biscuit dough.

VARIATIONS
Other soft red summer berries, such as mulberries, loganberries and tayberries, would be equally good in this dessert.

COOK'S TIP
For best results, serve the shortcakes as soon as possible after assembling them. Otherwise, they are likely to turn soggy from the berries' liquid.

2 Gently knead the dough on a lightly floured surface until smooth. Roll out quite thinly and prick all over with a fork. Using a 7.5cm/3in fluted cutter, cut out 12 rounds. Place these on a baking sheet and chill for 30 minutes.

3 Meanwhile, make the filling. Whisk the cream with the icing sugar until soft peaks form. Fold in the rosewater and chill until required.

4 Preheat the oven to 180°C/350°F/ Gas 4. To make the decoration, paint the roses and leaves with the egg white. Dust with sugar; dry on a wire rack.

5 Bake the shortcakes for 15 minutes or until lightly golden. Lift them off the baking sheet with a metal fish slice and cool on a wire rack.

6 To assemble the shortcakes, spoon the rosewater cream on to half the biscuits. Add a layer of raspberries, then top with a second shortcake. Dust with icing sugar. Decorate with the frosted roses and mint sprigs.

FRESH CURRANT BREAD–
AND–BUTTER PUDDING

FRESH MIXED CURRANTS ADD A TART TOUCH TO THIS SCRUMPTIOUS HOT PUDDING.

SERVES SIX

INGREDIENTS
    8 medium-thick slices day-old bread,
      crusts removed
    50g/2oz/¼ cup butter, softened
    115g/4oz/1 cup redcurrants
    115g/4oz/1 cup blackcurrants
    4 eggs, beaten
    75g/3oz/6 tbsp caster sugar
    475ml/16fl oz/2 cups creamy milk
    5ml/1 tsp pure vanilla essence
    a large pinch of grated nutmeg
    30ml/2 tbsp demerara sugar
    single cream, to serve

1 Preheat the oven to 160°C/325°F/
Gas 3. Generously butter a 1.2 litre/
2 pint/5 cup oval baking dish.

VARIATION
A mixture of blueberries and raspberries
would work just as well as the currants.

2 Spread the slices of bread generously
with the butter, then cut them in half
diagonally. Layer the slices in the dish,
buttered side up, scattering the currants
between the layers.

3 Beat the eggs and caster sugar
lightly together in a large mixing bowl,
then gradually whisk in the milk, vanilla
essence and a large pinch of freshly
grated nutmeg.

4 Pour the milk mixture over the bread,
pushing the slices down. Scatter the
demerara sugar and a little nutmeg over
the top. Place the dish in a baking tin
and fill with hot water to come halfway
up the sides of the dish. Bake for
40 minutes, then increase the oven
temperature to 180°C/350°F/Gas 4 and
bake for 20–25 minutes more or until
the top is golden. Cool slightly, then
serve with single cream.

CRANBERRY AND BLUEBERRY STREUSEL CAKE

CRANBERRIES ARE SELDOM USED IN SWEET DISHES BUT ONCE THEY ARE SWEETENED, THEY HAVE A GREAT FLAVOUR AND ARE PERFECT WHEN PARTNERED WITH BLUEBERRIES.

MAKES TEN SLICES

INGREDIENTS
175g/6oz/¾ cup butter, softened
115g/4oz/½ cup caster sugar
350g/12oz/3 cups plain flour
2 large eggs, beaten
5ml/1 tsp baking powder
5ml/1 tsp pure vanilla essence
115g/4oz/1 cup cranberries
115g/4oz/1 cup blueberries
50g/2oz/⅓ cup light muscovado sugar
2.5ml/½ tsp crushed cardamom seeds
icing sugar, for dusting

1 Preheat the oven to 190°C/375°F/ Gas 5. Grease and base-line a 21cm/ 8½in round springform cake tin.

2 Cream the butter and caster sugar together until smooth, then blend in the flour with your fingers until the mixture resembles fine breadcrumbs. Take out 200g/7oz/generous 1 cup of the mixture and set this aside.

3 Beat the eggs, baking powder and vanilla essence into the remaining mixture until soft and creamy. Spoon on to the base of the prepared tin and spread evenly. Arrange the cranberries and blueberries on top, then sprinkle the muscovado sugar over.

4 Stir the cardamom seeds into the reserved flour mixture, then scatter evenly over the top of the fruit. Bake for 50–60 minutes or until the topping is golden. Cool the cake in the tin for 10 minutes, then remove the sides of the tin. Slide it on to a wire rack, lifting it off its base at the same time. Cool the cake completely, then dust with icing sugar and serve with whipped cream.

BERRY BRÛLÉE TARTS·

THIS QUANTITY OF PASTRY IS ENOUGH FOR EIGHT TARTLETS, SO FREEZE HALF FOR ANOTHER DAY.
THE BRÛLÉE TOPPING IS BEST ADDED NO MORE THAN TWO HOURS BEFORE SERVING THE TARTS.

MAKES FOUR

INGREDIENTS
   250g/9oz/2¼ cups plain flour
   a pinch of salt
   25g/1oz/¼ cup ground almonds
   15ml/1 tbsp icing sugar
   150g/5oz/⅔ cup unsalted butter,
      chilled and diced
   1 egg yolk
   about 45ml/3 tbsp cold water
For the filling
   4 egg yolks
   15ml/1 tbsp cornflour
   50g/2oz/¼ cup caster sugar
   a few drops of pure vanilla essence
   300ml/½ pint/1¼ cups creamy milk
   225g/8oz/2 cups mixed berry fruits,
      such as small strawberries,
      raspberries, blackcurrants
      and redcurrants
   50g/2oz/½ cup icing sugar

1 Mix the flour, salt, ground almonds and icing sugar in a bowl. Rub in the butter by hand or in a food processor until the mixture resembles fine breadcrumbs. Add the egg yolk and enough cold water to form a dough. Knead the dough gently, then cut it in half and freeze half for use later.

2 Cut the remaining pastry into four equal pieces and roll out thinly.

COOK'S TIP
If you possess a culinary blowtorch – and are confident about operating it safely – it will easily melt and caramelize the brûlée topping.

3 Use the pastry rounds to line four individual tartlet tins, letting the excess pastry hang over the edges. Chill for 30 minutes.

4 Preheat the oven to 200°C/400°F/Gas 6. Line the pastry with non-stick baking paper and baking beans. Bake blind for 10 minutes. Remove the paper and beans and return the tartlet cases to the oven for 5 minutes until golden. Allow the pastry to cool, then carefully trim off the excess pastry.

5 Beat the egg yolks, cornflour, caster sugar and vanilla essence in a bowl.

6 Warm the milk in a heavy-based pan, pour it on to the egg yolks, whisking constantly, then return the mixture to the clean pan.

7 Heat, stirring, until the custard thickens, but do not let it boil. Remove from the heat, press a piece of clear film directly on the surface of the custard and allow to cool.

8 Scatter the berries in the tartlet cases and spoon over the custard. Chill the tarts for 2 hours.

9 To serve, sift icing sugar generously over the tops of the tartlets. Preheat the grill to the highest setting. Place the tartlets under the hot grill until the sugar melts and caramelizes. Allow the topping to cool and harden for about 10 minutes before serving the tarts.

BRAMBLE JELLY

THIS JELLY IS ONE OF THE BEST. IT HAS TO BE MADE WITH HAND-PICKED WILD BLACKBERRIES FOR THE BEST FLAVOUR. MAKE SURE YOU INCLUDE A FEW RED UNRIPE BERRIES FOR A GOOD SET.

MAKES 900G/2LB

INGREDIENTS
    900g/2lb/8 cups blackberries
    300ml/½ pint/1¼ cups water
    juice of 1 lemon
    about 900g/2lb/4 cups caster sugar
    hot buttered toast or English muffins,
        to serve

VARIATION
Redcurrant jelly is made in the same way, but with less sugar. Reduce the quantity to 350g/12oz/1½ cups for every 600ml/1 pint/2½ cups juice.

1 Put the fruit, water and lemon juice into a large saucepan. Cover the pan and cook for 15–30 minutes or until the blackberries are very soft.

2 Ladle into a jelly bag or a large sieve lined with muslin and set over a large bowl. Leave to drip overnight to obtain the maximum amount of juice.

3 Discard the fruit pulp. Measure the exuded juice and allow 450g/1lb/2 cups sugar to every 600ml/1 pint/2½ cups juice. Place both in a large heavy-based pan and bring the mixture slowly to the boil, stirring all the time until the sugar has dissolved.

4 Boil rapidly until the jelly registers 105°C/220°F on a sugar thermometer or test for setting by spooning a small amount on to a chilled saucer. Chill for 3 minutes, then push the mixture with your finger; if wrinkles form on the surface, it is ready. Cool for 10 minutes.

5 Skim off any scum and pour the jelly into warm sterilized jars. Cover and seal while the jelly is still hot and label when the jars are cool. Serve the jelly with hot buttered toast or English muffins.

STRAWBERRY JAM

CAPTURE THE VERY ESSENCE OF SUMMER IN A JAR OF DELICIOUS HOME-MADE STRAWBERRY JAM.

MAKES ABOUT 1.4KG/3LB

INGREDIENTS
1kg/2¼lb/8 cups small strawberries
900g/2lb/4 cups granulated sugar
juice of 2 lemons
scones and clotted cream, to serve

1 Layer the strawberries and sugar in a large bowl. Cover and leave overnight.

2 The next day, scrape the strawberries and their juice into a large heavy-based pan. Add the lemon juice. Gradually bring to the boil over a low heat, stirring until the sugar has dissolved.

COOK'S TIPS
For best results when making jam, don't wash the strawberries unless absolutely necessary. Instead, brush off any dirt, or wipe the strawberries with a damp cloth. If you have to wash any, pat them dry and then spread them out on a clean dish towel to dry further.

To sterilize jam jars, wash in hot soapy water, then rinse thoroughly and drain. Place the jars on a baking sheet and dry in a warm oven for 15–20 minutes.

3 Boil steadily for 10–15 minutes or until the jam registers 105°C/220°F on a sugar thermometer. Alternatively, test for setting by spooning a small amount on to a chilled saucer. Chill for 3 minutes, then push the jam with your finger; if wrinkles form on the surface, it is ready. Cool for 10 minutes.

4 Pour the strawberry jam into warm sterilized jars, filling them right to the top. Cover and seal while the jam is still hot and label when the jars are cool. Serve the jam with scones and clotted cream. This strawberry jam can be stored in a cool dark place and should keep for up to one year.

CITRUS FRUITS

No family of fruits seems to store up sunshine more successfully than citrus fruits. Golden oranges and tangerines, yellow lemons, deep green limes — their glowing colours light up a room, and the delicious scent of their essential oils tempts the tastebuds. Wonderfully versatile, they can be juiced, enjoyed just as they are or used in both sweet and savoury dishes. All citrus fruits have tough, bitter peel that is highly scented and contains aromatic essential oils. Inside, the fruit is segmented and encloses juicy flesh, with a more or less acid flavour. The fruits ripen on the tree and do not continue to develop after picking, so they have excellent keeping qualities.

GRAPEFRUIT

One of the largest citrus fruits, grapefruit can vary in diameter from 10–18cm/4–7in. Most have deep yellow skins, but the flesh can range from very pale yellow (confusingly called "white"), through rosy pink to deep pink (known as "ruby"). Generally speaking, the pinker the flesh, the sweeter the grapefruit will be.

History

Grapefruit are descended from the original West Indian **pomelo** or **shaddock**, a large sour fruit (the pomelos sold today are a cross between a grapefruit and a shaddock). These fruits were brought to Europe from the West Indies in the seventeenth century and are now grown in every sub-tropical country of the world.

Varieties

The main varieties of grapefruit are white, pink or ruby, but you may also find the green-skinned **Sweetie,** whose flesh, as the name implies, is so sweet that it needs no sugar.

Nutrition

One of the most filling fruits, yet very low in calories (about 43 kilocalories per 100g/3¾oz), grapefruit are an excellent source of dietary fibre and vitamin C; one fruit provides one-and-a-half times the adult daily requirement.

Above: Sweetie is a very sweet variety of grapefruit that needs no sugar.

Buying and Storing

Choose fruits that feel heavy for their size; they will be juicy. The skin can be thin or thick, depending on the variety, but it should be plump and firm; if it is puffy and coarse, the flesh will be dry. Avoid grapefruit with bruised or damaged skin. You cannot ripen grapefruit once they have been picked, but they can be kept in a cool place or in the fridge for a week or more.

Preparing and Serving

Grapefruit are best eaten raw and chilled, although in the 1960s it was fashionable to sprinkle them with brown sugar or brush with melted butter and caramelize them under the grill. They constitute the perfect breakfast food; perhaps the easiest way to enjoy them is freshly squeezed into a glass, but half a grapefruit on its own or with a little sugar is more satisfying. The fruits can also be used to make delicious marmalade to round off your breakfast.

Grapefruit can be used to start or finish a main meal. The tart flavour goes well with

Above: White grapefruit have pale yellow flesh.

Segmenting grapefruit

1 Cut the grapefruit in half and remove the pips.

2 Using a curved, serrated grapefruit knife, cut between the skin and flesh.

3 Using a small, sharp paring knife, cut carefully between the membrane that separates the segments. Start at the centre, work out to the skin, then around the segment and back to the centre again.

4 Finally, cut out the central core of the grapefruit with a sharp knife and remove the membrane.

seafood; grapefruit segments mixed with prawns and avocado make a refreshing starter. They combine well with smoked fish and poultry, and segments are sometimes served as a garnish to cut the richness of liver or sweetbreads. The segments can also be used in fruit salads, mousses and sorbets. Grapefruit juice makes an unusual addition to salad dressings, and the peel, without the pith, can be candied to be used in cakes or coated with chocolate.

Left: The flesh of pink grapefruit can range from rosy pink to deep pink. As a rule of thumb, the pinker the colour, the sweeter the grapefruit.

Below: Chocolate-coated grapefruit peel – a delectable sweet treat.

POMELOS

Although they resemble grapefruit, true pomelos are not a hybrid of the grapefruit, but a species in their own right. They are sometimes known as "shaddocks" after the sea captain who brought them from Polynesia to the West Indies. They are much larger than grapefruit, with thick yellow dimpled skin, pinkish-yellow flesh and a sharp, refreshing flavour, which often needs a little sugar to make it palatable.

Below: Pomelos sold today are a smaller, rounder and smoother-skinned cross between the original pomelo or shaddock and grapefruit.

UGLI FRUIT

Despite its large size, baggy shape and mottled green skin, the Ugli is a hybrid of the grapefruit, orange and tangerine. It may not be the beauty of the citrus family, but the flavour is sweet and delicious – a cross between grapefruit and tangerine. The peel can be candied like grapefruit.

LEMONS

Arguably the most useful of all fruit, the distinctively shaped lemon can be very large or quite small, with thick or thin, smooth or knobbly skin. The skin contains aromatic essential oils, and a good lemon will perfume the air with its fragrance. The juicy, pale yellow, acid flesh enhances almost any other food and never fails to awaken and refresh the tastebuds.

History

Originally from India or Malaysia, lemons were introduced into Assyria where they were discovered by the soldiers serving Alexander the Great. They took them back to Greece, where the lemons were used as a condiment and for medicinal and cosmetic purposes. The Crusaders brought lemons to Europe from Palestine, and their cultivation became widespread. Like limes, lemons became invaluable as a protection against scurvy and were carried by sailors on every sea voyage.

Nutrition

Rich in vitamin C and very low in calories, lemons only provide about 22 kilocalories per 100g/3¾oz.

Buying and Storing

Choose lemons that are firm and heavy for their size. Smooth-skinned lemons are best for juicing and cooking, while the knobbly skinned varieties are easier to grate. Lemons become paler as they ripen and lose some juiciness and acidity, so avoid light yellow fruit; look instead for deep yellow specimens with glossy unblemished skins. Do not buy lemons with patches of mould, or those with hard, shrivelled skins.

Lemons have often been treated with diphenyl, an ethylene gas that keeps the skins yellow and fresh-looking. If you are going to use the lemon rind, buy untreated or "unwaxed" fruit.

Lemons do not ripen once picked. They can be kept in a cool room or the fridge for at least a week.

Preparing and Cooking

Although few people would choose to eat a lemon raw, these citrus fruits are infinitely versatile. Their high ascorbic acid (vitamin C) content prevents oxidization, so lemon juice is often brushed over cut fruit or white vegetables, such as potatoes, celeriac or artichokes, to stop them from turning brown. Lemons can be distilled into alcoholic drinks, such as *limoncello,* a sweet *digestivo,* which is served straight from the freezer.

Every part of the lemon can be used in sweet and savoury cooking, from the juice to the zest. Lemon wedges are traditionally served as an accompaniment to fish dishes, particularly fried fish; their acidity counteracts the fattiness of all fried

Left: Smooth-skinned lemons are best for juicing and cooking.

Zesting or grating a lemon
1 Choose an unwaxed lemon. Hold it firmly in one hand.

2 Scrape a zester down the length of the lemon to pare off fine slivers of zest.

3 Chop the pared zest finely with a sharp knife if desired.

4 For grating, choose a knobbly skinned lemon if possible. Grate it on the fine side of a grater, taking care to remove only the yellow zest. Work over a bowl or, if you prefer, work over a piece of foil – this makes it easy to transfer the grated rind to a bowl or pan with the aid of a pastry brush.

foods. Lemon slices are a popular addition to tea and cold drinks, or can be used to garnish any number of sweet or savoury dishes. Whole lemons can be preserved in salt and are widely used in North African dishes, such as Moroccan *tagines.*

Lemons give a wonderful flavour to sweet dishes. They can be used for jellies, jams and lemon curd or lemon cheese and make refreshing mousses, sorbets and ice creams.

Lemon juice Lemon juice can be drunk on its own, with added sugar, or as a refreshing long drink, such as lemonade. It enhances the flavour of most other foods and can be used as a healthy substitute for salt. Use it in dressings, sauces and marinades; marinating fish for a long time in lemon juice will even "cook" the fish without heat, as in the South American dish

Above: Knobbly-skinned lemons are easier to grate.

ceviche. Lemon juice will also tenderize meat. A few drops added to the cooking water helps poached eggs to coagulate, and a couple of spoonfuls will turn fresh cream into soured cream.

Lemon juice has non-culinary uses, too. It acts as a bleach and can be used as a household cleaner or cosmetically, to whiten the skin or lighten blonde hair.

Lemons yield more juice if they are warmed before squeezing; roll them between the palms of your hands for a minute or two, cover with boiling water or microwave on High for 30 seconds before squeezing. Do not squeeze lemons too hard, or the juice will become bitter.

Lemon zest and peel
The essential oils in lemon zest have an aromatic flavour that enhances many dishes. The zest can be obtained by grating or peeling into strips with a zester or canelle knife. Use it as a flavouring for butter, sauces, custards, mousses, cakes, biscuits and tarts. For a milder lemon flavour, rub a lump of sugar over the surface of a lemon so that it absorbs the oils, then add the sugar cube to a sauce or pudding.

Lemon peel (including the white pith) contains pectin, which helps to set jams and jellies. Strips of peel (minus pith) can be added to casseroles, or candied to serve with coffee or to add to cakes and puddings.

Below: Lemon juice enhances the flavour of most other fruits.

CITRON

A lemon or pear-shaped citrus fruit originally from China, citrons are large fruit, sometimes up to 20cm/8in long, with thick, knobbly, greenish skin. They give very little juice, but this can be used like lemon juice. Citron flesh is very bitter and unpalatable, but the attractive green peel can be candied and used like candied lemon peel; it develops a lovely translucency. The peel can also be used for marmalade and jams. In Corsica, citrons are used to make a liqueur called *Cédratine.*

Right: Citrons are large fruit with bitter, unpalatable flesh.

TANGERINES OR MANDARINS

Sometimes known as "easy peelers", tangerines or mandarins are part of a large family of small citrus fruit. They resemble slightly flattened oranges with loose orange skin and have a fragrant aroma, which is inextricably bound up with Christmas. Who can forget the childhood delight of finding a tangerine in the toe of a Christmas stocking? The tangerine family all have aromatic skins, which can easily be detached from the segments (unlike oranges and lemons) and segments that separate easily. The flesh is sweet and perfumed, but often contains a large number of pips.

History

As the name suggests, tangerines or mandarins almost certainly originated in China and were brought to Italy in Roman times by Arab traders. Like oranges, they were regarded as a

Right: Easy to peel, satsumas have a refreshing tart flavour.

Right: These tangerines, grown in Italy, have sweet flesh, but often contain a large number of pips.

symbol of luxury and prosperity. They are now grown throughout North Africa and the Mediterranean.

Varieties

The names of many types of tangerine are commonly interchanged, so you may find a bewildering variety of fruits that are essentially the same.

Clementine The smallest of the tangerines, with bright orange skin and no pips. This, and their sweet, aromatic flesh, make clementines the most popular variety of tangerine. They are sometimes sold with the leaves still attached, which makes the fruit particularly attractive.

Mandarin Most commonly sold canned, tiny peeled tangerine segments are sold as mandarin oranges, although they are usually small satsumas. The deliciously sweet, vibrant segments make an attractive decoration for a dessert.

Satsuma These largish tangerines from Japan have loose skin and a refreshing, rather tart flavour. Satsumas contain very few pips.

Making tangerine shells

1 Choose attractive, well-shaped fruit. Cut off the top of each to make a lid.

2 Carefully scoop out the segments with a teaspoon, a few at a time. Scrape out any pith or membrane, taking care to avoid breaking the skin. Fill the shells with iced tangerine pulp.

Right: The cementine is the smallest and most popular variety of tangerine.

Ortanique Also known as "honey tangerines" because of their delicious sweetness, ortaniques are a hybrid, which can be found growing on the same trees as tangerines or oranges.

Tangelo These are a cross between a tangerine and a grapefruit, and have the easy-peeling qualities of the former. Tangelos are irregularly shaped and have a refreshing, tart flavour, rather like an orange.

Minneola Another tangerine–grapefruit hybrid, minneolas can be recognized by the distinctive bulge at their stalk end. They have bright orange skin and are very easy to peel. The sweet, juicy flesh has no pips.

Nutrition

All tangerines and their hybrids are extremely good sources of vitamin C and beta-carotene. They provide about 40 kilocalories per 100g/3³⁄₄oz.

Buying and Storing

Many varieties of tangerine have loose, puffy skins, which are no indication of quality. Choose fruits that feel heavy for their size; they will contain more juice. Avoid fruits with damaged skins and, if you are buying pre-packed fruits, check that none is mouldy or it will quickly taint all the other fruit.

Tangerines do not keep as long as other citrus fruit, but can be stored in the fridge for up to a week.

Canned mandarin oranges are a very useful store-cupboard item. Use them in trifles, chocolate slices and also on cheesecakes. Children love them set in orange or mandarin jelly.

It is also possible to buy canned peeled whole mandarins in syrup – the lazy cook's answer for a simply sensational dessert. Just make a caramel sauce, add the drained fruit and decorate with some fresh orange or mandarin zest. A dash of orange liqueur gilds the lily.

Preparing and Serving

All varieties of tangerine can be used in the same way as oranges. The peel is as useful as the flesh, and the zest can be candied or used to flavour sweet liqueurs. Strips of peel can be dried and used in savoury stews or included with herbs to make a bouquet garni.

Tangerine segments can be eaten on their own. Dipped in melted chocolate or crystallized, they make a delicious after-dinner sweet. Tangerine juice adds a distinctive flavour to marinades for pork and poultry; combine it with oriental aromatics like five-spice powder, ginger and soy sauce.

CITRUS FRUIT RECIPES

Put the squeeze on citrus fruit for some of the finest puddings and preserves in any good cook's repertoire. Lemon Surprise Pudding, Moist Orange and Almond Cake, Key Lime Pie and Lemon Meringue Pie are perennially popular, while new delights include Lemon Coeur à la Crème with Cointreau Oranges.

RUBY ORANGE SHERBET IN GINGER BASKETS

THIS SUPERB FROZEN DESSERT IS PERFECT FOR PEOPLE WITHOUT ICE CREAM MAKERS WHO CAN'T BE BOTHERED WITH THE FREEZING AND STIRRING THAT HOME-MADE ICES NORMALLY REQUIRE. IT IS ALSO IDEAL FOR SERVING AT A SPECIAL DINNER PARTY AS BOTH THE SHERBET AND GINGER BASKETS CAN BE MADE IN ADVANCE AND THE DESSERT SIMPLY ASSEMBLED BETWEEN COURSES.

SERVES SIX

INGREDIENTS
grated rind and juice of
  2 blood oranges
175g/6oz/1½ cups icing sugar
300ml/½ pint/1¼ cups double cream
200g/7oz/scant 1 cup Greek-style
  natural yogurt
blood orange segments, to
  decorate (optional)
For the ginger baskets
  25g/1oz/2 tbsp unsalted butter
  15ml/1 tbsp golden syrup
  30ml/2 tbsp caster sugar
  1.5ml/¼ tsp ground ginger
  15ml/1 tbsp finely chopped mixed
    citrus peel
  15ml/1 tbsp plain flour

2 Whisk the double cream in a large bowl until the mixture forms soft peaks, then fold in the yogurt.

3 Gently stir in the orange juice mixture, then pour into a freezerproof container. Cover and freeze until firm.

6 Lightly grease two baking sheets. Using about 10ml/2 tsp of the mixture at a time, drop three portions of the ginger dough on to each baking sheet, spacing them well apart. Spread each one to a 5cm/2in circle, then bake for 12–14 minutes or until the biscuits are dark golden in colour.

1 Place the orange rind and juice in a bowl. Sift the icing sugar over the top and set aside for 30 minutes, then stir until smooth.

COOK'S TIP
When making the ginger baskets it is essential to work quickly. Have the greased tins or cups ready before you start. If the biscuits cool and firm up before you have time to drape them all, return them to the oven for a few seconds to soften them again.

4 Make the baskets. Preheat the oven to 180°C/350°F/Gas 4. Place the butter, syrup and sugar in a heavy-based saucepan and heat gently until melted.

5 Add the ground ginger, mixed citrus peel and flour and stir until the mixture is smooth.

7 Remove the biscuits from the oven and allow to stand on the baking sheets for 1 minute to firm slightly. Lift off with a fish slice and drape over six greased mini pudding tins or upturned cups; flatten the top (which will become the base) and flute the edges to form a basket shape.

8 When cool, lift the baskets off the tins or cups and place on individual dessert plates. Arrange small scoops of the frozen orange sherbet in each basket. Decorate each portion with a few orange segments, if you like.

LEMON SURPRISE PUDDING

THIS IS A MUCH-LOVED DESSERT MANY OF US REMEMBER FROM CHILDHOOD. THE SURPRISE IS THE UNEXPECTED SAUCE CONCEALED BENEATH THE DELECTABLE SPONGE.

SERVES FOUR

INGREDIENTS
   50g/2oz/¼ cup butter, plus extra
      for greasing
   grated rind and juice of 2 lemons
   115g/4oz/½ cup caster sugar
   2 eggs, separated
   50g/2oz/½ cup self-raising flour
   300ml/½ pint/1¼ cups milk

1 Preheat the oven to 190°C/375°F/ Gas 5. Use a little butter to grease a 1.2 litre/2 pint/5 cup baking dish.

2 Beat the lemon rind, remaining butter and caster sugar in a bowl until pale and fluffy. Add the egg yolks and flour and beat together well. Gradually whisk in the lemon juice and milk (don't be alarmed if the mixture curdles horribly!). In a grease-free bowl whisk the egg whites until they form stiff peaks.

3 Fold the egg whites lightly into the lemon mixture, then pour into the prepared baking dish.

4 Place the dish in a roasting tin and pour in hot water to come halfway up the side of the dish. Bake for about 45 minutes until golden. Serve at once.

CRÊPES SUZETTE

SIMPLY SUPERB — THAT'S THE VERDICT ON THIS PERENNIALLY POPULAR DESSERT. THESE CRÊPES DESERVE NOTHING LESS THAN THE BEST QUALITY VANILLA ICE CREAM YOU CAN FIND.

SERVES FOUR

INGREDIENTS
   8 crêpes (see Summer Berry Crêpes,
      page 116, for method)
   25g/1oz/2 tbsp unsalted butter
   50g/2oz/¼ cup caster sugar
   juice of 2 oranges
   juice of ½ lemon
   60ml/4 tbsp Cointreau or other
      orange liqueur
   best quality vanilla ice cream,
      to serve

COOK'S TIP
Crêpes freeze well and can be reheated by the method described in step 1, or simultaneously thawed and reheated in the microwave. A stack of eight crêpes, interleaved with greaseproof paper, will take 2–3 minutes on High. Be sure to cover the top crêpe with a piece of paper as well.

1 Warm the cooked crêpes between two plates placed over a saucepan of simmering water.

2 Melt the butter in a heavy-based frying pan. Stir in the caster sugar and cook over a medium heat, tilting the pan occasionally, until the mixture is golden brown. Add the orange and lemon juices and stir until the caramel has completely dissolved.

3 Add a crêpe to the pan. Using kitchen tongs, fold it in half, then in half again. Slide to the side of the pan. Repeat with the remaining crêpes.

4 When all the crêpes have been folded in the sauce, pour over the Cointreau and set it alight. Shake the pan until the flames die down. Divide the crêpes and sauce among dessert plates and serve at once with vanilla ice cream.

CITRUS FRUIT FLAMBÉ
WITH PISTACHIO PRALINE

A FRUIT FLAMBÉ MAKES A DRAMATIC FINALE FOR A DINNER PARTY. TOPPING THIS REFRESHING CITRUS FRUIT DESSERT WITH CRUNCHY PISTACHIO PRALINE MAKES IT EXTRA SPECIAL.

SERVES FOUR

INGREDIENTS
   4 oranges
   2 ruby grapefruit
   2 limes
   50g/2oz/¼ cup butter
   50g/2oz/⅓ cup light muscovado sugar
   45ml/3 tbsp Cointreau
   fresh mint sprigs, to decorate
For the praline
   oil, for greasing
   115g/4oz/½ cup caster sugar
   50g/2oz/½ cup pistachio nuts

4 Heat the butter and muscovado sugar together in a heavy-based frying pan until the sugar has melted and the mixture is golden. Strain the citrus juices into the pan and continue to cook, stirring occasionally, until the juice has reduced and is syrupy.

5 Add the fruit segments and warm through without stirring. Pour over the Cointreau and set it alight. As soon as the flames die down, spoon the fruit flambé into serving dishes. Scatter some praline over each portion and decorate with mint. Serve at once.

1 First, make the pistachio praline. Brush a baking sheet lightly with oil. Place the caster sugar and nuts in a small heavy-based saucepan and cook gently, swirling the pan occasionally until the sugar has melted.

2 Continue to cook over a fairly low heat until the nuts start to pop and the sugar has turned a dark golden colour. Pour on to the oiled baking sheet and set aside to cool. Using a sharp knife, chop the praline into rough chunks.

3 Cut off all the rind and pith from the citrus fruit. Holding each fruit in turn over a large bowl, cut between the membranes so that the segments fall into the bowl, with any juice.

COOK'S TIP
If desired, use a rolling pin or toffee hammer to break up the praline.

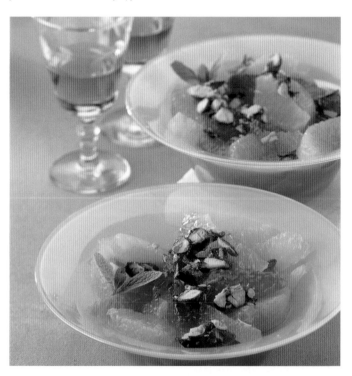

COLD LEMON SOUFFLÉ <u>WITH</u> CARAMELIZED ALMOND TOPPING

THIS TERRIFIC TO LOOK AT, REFRESHING DESSERT SOUFFLÉ IS LIGHT AND LUSCIOUS.

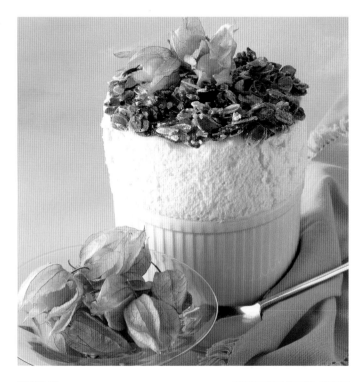

2 Put the lemon rind and egg yolks in a bowl. Add 75g/3oz/6 tbsp of the caster sugar and whisk until light and creamy.

3 Place the lemon juice in a small heatproof bowl and sprinkle over the gelatine. Set aside for 5 minutes, then place the bowl in a pan of simmering water. Heat, stirring occasionally, until the gelatine has dissolved. Cool slightly, then stir the gelatine mixture into the egg yolk mixture.

4 In a separate bowl, lightly whip the cream to soft peaks. Fold into the egg yolk mixture and set aside.

5 Whisk the egg whites in a grease-free bowl until stiff peaks form. Gradually whisk in the remaining caster sugar until the mixture is stiff and glossy. Quickly and lightly fold the whites into the yolk mixture. Pour into the prepared dish, smooth the surface and chill for 4–5 hours or until set.

SERVES SIX

INGREDIENTS
  oil, for greasing
  grated rind and juice of
    3 large lemons
  5 large eggs, separated
  115g/4oz/½ cup caster sugar
  25ml/1½ tbsp powdered gelatine
  450ml/¾ pint/scant 2 cups
    double cream
For the decoration
  75g/3oz/¾ cup flaked almonds
  75g/3oz/¾ cup icing sugar
  3 physalis

COOK'S TIP
When peeling off the soufflé collar, hold the blade of a knife against the set soufflé so that it keeps its shape.

1 Make the soufflé collar. Cut a strip of non-stick baking paper long enough to fit around a 900ml/1½ pint/3¾ cup soufflé dish and wide enough to extend 7.5cm/3in above the rim. Fit the strip around the dish, tape, then tie it around the top of the dish with string. Brush the inside of the paper lightly with oil.

6 Make the decoration. Brush a baking sheet lightly with oil. Preheat the grill. Scatter the almonds over the sheet and sift the icing sugar over. Grill until the nuts are golden and the sugar has caramelized. Allow to cool, then remove the mixture from the tray with a palette knife and break it into pieces.

7 When the soufflé has set, carefully peel off the paper. Pile the caramelized almonds on top of the soufflé and decorate with the physalis.

LEMON ROULADE ^{WITH} LEMON CURD CREAM

THIS FEATHERLIGHT ROULADE FILLED WITH A RICH LEMON CURD CREAM MAKES A MARVELLOUS DESSERT OR TEA-TIME TREAT. THE LEMON CURD CAN BE MADE AHEAD AND KEPT IN THE FRIDGE.

MAKES EIGHT SLICES

INGREDIENTS

4 eggs, separated
115g/4oz/½ cup caster sugar
finely grated rind of 2 lemons
5ml/1 tsp pure vanilla essence
25g/1oz/¼ cup ground almonds
40g/1½oz/⅓ cup plain flour, sifted
45ml/3 tbsp icing sugar, for dusting
For the lemon curd cream
300ml/½ pint/1¼ cups double cream
60ml/4 tbsp fresh lemon curd
(see recipe below right)

1 Preheat the oven to 190°C/375°F/ Gas 5. Grease a 33 × 23cm/13 × 9in Swiss roll tin and line with non-stick baking paper.

2 In a large bowl, beat the egg yolks with half the caster sugar until light and foamy. Beat in the lemon rind and vanilla essence, then lightly fold in the ground almonds and flour using a large metal spoon or spatula.

COOK'S TIP
Having filled and rolled the roulade, keep it wrapped in the non-stick baking paper and hold it together for about a minute to allow the shape to set before removing the paper and transferring the roulade to a plate.

3 Whisk the egg whites in a grease-free bowl until they form stiff, glossy peaks. Gradually whisk in the remaining caster sugar to form a stiff meringue. Stir half the meringue mixture into the egg yolk mixture and fold in the rest.

4 Pour into the prepared tin, level the surface with a palette knife and bake for 10 minutes or until risen and spongy to the touch. Cover loosely with a sheet of non-stick baking paper and a damp dish towel. Leave to cool in the tin.

5 Make the lemon curd cream. Whip the cream; then lightly fold in the lemon curd.

6 Sift the icing sugar liberally over a piece of non-stick baking paper. Turn the sponge out on to it. Peel off the lining paper and spread the lemon curd cream over the surface of the sponge, leaving a border around the edge.

7 Using the paper underneath as a guide, roll up the sponge from one of the long sides. Place on a serving platter, with the seam underneath. Cut the roulade into slices to serve.

FRESH LEMON CURD
Put the grated rind and juice of 3 lemons into a pan with 115g/4oz/ ½ cup caster sugar. Bring to the boil, stirring until the sugar has dissolved. Stir in 15ml/1 tbsp cornflour mixed to a paste with 15ml/1 tbsp cold water. Off the heat, whisk in 2 egg yolks. Return to a low heat, whisk for about 2 minutes; remove from the heat. Gradually whisk in 50g/2oz/¼ cup butter, at room temperature. Pour into a sterilized jar, cover and seal at once. Leave to cool, then chill. Use within 2–3 weeks. Makes 450g/1lb.

LEMON MERINGUE PIE

CRISP SHORTCRUST IS FILLED WITH A MOUTHWATERING LEMON CREAM FILLING AND HEAPED WITH
SOFT GOLDEN-TOPPED MERINGUE. THIS CLASSIC OPEN TART NEVER FAILS TO PLEASE. POPULAR WITH
ADULTS AND CHILDREN, IT IS THE ESSENTIAL SUNDAY LUNCH DESSERT.

2 Meanwhile make the filling. Place all the ingredients in a bowl, mix lightly and leave to soak for 1 hour.

3 Preheat the oven to 200°C/400°F/Gas 6. Beat the filling until smooth and pour into the chilled pastry case. Bake for 20 minutes or until the filling has just set and the pastry is golden. Remove from the oven and cool on a wire rack for 30 minutes or until a skin has formed on the surface. Lower the oven temperature to 180°C/350°F/Gas 4.

4 Make the topping. Whisk the egg whites in a grease-free bowl until they form stiff peaks. Whisk in the caster sugar to form a glossy meringue. Spoon on top of the set lemon filling and spread over, making sure you spread the meringue right to the rim of the pie shell. Swirl the meringue slightly.

SERVES SIX

INGREDIENTS
  115g/4oz/1 cup plain flour
  a pinch of salt
  50g/2oz/¼ cup butter
  50g/2oz/¼ cup lard
  15ml/1 tbsp caster sugar
  about 15ml/1 tbsp iced water
For the filling
  3 large egg yolks
  30ml/2 tbsp caster sugar
  grated rind and juice of 1 lemon
  25g/1oz/½ cup fresh
    white breadcrumbs
  250ml/8fl oz/1 cup milk
For the topping
  3 large egg whites
  115g/4oz/½ cup caster sugar

1 Sift the flour and salt into a bowl. Rub in the butter and lard until the mixture resembles fine breadcrumbs. Stir in the sugar and add enough iced water to make a soft dough. Roll out the pastry on a lightly floured surface and line a 21cm/8½in pie plate or tin. Chill until required.

5 Bake the pie for 20–25 minutes or until the meringue is crisp and golden brown. Allow to cool on a wire rack for 10 minutes before serving.

FRESH LEMON TART

MADE FAMOUS BY ITS FRENCH TITLE – TARTE AUX CITRON – THIS TART SHOULD BE SERVED AT ROOM TEMPERATURE IF THE ZESTY LEMON FLAVOUR IS TO BE ENJOYED TO THE FULL.

SERVES SIX TO EIGHT

INGREDIENTS
350g/12oz packet ready-made rich
    sweet shortcrust pastry, thawed
    if frozen
For the filling
    3 eggs
    115g/4oz/½ cup caster sugar
    115g/4oz/1 cup ground almonds
    105ml/7 tbsp double cream
    grated rind and juice of 2 lemons
For the topping
    2 thin-skinned unwaxed lemons,
    thinly sliced
    200g/7oz/scant 1 cup caster sugar
    105ml/7 tbsp water

COOK'S TIP
If you prefer not to candy the lemons,
simply dust the tart with icing sugar.

1 Roll out the pastry and line a deep 23cm/9in fluted flan tin. Prick the base and chill for 30 minutes.

2 Preheat the oven to 200°C/400°F/ Gas 6. Line the pastry with non-stick baking paper and baking beans and bake blind for 10 minutes. Remove the paper and beans and return the pastry case to the oven for 5 minutes more.

3 Meanwhile, make the filling. Beat the eggs, caster sugar, almonds and cream in a bowl until smooth. Beat in the lemon rind and juice. Pour the filling into the pastry case. Lower the oven temperature to 190°C/375°F/Gas 5 and bake for 20 minutes or until the filling has set and the pastry is golden.

4 Make the topping. Place the lemon slices in a pan and pour over water to cover. Simmer for 15–20 minutes or until the skins are tender, then drain.

5 Place the sugar in a saucepan and stir in the measured water. Heat gently until the sugar has dissolved, stirring constantly, then boil for 2 minutes. Add the lemon slices and cook for 10–15 minutes until the skins become shiny and candied.

6 Lift out the candied lemon slices and arrange them over the top of the tart. Return the syrup to the heat and boil until reduced to a thick glaze. Brush this over the tart and allow to cool completely before serving.

KEY LIME PIE

THIS IS ONE OF AMERICA'S FAVOURITES. AS THE NAME SUGGESTS, IT ORIGINATED IN THE FLORIDA KEYS.

MAKES TEN SLICES

INGREDIENTS
225g/8oz/2 cups plain flour
115g/4oz/½ cup chilled
   butter, diced
30ml/2 tbsp caster sugar
2 egg yolks
a pinch of salt
30ml/2 tbsp cold water
thinly pared lime rind and mint
   leaves, to decorate
For the filling
4 eggs, separated
400g/14oz can condensed milk
grated rind and juice of 3 limes
a few drops of green food
   colouring (optional)
30ml/2 tbsp caster sugar
For the topping
300ml/½ pint/1¼ cups double cream
2–3 limes, thinly sliced

1 Sift the flour into a mixing bowl and rub in the butter using your fingertips until the mixture resembles fresh breadcrumbs. Add the sugar, egg yolks, salt and water. Mix to a soft dough.

2 Roll out the pastry on a lightly floured surface and use to line a deep 21cm/8½in fluted flan tin, allowing the excess pastry to hang over the edge. Prick the pastry base and chill for at least 30 minutes.

3 Preheat the oven to 200°C/400°F/ Gas 6. Trim off the excess pastry from around the edge of the pastry case using a large sharp knife and line the pastry case with non-stick baking paper and baking beans.

4 Bake the pastry case blind for 10 minutes. Remove the paper and beans and return the pastry case to the oven for 10 minutes more.

5 Meanwhile, make the filling. Beat the egg yolks in a large bowl until light and creamy, then beat in the condensed milk, with the lime rind and juice until well combined. Add the food colouring, if using, and continue to beat until the mixture is thick.

COOK'S TIP
You can make the pastry in a food processor, but take care not to overprocess the dough. Use the pulse button and process for a few seconds at a time; switch off the motor the moment the dough clumps together.

6 In a grease-free bowl, whisk the egg whites to stiff peaks. Whisk in the caster sugar, then fold into the lime mixture.

7 Lower the oven temperature to 160°C/325°F/Gas 3. Pour the lime filling into the pastry case. Bake for 20–25 minutes or until it has set and is starting to brown. Cool, then chill.

8 Just before serving, whip the double cream for the topping and spoon it around the edge of the pie. Cut the lime slices once from the centre to the edge, then twist each slice and arrange between the spoonfuls of cream. Decorate with lime rind and mint leaves.

MOIST ORANGE AND ALMOND CAKE

THE KEY TO THIS RECIPE IS TO COOK THE ORANGE SLOWLY FIRST, SO IT IS FULLY TENDER BEFORE BEING BLENDED. DON'T USE A MICROWAVE TO SPEED THINGS UP — THIS MAKES ORANGE SKIN TOUGH.

SERVES EIGHT

INGREDIENTS
    1 large orange
    3 eggs
    225g/8oz/1 cup caster sugar
    5ml/1 tsp baking powder
    225g/8oz/2 cups ground almonds
    25g/1oz/¼ cup plain flour
    icing sugar, for dusting
    whipped cream and orange slices
    to serve (optional).

1 Wash the orange and pierce it with a skewer. Put it in a deep saucepan and pour over water to cover completely. Bring to the boil then lower the heat, cover and simmer for 1 hour or until the skin is very soft. Drain, then cool.

COOK'S TIP
For a treat, serve this cake with spiced poached kumquats.

2 Preheat the oven to 180°C/350°F/ Gas 4. Grease a 20cm/8in round cake tin and line it with non-stick baking paper. Cut the cooled orange in half and discard the pips. Place the orange, skin and all, in a blender or food processor and purée until smooth and pulpy.

3 In a bowl, whisk the eggs and sugar until thick. Fold in the baking powder, almonds and flour. Fold in the purée.

4 Pour into the prepared tin, level the surface and bake for 1 hour or until a skewer inserted into the centre comes out clean. Cool the cake in the tin for 10 minutes, then turn out on to a wire rack, peel off the lining paper and cool completely. Dust the top liberally with icing sugar and serve as a dessert with whipped cream, if you like. You could tuck thick orange slices under the cake just before serving.

LEMON <u>AND</u> LIME SYRUP CAKE

THIS CAKE IS PERFECT FOR BUSY COOKS AS IT CAN BE MIXED IN MOMENTS AND NEEDS NO ICING.
THE SIMPLE TANGY LIME TOPPING TRANSFORMS IT INTO A FABULOUSLY MOIST CAKE.

SERVES EIGHT

INGREDIENTS
    225g/8oz/2 cups self-raising flour
    5ml/1 tsp baking powder
    225g/8oz/1 cup caster sugar
    225g/8oz/1 cup butter, softened
    4 eggs, beaten
    grated rind of 2 lemons
    30ml/2 tbsp lemon juice
For the topping
    finely pared rind of 1 lime
    juice of 2 limes
    150g/5oz/⅔ cup caster sugar

1 Make the cake. Preheat the oven to 160°C/325°F/Gas 3. Grease and line a 20cm/8in round cake tin. Sift the flour and baking powder into a large bowl. Add the caster sugar, butter and eggs and beat together well until the mixture is smooth, creamy and fluffy.

2 Beat in the lemon rind and juice. Spoon the mixture into the prepared tin, then smooth the surface and make a shallow indentation in the top with the back of a spoon.

3 Bake for 1¼–1½ hours or until the cake is golden on top and spongy when lightly pressed, and a skewer inserted into the centre comes out clean.

4 Meanwhile, mix the topping ingredients together. As soon as the cake is cooked, remove it from the oven and pour the topping over the surface. Allow the cake to cool in the tin.

VARIATION
Use lemon rind and juice instead of lime for the topping if you prefer. You will need only one large lemon.

EXOTIC FRUITS

Thanks to modern transportation methods, tropical fruits are no longer merely the stuff of travellers' tales. Rambutans, carambolas, guavas, passion fruit and pomegranates are stocked on greengrocers' shelves alongside recent rarities, which have now become commonplace, such as mangoes, fresh dates and kiwi fruit. Most supermarkets now label tropical fruits with preparation and serving suggestions, so it is easy to venture into the realms of the exotic.

Peeling plantains

1 Using a sharp knife, top and tail the fruit. Cut in half horizontally.

2 Slit the plantain skin with a sharp knife, along the natural ridge. Take care not to cut through the flesh.

3 Ease up the edge of the skin and run your thumb tip underneath to lift up the skin. Lift off and discard the skin.

Right: Plantains are almost always used in savoury dishes and can be cooked like potatoes.

Cooking

Peel bananas just before using, removing the white threads from the flesh. Slice the bananas and, if not serving immediately, brush with lemon juice to prevent discoloration.

Dessert bananas are delicious eaten raw, but cooking brings out the sweetness and enhances the flavour. Raw bananas can be made into ice cream, milk shakes and trifles. Sliced bananas can be added to fruit salads or used to garnish sweet and savoury dishes. In Indonesia and the Far East, they are served as an accompaniment to rice dishes such as *nasi goreng* and curries. They combine well with other tropical ingredients, especially brown sugar, coconut, exotic fruits like pineapple, passion fruit and mango, and rum.

Bananas can be baked in their skins, then split and served with melted butter and lemon juice. Alternatively, cook them over the dying embers of a barbecue until the skins turn black. Split them, sprinkle with rum and serve with double cream. Another rich dessert is banoffi pie, a very sweet concoction of bananas and toffee. A less sweet, but equally delicious combination is grilled bananas wrapped in bacon. Banana fritters are always popular; cut the fruit into chunks, coat in batter and deep fry, or wrap in filo

Above: Dried bananas are dark brown, sticky and very sweet.

pastry, brush with melted butter and deep fry. Mashed bananas make deliciously moist cakes and teabreads.

Green bananas and plantains are starchier than sweet bananas and contain less sugar, so they are served as a vegetable. They can be boiled, baked, mashed, fried or grilled, and are an essential ingredient of many African and West Indian dishes. Banana leaves are often used as a wrapping for savoury fillings and add a pleasant aromatic flavour to both chicken and fish.

BABACOS

The babaco is a hybrid of the papaya. Pointed at the stem end and blunt at the other, this large five-sided fruit reveals a soft white core when halved. When unripe, the waxy skin is pale green, maturing to yellow. When ripe, the pale orangey-pink flesh is succulent and juicy, with a faint aroma of fresh strawberries, and the flavour resembles that of a rather bland papaya.

History

The babaco is native to Ecuador. European botanists discovered it about seventy years ago, and it is now widely grown in New Zealand, and in the Channel Islands.

Nutrition

The fruit contains valuable enzymes that help to digest fat and proteins and can be used to tenderize meat. It is a good source of vitamin C.

Buying and Storing

Babacos keep well. Yellow fruit are ready to eat straight away and should be stored in the fridge, where they will keep for about five days. Pale green babacos can be kept for a few days at room temperature until yellow and ripe.

Preparing and Cooking

Babacos can be sliced, skin and all, and eaten raw. The delicate flavour can be livened up with lemon or lime juice and sugar. The flesh can be diced and used raw in salads, or squeezed to make a refreshing juice. Babacos can also be poached in syrup and served as a dessert with cream, custard or vanilla or stem ginger ice cream, but you will need to flavour the syrup with lime juice and aromatics. On a savoury note, the fruit makes excellent sauces, chutneys and relishes. Stewed babaco can be served as an accompaniment to roast chicken, pork and ham.

Babaco for breakfast

For a deliciously different breakfast experience, try serving your favourite cereal with chilled cooked babaco. Make a syrup by boiling equal quantities of water and sugar with the juice of a lemon or lime and a split vanilla pod, a cinnamon stick or a grating of nutmeg. Dice the babaco (there is no need to peel it) and poach gently in the syrup for about 10 minutes, until tender. Chill well before using.

Right:
Babacos are ripe
when yellow all over
– keep fruits that are
still mottled green (as here)
at room temperature for a few days until
they turn completely yellow.

DRAGON FRUIT

Dragon fruit, or pitihayas, come in both yellow and pink versions. Pink dragon fruit are large, fuschia-pink fruit about 10cm/4in long, covered with pointed green-tipped scales, rather like the leaves of a globe artichoke. Inside, they are spectacularly beautiful, with translucent pearly-white flesh dotted with a mass of edible black seeds, which add an appealing crunch. The flesh is sweet and refreshing, with a slightly acidic melon-like flavour. It has the texture of kiwi fruit.

Yellow dragon fruit look more like prickly pears or mini-pineapples. They taste exactly like the pink variety.

Nutrition

Dragon fruit are rich in vitamin C and dietary fibre.

Buying and Storing

Yellow dragon fruit are ripe when golden all over. Both pink and yellow varieties should yield when gently squeezed in the hand. They are best eaten as soon as they are ripe, but the fruits can be kept in the fridge for up to three days.

Preparing and Serving

Dragon fruit are best eaten on their own, sprinkled with lemon or lime juice to enhance the flavour. They should be served chilled. Cut them in half lengthways, then scoop out the flesh from the shell. The shells can be used as unusual serving dishes.

Above: Brightly coloured dragon fruit have sweet refreshing flesh.

DURIANS

The disgusting, all-pervading, sewage-like smell is legendary and has given rise to the alternative name: civet fruit. When ripe, the flavour of the flesh, however, is delicious.

Durians are large fruit, which can weigh up to 4.5kg/10lb. Round or oval, they have a woody, olive green outer layer covered with stubby, sharp spikes, which turns yellow as they ripen. They consist of three to five segments containing aromatic creamy-white flesh with the texture of rich custard; the flavour is sweet, a little like strawberries, with a creamy after-taste. The large brown seeds are edible if cooked.

History

Durians originated in Malaysia or Borneo and from there spread to South-east Asia in prehistoric times. Despite their unspeakable smell, they have always been considered an aphrodisiac.

Nutrition

Durians are starchy fruits. They contain a small amount of fat and are a good source of potassium and vitamin C.

Buying and Storing

It is essential to eat durians very fresh; don't attempt to store them, however briefly, or your house will smell of blocked drains. Never buy fruit with damaged skin, or the smell will be

unbearable. Do not buy durians abroad and attempt to bring them home, as they are banned by most airlines! Take care not to drip juice on to clothing or table linen as it stains indelibly. Despite all these dire warnings, don't be put off trying this exotic fruit; it really does taste wonderful.

Preparing and Serving

Durians are best eaten raw. Use a large sharp knife to slit the skin at the segment joints, press out the segments and scoop out the flesh and seeds with a spoon. The rich, custardy flesh can be eaten just as it is, or puréed to make ice cream or milk shakes. Durian flesh is also used for making jam and cakes, and is available canned. The richness of the pulp also makes an excellent foil to hot, spicy foods like curries and chilli dishes. Durian seeds can be roasted or boiled and eaten like nuts.

Left: The horrible, all-pervading sewage-like smell of Durians is legendary, however, when ripe, the flavour of the flesh is delicious.

FEIJOAS

Although a distant member of the guava family, feijoas resemble small slightly pear-shaped passion fruit, with a dark green skin that yellows as the fruit ripens. The thin, tough skin protects a soft jelly-like pulp containing tiny hard seeds, which are edible. Despite its alternative name of "pineapple guava", the feijoa tastes more like an aromatic strawberry. Treat it like guava.

History

Originally from South America, the feijoa takes its name from the Portuguese botanist Dom da Silva Feijoa, who discovered it in Brazil. It is also nowadays cultivated in New Zealand.

Nutrition

Feijoas are an excellent source of vitamin C and are rich in iodine. They provide 20 kilocalories per 100g/3¾oz.

Right: Feijoas taste a little like aromatic fresh strawberries.

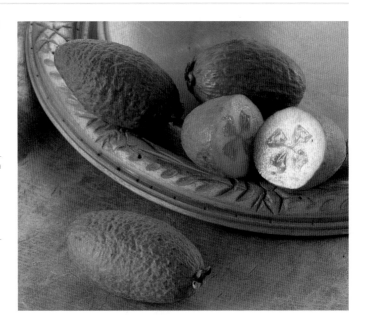

GINUP

The bright green dimpled skin of the ginup gives rise to its alternative name of "Spanish lime", but it is related to neither the lime nor the lychee, which it resembles in flavour. Ginups are small round tropical fruits, about 3cm/1¼in in diameter, which grow on trees in bunches like grapes. The tough green skin protects a jelly-like pink pulp containing a large central seed. The flesh is juicy and sweet, with a slightly acidic note. Despite its pale colour, ginup juice stains horribly and if you get it on your clothes or table linen, it will never come out.

GRANADILLAS

Granadillas, or grenadillas, are the largest members of the passion fruit family and can weigh several pounds. In their unripe state, these large specimens are used as vegetables, but they are seldom exported. The granadillas you will find in the shops are smooth, round, orange-skinned fruits, with greyish pulp containing small hard seeds. They look more attractive than passion fruit, but taste less fragrant. Granadillas can be eaten and used in exactly the same way as passion fruit.

Right: Granadillas

MANGOSTEENS

Despite their name, mangosteens have nothing to do with mangoes. Nor are they related to lychees, although their pearly white flesh looks very similar.

Mangosteens are apple-shaped with rather leathery, reddish-brown skin, which is deep purple when ripe. The flesh is divided into five segments, each containing a large seed. The segments are enclosed in dark pink pith, which should be removed before eating. Mangosteens have a sweet, refreshing flavour, rather like that of a plum, but more highly perfumed.

History

Mangosteens are indigenous to Southeast Asia. The trees are slow to grow; it is fifteen years before they bear fruit. They are now grown commercially in parts of Thailand, Central America and Australia.

Preparing and Serving

The flavour of mangosteens is too fragrant and delicate to be impaired by cooking. Eat them just as they are, or add to fruit salad. Peeled mangosteens look spectacular surrounded by a ribbon of strawberry or raspberry coulis.

Serving a mangosteen

1 Using a small sharp knife, cut the skin around the equator of the shell, then lift off the top half of the shell and spoon out the flesh.

2 Alternatively, simply cut the mangosteens in half and scoop out the flesh with a spoon

Above: Mangosteens have a highly perfumed flavour. Eat the pearly white fruit segments just as they are, or add them to fruit salad.

MARACOYAS

Also known as yellow passion fruit, the maracoya is a largish fruit with vibrant green, thick shiny skin that turns yellow as it ripens. Inside is a mass of translucent orange pulp enclosing hard grey seeds, just like a passion fruit, but sharper and less aromatic. Use in exactly the same way as passion fruit, adding plenty of sugar.

Right: Maracoyas

PASSION FRUIT

Passion fruit takes its name from its exotic flower, which is said to symbolize the Passion of Christ. Native to the Americas, these round or oval fruits have a leathery purplish-brown skin (some, like those from Brazil, are yellow in colour), which wrinkles when the fruits are fully ripe. Inside, the edible seeds are surrounded by intensely fragrant, translucent, greenish-orange pulp with a distinctive sour-sweet flavour and a wonderful scent. The fruits can be as small as a cherry or as large as an orange, but the ones most commonly available in the shops are about 7.5cm/3in long.

Left: Passion fruit

Nutrition

The fruits contain vitamins A and C and are a good source of dietary fibre. They contain 34 kilocalories per 100g/3³/₄oz.

Buying and Storing

Choose fruit that feel heavy for their size, with firm, slightly wrinkled skins. Very wrinkly passion fruit with extremely dark skins will have dried out. Passion fruit can be ripened at room temperature; do not keep them in the fridge. The pulp can be frozen in ice cube trays, then packed into plastic bags. The juice is sold in cartons.

Preparing and Serving

The simplest way to eat passion fruit is on its own; cut the fruit in half and scoop out the pulp and seeds with a spoon. Both are edible, but the pulp can be sieved to make a smooth coulis or refreshing drink. Passion fruit enhances the flavour of all other fruits and makes a delicious topping for a pavlova or cheesecake.

Sieved pulp can be made into ice creams and sorbets, or added to yogurt. Passion fruit jelly goes well with roast meats, or it can be spread on bread or toast. The juice makes an excellent marinade for rich meats like venison and game birds.

PAPAYAS

The papaya, or paw-paw, is native to tropical America, but it is now grown in most tropical or sub-tropical regions of the world. The large pear-shaped fruits grow to about 20cm/8in in length. Some varieties remain green when ripe, but most turn deep yellow or orange. Papayas have beautiful deep salmon-pink flesh, with an abundance of grey-black seeds in the central cavity, which are edible. The soft, juicy, sweet flesh tastes like a cross between melons and peaches.

Right: Papayas

PINEAPPLES

Pineapples are probably the most recognizable of all fruit. In fact, they are multiple fruits consisting of dozens of lozenge-shaped protuberances, each one being the fruit of a single flower, which together make up a single pineapple. Resembling a large pine cone topped with a spiky grey-green plume of leaves, a whole pineapple makes a spectacular addition to a fruit

Above: Crystallized pineapple

platter. The warm, distinctive aroma of the fruit is also very pleasing.

Pineapples are very versatile fruit, their sweet, acidic taste lending itself to sweet and savoury dishes.

History

Native to South and Central America, pineapples had been cultivated for centuries before Christopher Columbus "discovered" them on his voyage to the West Indies in 1493. Astonished by the extraordinary appearance and flavour of the fruit, he brought some back to Europe, where they were regarded with wonder and awe. Due to their rarity and high cost, they became a symbol of hospitality, and stone pineapples often featured on the gateposts of houses to welcome guests.

The first pineapples, ripened in glasshouses, were presented to Louis XV of France, whose passion for the fruit made them even more

highly prized. Pineapples are now grown in every tropical region of the world.

Varieties

There are hundreds of pineapple varieties, ranging from very large to miniature fruits. They are seldom sold by name, although **Sweet Gold** is becoming familiar in some stores and markets. The colour of the skin varies from orange to greenish-yellow, while the degree of juiciness and sweetness depends upon the season.

Nutrition

Pineapples, which are rich in both vitamin C and dietary fibre, provide about 46 kilocalories per 100g/3¾oz. They contain bromelain, an enzyme that aids digestion, so are the perfect

Left: Large, small and baby pineapples

Making pineapple wedges with plumes

1 Place the fruit upright, hold it firmly and slice it in half vertically with a sharp serrated knife, cutting down through the plume into the flesh. Cut each piece in half again to make four wedges.
2 Run a small sharp knife between the rind and flesh. Slice off the core on each wedge, then slice the fruit into neat pieces, leaving these in place.

---

fruit to finish a rich meal. The enzyme breaks down protein so can be used to tenderize meat, but will prevent gelatine from setting.

Buying and Storing

Choose a plump pineapple that feels heavy for its size, with a fresh, stiff plume. To test for ripeness, gently pull out one of the bottom leaves; it should come out easily. Avoid lifeless-looking, bruised or withered fruit with browning leaves. Use the fruit as soon as possible after purchase. Do not store whole pineapples in the fridge, although peeled, sliced or cubed pineapple can be chilled in an airtight container for up to three days. Fresh, peeled and sliced pineapple is available and should also be kept chilled.
Dried and crystallized pineapple Both can be eaten as a snack or used to make cakes and puddings.
Canned pineapple Chunks and rings are available in syrup or juice. They are useful store cupboard items, but lack the aromatic flavour of fresh pineapple. Crushed pineapple is also available.

Preparing and Cooking

Pineapples are delicious on their own, served in wedges or rings. Some people like to add a splash of Kirsch, but a good pineapple should need no enhancement (although, surprisingly, a grinding of black pepper does wonders for the flavour). They go very well with other fruits; a hollowed-out pineapple shell complete with plume makes a spectacular container for fruit salad or tropical fruit sorbets.

Sliced pineapple can be made into a variety of hot desserts. Sauté in butter and brown sugar, make crisp fritters or combine with other fruits on skewers to make grilled fruit kebabs.

Tropical flavours, such as ginger, vanilla, cinnamon, allspice, coconut and rum, go extremely well with pineapple. Perhaps the most famous combination of pineapple, coconut and rum is the pina colada cocktail.

Pineapples' refreshing sweet-sour flavour makes them perfect for savoury dishes and they are often used in Chinese cooking. Traditionally, pineapple is cooked with gammon and pork, but it also goes well with lamb, poultry and fish, particularly in spicy dishes and curries.

Below: Dried pineapple can be eaten as a snack or chopped to use in cake and pudding recipes.

Peeling a pineapple

1 Cut the pineapple across into slices of the desired width.

2 Use a small, sharp knife to cut off the rind.

3 Hold each slice upright and cut out the "eyes".

4 Remove the central core of each slice with an apple corer.

POMEGRANATES

This attractive, apple-shaped fruit has leathery reddish-gold skin and a large calyx or crown. Inside is a mass of creamy-white edible seeds, each encased in a translucent sac of deep pink or crimson pulp and held together by segments of bitter, inedible, yellow membrane that extend outwards to the skin. The seeds gave the fruit its name, which means "grain apple". Eating a pomegranate is quite hard work, as each fleshy seed must be picked out individually, but their delicate, slightly tart flavour and refreshing, juicy texture make the effort worthwhile. Be warned, however, that pomegranate juice stains indelibly.

History

Originally from Persia, pomegranates have been linked with many cultures and religions for centuries and have been a symbol of fertility since ancient times because of their numerous seeds. Venus, the goddess of Love, was said to have given pomegranates as presents to her favourites.

Until the Renaissance, pomegranates were used primarily for medicinal purposes in Europe, although they have always featured in the cooking of Middle Eastern countries. Nowadays, they are widely cultivated, from France, Spain and Israel to America and all over Asia.

Nutrition

Pomegranate seeds are rich in vitamin C and are a good source of dietary fibre. They provide about 72 kilocalories per 100g/3¾oz.

Buying and Storing

A pomegranate that feels heavy for its size is likely to be full of juice. Choose glossy fruit and avoid those whose skin looks hard and dry. They will keep in the fridge for up to a week. Dried pomegranate seeds are used in Middle Eastern cooking.

Preparing and Serving

If you have the patience, pomegranates are fun to eat raw; cut them open and pick out the seeds with a pin. Either suck out the juice and discard the

Below: Inside pomegranates is a mass of seeds, each encased in deep pink pulp.

Preparing a pomegranate

1 Cut off a thin slice from one end.

2 Stand the fruit upright. Cut downwards through the skin at intervals, using a small sharp knife.

3 Bend back the segments and use your fingers to push the seeds into a bowl.

4 Remove all the bitter pith and membrane from the seeds.

Extracting pomegranate juice
Heat the fruit for 30 seconds on High in a microwave, then roll gently on the work surface to burst, but not crush the seeds. Make a hole in the bottom, stand over a jug and let the juice drain out, squeezing the pomegranate occasionally. Another method is to put the seeds in a sieve set over a bowl and press down gently with the back of a wooden spoon.

seeds or eat the jelly-like cells, seeds and all. The seeds make a decorative addition to fruit salads and can be used as a pretty topping for creamy desserts, ice cream or cheesecake. They have a particular affinity with almonds and make a jewel-like garnish for couscous. In India and Pakistan, the seeds are used in meat dishes.

Pomegranate juice Pomegranate juice must be extracted gently; electric or mechanical juicers will over-crush the seeds and make the juice bitter. The juice is delicious in some refreshing

long drinks, such as pomegranate-flavoured lemonade, or it can be used to make a syrup to colour and flavour alcoholic drinks and cocktails. Commercially produced pomegranate syrup is called grenadine.

The juice can also be used for sorbets and sauces, and makes a delicious pink jelly for savoury dishes, particularly those from the Middle East. Use it to marinate pheasant, turkey or chicken, or to make a sauce for chicken or turkey, which can then be garnished with pomegranate seeds.

PRICKLY PEARS

Sometimes known as "Indian figs", prickly pears are the fruit of a cactus. They certainly live up to their name, the skin being covered in tiny, painful prickles. Prickly pears are generally 7.5cm/3in long, with greenish-orange skin and orangey-pink flesh with a melon-like texture. The flavour is sweet and aromatic. The small seeds can be eaten raw, but become hard when they are cooked.

Buying and Storing

Prickly pears are orangey-yellow when ripe. Choose unblemished fruit and ripen at room temperature if necessary.

Preparing and Cooking

Prickly pears are usually peeled and eaten raw with a squeeze of lime or lemon and perhaps a little cream.

Prickly pears go well with other fruit and are good in fruit salads. They can be made into jams or mixed with oranges to make an unusual marmalade. Mix raw sieved pulp with ginger to make a sauce for gammon or cooked ham, or serve slices of prickly pear instead of melon with cured meats like Parma ham. Try adding stewed prickly pear segments to a fruit compote, or make a sauce or ice cream with the sieved purée. Candied or crystallized slices of prickly pear can be used to decorate cakes and many desserts, such as cheesecake.

Right: Prickly pears have a sweet and aromatic flavour.

Preparing prickly pears

1 The pear prickles are usually removed before the fruits are sold, but if not, wearing gloves, scrub each fruit with a stiff brush.

2 Using a sharp knife, cut a thin slice from each end of the prickly pear, then make a shallow cut just through the skin from end to end on either side of the fruit.

3 Now simply peel off the skin.

RAMBUTANS

Rambutans are related to lychees and are sometimes referred to as "hairy lychees". Originally from Malaysia, but now grown in tropical Central America and South-east Asia, they are larger than lychees (about 5cm/2in in diameter) and look quite different, but have a similar texture. Their taste is similar, too, but slightly sharper. Rambutans resemble small hairy animals, their reddish-brown leathery skins being covered with soft curly spines or hairs.

Preparing and Serving

Rambutans can be used in exactly the same way as lychees. To prepare, cut around the equator of the rambutan with a sharp knife, penetrating the skin only. Lift off the top half of the skin, leaving the fruit on the half shell, like an egg in a (rather hairy) egg cup. They can be added to fruit salads, served with ice cream (coffee ice cream is particularly compatible) or made into

jams or jellies, but are best eaten on their own. For an unusual appetizer, wrap peeled and stoned rambutans in Parma ham and serve speared on

Above: Rambutans

cocktail sticks. Rambutans are also available canned in syrup.

SAPODILLAS

The unprepossessing appearance of this drab oval fruit from Central America belies its delicious taste, which resembles that of vanilla-flavoured banana custard. Inside the rough, light brown skin of the ripe fruit, the honey-coloured flesh is sweet and luscious, with a core containing inedible, hard black pips.

Right: Sapodillas are sweet and luscious – like vanilla-flavoured banana custard.

Buying and Storing

Ripe sapodillas should have wrinkled brown skins and "give" slightly when pressed. Unripe fruit has smooth skin with a greenish tinge. Avoid this – unripe fruit is full of tannin and the flesh is unpleasantly grainy and mouth-puckeringly unpalatable. Instead, leave the fruit to ripen for up to a week in a fruit bowl. Ripe sapodillas can be kept in the fridge for up to a month.

Preparing and Serving

Sapodillas can be eaten just as they are – simply cut them in half, scoop out the flesh and discard the pips. A squeeze of lime or lemon enhances the flavour. The flesh can be mashed and stirred into cream or custard, or made into ice creams, fools and mousses. It can be added to cakes and teabreads and

makes an unusual pancake filling. Mix puréed sapodilla flesh with home-made mayonnaise or lime vinaigrette to make a sauce or dressing to be served with cold fish or chicken.

The milky sap of the sapodilla tree is used to make chicle gum, the main component of chewing gum.

SNAKE FRUIT

Also known as salak, this large member of the lychee family acquired its nickname from its beautifully patterned scaly brown snake-like skin. The creamy flesh is divided into four segments, each enclosing a very large inedible brown stone. The flesh is denser and less juicy than a lychee and has a distinctive apple flavour. Although the hard shells protect the fruit, the flesh quickly dries out, so eat them as soon as possible after purchase.

Snake fruit can be peeled and then eaten just as they are, or added to fruit salads. They are delicious poached in a light lemon- or vanilla-scented syrup and served chilled, alone or with vanilla ice cream or sorbet as a refreshing end to a meal.

Right: Snake fruit – so named because the patterned, scaly brown shell resembles snake skin.

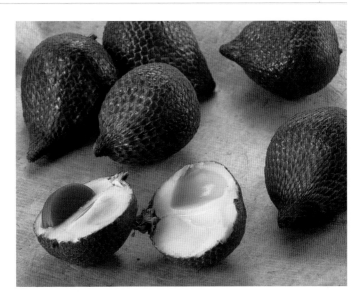

TAMARILLOS

Also known as "tree tomatoes", tamarillos look like large egg-shaped tomatoes with thick, smooth, wine-red skins. Each fruit has two lobes containing a multitude of black seeds.

Buying and Storing

Tamarillos with a greenish tinge will be unripe. Ripe fruit is bright purplish- or orangey-red and is soft to the touch. The fruit will keep in the fridge for several days.

Preparing and Cooking

Tamarillos can only be eaten raw when they are completely ripe. At this stage the flavour is tangy, sweet and sour, while unripe fruit has a quite unpleasant tannin taste.

To enjoy tamarillos at their best, cut them in half, sprinkle with a little sugar and leave overnight in the fridge. The next day, scoop out the chilled pulp with a spoon. Do not attempt to eat the skin, which is horribly bitter. Remove it by plunging the fruit into boiling water for about a minute, then slipping it off, or peel the fruit with a sharp vegetable peeler or knife.

Raw tamarillos can be used in fruit salads or puréed and made into jam and ice cream. They can be stewed or dredged with brown sugar and grilled. They make excellent chutney and a delicious sweet-sour sauce to go with fish or poultry.

Above: Tamarillos are members of the same family as tomatoes, aubergines and potatoes.

EXOTIC FRUIT RECIPES

Who can resist the colours, textures and flavours of exotic fruits? Now that many varieties are widely available all year, there's every excuse for taking the taste trip and trying such delights as Lychee and Elderflower Sorbet, Passion Fruit Crème Caramels with Dipped Physalis or Exotic Fruit Sushi.

LEMON GRASS SKEWERS WITH LIME CHEESE

GRILLED FRUITS MAKE A FINE FINALE TO ANY MEAL, AND THE LEMON GRASS SKEWERS NOT ONLY LOOK GOOD, BUT GIVE THE FRUIT A SUBTLE LEMON TANG. THE FRUITS USED HERE MAKE AN IDEAL EXOTIC MIX, BUT ALMOST ANY SOFT FRUIT CAN BE SUBSTITUTED.

SERVES FOUR

INGREDIENTS
  4 long fresh lemon grass stalks
  1 mango, peeled, stoned and cut
    into chunks
  1 papaya, peeled, seeded and cut
    into chunks
  1 star fruit, cut into thick slices
    and halved
  8 fresh bay leaves
  a nutmeg
  60ml/4 tbsp maple syrup
  50g/2oz/⅓ cup demerara sugar
For the lime cheese
  150g/5oz/⅔ cup curd cheese or
    low-fat soft cheese
  120ml/4fl oz/½ cup double cream
  grated rind and juice of ½ lime
  30ml/2 tbsp icing sugar

1 Prepare the barbecue or preheat the grill. Cut the top of each lemon grass stalk into a point with a sharp knife. Discard the outer leaves, then use the back of the knife to bruise the length of each stalk to release the aromatic oils. Thread each stalk, skewer-style, with the fruit pieces and bay leaves.

2 Support a piece of foil on a baking sheet and roll up the edges to make a rim. Grease the foil, lay the kebabs on top and grate a little nutmeg over each. Drizzle the maple syrup over and dust liberally with the demerara sugar. Grill for 5 minutes, until lightly charred.

3 Meanwhile, make the lime cheese. Mix together the cheese, cream, grated lime rind and juice and icing sugar in a bowl. Serve at once with the lightly charred fruit kebabs.

COOK'S TIP
Only fresh lemon grass will work as skewers for this recipe. It is now possible to buy lemon grass stalks in jars. These are handy for curries and similar dishes, but are too soft to use as skewers.

COCONUT JELLY WITH STAR ANISE FRUITS

SERVE THIS DESSERT AFTER ANY ORIENTAL-STYLE MEAL WITH PLENTY OF REFRESHING EXOTIC FRUIT.

SERVES FOUR

INGREDIENTS
  250ml/8fl oz/1 cup cold water
  75g/3oz/⅓ cup caster sugar
  15ml/1 tbsp powdered gelatine
  400ml/14fl oz/1⅔ cups coconut milk
For the syrup and fruit
  250ml/8fl oz/1 cup water
  3 star anise
  50g/2oz/¼ cup caster sugar
  1 star fruit, sliced
  12 lychees, peeled and stoned
  115g/4oz/1 cup blackberries

1 Pour the water into a saucepan and add the caster sugar. Heat gently until the sugar has dissolved. Sprinkle over the gelatine and continue to heat the mixture gently until the gelatine has dissolved, stirring occasionally. Stir in the coconut milk, remove from the heat and set aside to cool.

2 Grease an 18cm/7in square cake tin. Line with clear film. Pour in the coconut milk mixture and chill until set.

3 To make the syrup, combine the water, star anise and sugar in a pan. Bring to the boil, stirring, then lower the heat and simmer for 10–12 minutes until syrupy. Place the prepared fruit in a heatproof bowl and pour over the hot syrup. Cool, then chill.

4 To serve, cut the coconut jelly into diamonds and remove from the tin. Arrange the coconut jelly on individual plates, adding a few of the fruits and their syrup to each portion.

COOK'S TIP
Coconut milk is available in cans or as a powder. If using the coconut powder, reconstitute it with cold water according to the packet instructions.

PAPAYA BAKED <u>WITH</u> GINGER

*GINGER ENHANCES THE FLAVOUR OF PAPAYA IN THIS RECIPE, WHICH TAKES NO MORE THAN
TEN MINUTES TO PREPARE! DON'T OVERCOOK PAPAYA OR THE FLESH WILL BECOME VERY WATERY.*

SERVES FOUR

INGREDIENTS

2 ripe papayas
2 pieces stem ginger in syrup,
   drained, plus 15ml/1 tbsp syrup
   from the jar
8 amaretti or other dessert biscuits,
   coarsely crushed
45ml/3 tbsp raisins
shredded, finely pared rind and juice
   of 1 lime
25g/1oz/¼ cup pistachio
   nuts, chopped
15ml/1 tbsp light muscovado sugar
60ml/4 tbsp crème fraîche, plus
   extra to serve

VARIATION
Use Greek yogurt and almonds instead of
crème fraîche and pistachio nuts.

1 Preheat the oven to 200°C/400°F/
Gas 6. Cut the papayas in half and
scoop out their seeds. Place the halves
in a baking dish and set aside. Cut the
stem ginger into fine matchsticks.

2 Make the filling. Combine the
crushed amaretti biscuits, stem ginger
matchsticks and raisins in a bowl.

3 Stir in the lime rind and juice, two-
thirds of the nuts, then add the sugar
and the crème fraîche. Mix well.

4 Fill the papaya halves and drizzle
with the ginger syrup. Sprinkle with
the remaining nuts. Bake for about
25 minutes or until tender. Serve with
extra crème fraîche.

EXOTIC FRUIT SALAD WITH PASSION FRUIT DRESSING

PASSION FRUIT MAKES A SUPERB DRESSING FOR ANY FRUIT, BUT REALLY BRINGS OUT THE FLAVOUR OF EXOTIC VARIETIES. YOU CAN EASILY DOUBLE THE RECIPE, THEN SERVE THE REST FOR BREAKFAST.

SERVES SIX

INGREDIENTS
    1 mango
    1 papaya
    2 kiwi fruit
    coconut or vanilla ice cream, to serve
For the dressing
    3 passion fruit
    thinly pared rind and juice of 1 lime
    5ml/1 tsp hazelnut or walnut oil
    15ml/1 tbsp clear honey

COOK'S TIP
A clear golden honey scented with orange blossom or acacia blossom would be perfect for the dressing.

1 Peel the mango, cut it into three slices, then cut the flesh into chunks and place it in a large bowl. Peel the papaya and cut it in half. Scoop out the seeds, then chop the flesh.

2 Cut both ends off each kiwi fruit, then stand them on a board. Using a small sharp knife, cut off the skin from top to bottom. Cut each kiwi fruit in half lengthways, then cut into thick slices. Combine all the fruit in a large bowl.

3 Make the dressing. Cut each passion fruit in half and scoop the seeds out into a sieve set over a small bowl. Press the seeds well to extract all the juices. Lightly whisk the remaining dressing ingredients into the passion fruit juice, then pour the dressing over the fruit. Mix gently to combine. Leave to chill for 1 hour before serving with scoops of coconut or vanilla ice cream.

TROPICAL FRUIT GRATIN

THIS OUT-OF-THE-ORDINARY GRATIN IS STRICTLY FOR GROWN-UPS. A COLOURFUL COMBINATION
OF FRUIT IS TOPPED WITH A SIMPLE SABAYON BEFORE BEING FLASHED UNDER THE GRILL.

SERVES FOUR

INGREDIENTS
  2 tamarillos
  ½ sweet pineapple
  1 ripe mango
  175g/6oz/1½ cups blackberries
  120ml/4fl oz/½ cup sparkling
    white wine
  115g/4oz/½ cup caster sugar
  6 egg yolks

VARIATION
Although boiling drives off the alcohol
in the wine, children do not always
appreciate the flavour, so substitute
orange juice if making the gratin for
them. White grape juice or pineapple
juice would also work well.

1 Cut each tamarillo in half lengthways
and then into thick slices. Cut the rind
and core from the pineapple and take
spiral slices off the outside to remove
the eyes. Cut the flesh into chunks.
Peel the mango, cut it in half and cut
the flesh from the stone in slices.

2 Divide all the fruit, including the
blackberries, among four 14cm/5½in
gratin dishes set on a baking sheet and
set aside. Heat the wine and sugar in a
saucepan until the sugar has dissolved.
Bring to the boil and cook for 5 minutes.

3 Put the egg yolks in a large heatproof
bowl. Place the bowl over a pan of
simmering water and whisk until pale.
Slowly pour on the hot sugar syrup,
whisking all the time, until the mixture
thickens. Preheat the grill.

4 Spoon the mixture over the fruit.
Place the baking sheet holding the
dishes on a low shelf under the hot grill
until the topping is golden. Serve hot.

GRILLED PINEAPPLE WITH PAPAYA SAUCE

PINEAPPLE COOKED THIS WAY TAKES ON A SUPERB FLAVOUR AND IS SENSATIONAL WHEN SERVED WITH
THE PAPAYA SAUCE.

SERVES SIX

INGREDIENTS
  1 sweet pineapple
  melted butter, for greasing
    and brushing
  2 pieces drained stem ginger in
    syrup, cut into fine matchsticks,
    plus 30ml/2 tbsp of the syrup
    from the jar
  30ml/2 tbsp demerara sugar
  a pinch of ground cinnamon
  fresh mint sprigs, to decorate
For the sauce
  1 ripe papaya, peeled and seeded
  175ml/6fl oz/¾ cup apple juice

1 Peel the pineapple and take spiral
slices off the outside to remove the
eyes. Cut it crossways into six slices,
each 2.5cm/1in thick. Line a baking
sheet with a sheet of foil, rolling up the
sides to make a rim. Grease the foil with
melted butter. Preheat the grill.

2 Arrange the pineapple slices on the
lined baking sheet. Brush with butter,
then top with the ginger matchsticks,
sugar and cinnamon. Drizzle over the
stem ginger syrup. Grill for 5–7 minutes
or until the slices are golden and lightly
charred on top.

3 Meanwhile, make the sauce. Cut a
few slices from the papaya and set aside,
then purée the rest with the apple juice
in a blender or food processor.

4 Press the purée through a sieve
placed over a bowl, then stir in any
juices from cooking the pineapple.
Serve the pineapple slices with a little
sauce drizzled around each plate.
Decorate with the reserved papaya
slices and the mint sprigs.

COOK'S TIP
Try the papaya sauce with savoury dishes,
too. It tastes great with grilled chicken
and game birds as well as pork and lamb.

JAMAICAN FRUIT TRIFLE

THIS TRIFLE IS ACTUALLY BASED ON A CARIBBEAN FOOL THAT CONSISTS OF FRUIT STIRRED INTO THICK VANILLA-FLAVOURED CREAM. THIS VERSION IS NOT SO RICH, REDRESSING THE BALANCE WITH PLENTY OF FRUIT, AND WITH CRÈME FRAÎCHE REPLACING SOME OF THE CREAM.

2 Whip the double cream to very soft peaks, then lightly but thoroughly fold in the crème fraîche, sifted icing sugar, vanilla essence and rum.

3 Fold the drained chopped pineapple into the cream mixture. Place the chopped papayas and mangoes in a large bowl and pour over the lime juice. Gently stir the fruit mixture to combine. Shred the pared lime rind.

4 Divide the fruit mixture and the pineapple cream among eight dessert plates. Decorate with the lime shreds, toasted coconut and a few small pineapple leaves, if you like, and serve at once.

SERVES EIGHT

INGREDIENTS
1 large sweet pineapple, peeled and cored, about 350g/12oz
300ml/½ pint/1¼ cups double cream
200ml/7fl oz/scant 1 cup crème fraîche
60ml/4 tbsp icing sugar, sifted
10ml/2 tsp pure vanilla essence
30ml/2 tbsp white or coconut rum
3 papayas, peeled, seeded and chopped
3 mangoes, peeled, stoned and chopped
thinly pared rind and juice of 1 lime
25g/1oz/⅓ cup coarsely shredded or flaked coconut, toasted

1 Cut the pineapple into large chunks, place in a food processor or blender and process briefly until chopped. Tip into a sieve placed over a bowl and leave for 5 minutes so that most of the juice drains from the fruit.

COOK'S TIP
It is important to let the pineapple purée drain thoroughly, otherwise, the pineapple cream will be watery. Don't throw away the drained pineapple juice – mix it with fizzy mineral water for a wonderfully refreshing drink.

POMEGRANATE JEWELLED CHEESECAKE

THIS LIGHT CHEESECAKE IS FLAVOURED WITH COCONUT AND HAS A STUNNING POMEGRANATE GLAZE.

SERVES EIGHT

INGREDIENTS
  225g/8oz oat biscuits
  75g/3oz/⅓ cup unsalted
  butter, melted
For the filling
  45ml/3 tbsp orange juice
  15ml/1 tbsp powdered gelatine
  250g/9oz/generous 1 cup mascarpone
  cheese
  200g/7oz/scant 1 cup full-fat
  soft cheese
  75g/3oz/¾ cup icing sugar, sifted
  200ml/7fl oz/scant 1 cup coconut
  cream
  2 egg whites
For the topping
  2 pomegranates, peeled and
  seeds separated
  grated rind and juice of 1 orange
  30ml/2 tbsp caster sugar
  15ml/1 tbsp arrowroot, mixed to a
  paste with 30ml/2 tbsp Kirsch
  a few drops of red food colouring
  (optional)

2 For the filling, pour the orange juice into a heatproof bowl, then sprinkle the gelatine on top and set aside for 5 minutes until sponged. Place the bowl in a pan of hot water and stir until the gelatine has dissolved.

3 In a bowl, beat together both cheeses and the icing sugar, then gradually beat in the coconut cream. Whisk the egg whites in a grease-free bowl to soft peaks. Quickly stir the melted gelatine into the coconut mixture and fold in the egg whites. Pour over the biscuit base, level and chill until set.

4 Make the cheesecake topping. Place the pomegranate seeds in a saucepan and add the orange rind and juice and caster sugar. Bring to the boil, then lower the heat, cover and simmer for 5 minutes. Add the arrowroot paste and heat, stirring constantly, until thickened. Stir in the food colouring, if using. Allow to cool, stirring occasionally.

5 Pour the glaze over the top of the set cheesecake, then chill. To serve, run a knife between the edge of the tin and the cheesecake, then remove the side of the tin.

1 Grease a 23cm/9in springform cake tin. Crumb the oat biscuits in a food processor or blender. Add the melted butter and process briefly to combine. Spoon into the prepared tin, press the mixture in well, then chill.

COOK'S TIP
If you do not have a blender or a food processor, crumb the biscuits by placing them in a large, strong plastic bag and crushing them with a rolling pin. For the best results, crush the crumbs as finely as you possibly can.

BANANA AND MASCARPONE CREAMS

IF YOU ARE A FAN OF COLD BANANA CUSTARD, YOU'LL LOVE THIS RECIPE. IT IS A GROWN-UP VERSION OF AN OLD FAVOURITE. NO ONE WILL GUESS THAT THE SECRET IS READY-MADE CUSTARD.

SERVES FOUR TO SIX

INGREDIENTS
  250g/9oz/generous 1 cup mascarpone
    cheese
  300ml/½ pint/1¼ cups fresh ready-
    made custard
  150ml/¼ pint/⅔ cup Greek yogurt
  4 bananas
  juice of 1 lime
  50g/2oz/½ cup pecan nuts,
    coarsely chopped
  120ml/4fl oz/½ cup maple syrup

VARIATIONS
Use clear honey instead of maple syrup
and walnuts instead of pecans, if you
like. Also, try layering in some crumbled
biscuits, such as amaretti or ratafia,
shortbread crumbs or crushed meringues.
Or add a handful of finely grated dark or
white chocolate.

1 Combine the mascarpone, custard
and yogurt in a large bowl and beat
together until smooth. Make this mixture
up to several hours ahead, if you
like. Cover and chill, then stir before using.

2 Slice the bananas diagonally and
place in a separate bowl. Pour over the
lime juice and toss together until the
bananas are coated in the juice.

3 Divide half the custard mixture
among four or six dessert glasses and
top each portion with a generous
spoonful of the banana mixture.

4 Spoon the remaining custard mixture
into the glasses and top with the rest of
the bananas. Scatter the nuts over the
top. Drizzle maple syrup over each dessert
and chill for 30 minutes before serving.

BANANAS WITH LIME AND CARDAMOM SAUCE

SERVE THESE BANANAS SOLO, WITH VANILLA ICE CREAM, OR SPOON THEM OVER FOLDED CRÊPES.

SERVES FOUR

INGREDIENTS
  6 small bananas
  50g/2oz/¼ cup butter
  seeds from 4 cardamom
    pods, crushed
  50g/2oz/½ cup flaked almonds
  thinly pared rind and juice
    of 2 limes
  50g/2oz/⅓ cup light
    muscovado sugar
  30ml/2 tbsp dark rum
  vanilla ice cream, to serve

VARIATION
If you prefer not to use alcohol in your
cooking, replace the rum with orange
juice or even pineapple juice.

1 Peel the bananas and cut them in
half lengthways. Heat half the butter in
a large frying pan. Then add half the
bananas, and cook until the undersides
are golden. Turn carefully, using a fish
slice. Cook until golden.

2 As they cook, transfer the bananas to
a heatproof serving dish. Cook the
remaining bananas in the same way.

3 Melt the remaining butter, then add
the cardamom seeds and almonds.
Cook, stirring, until golden.

4 Stir in the lime rind and juice, and
then the sugar. Cook, stirring, until the
mixture is smooth, bubbling and slightly
reduced. Stir in the rum. Pour the
sauce over the bananas and serve
immediately, with vanilla ice cream.

TOFFEE BANANAS

ALTHOUGH THE METHOD FOR THIS RECIPE SOUNDS SIMPLE, IT CAN BE A BIT TRICKY TO MASTER.
YOU NEED TO WORK FAST, ESPECIALLY WHEN DIPPING THE FRUIT IN THE CARAMEL, AS IT WILL COOL
AND SET QUITE QUICKLY. THE LUSCIOUS RESULTS, HOWEVER, ARE WORTH THE EFFORT.

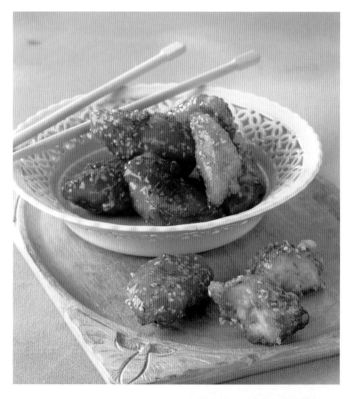

2 Heat the groundnut, sunflower or corn oil in a deep pan until it registers 180°C/350°F or until a cube of bread, added to the oil, turns pale brown in 45 seconds.

3 Using a fork, remove a piece of banana from the batter, allowing the excess batter to drain back into the bowl. Gently lower the piece of banana into the hot oil. Add more pieces of battered banana in the same way; do not overcrowd the pan. Fry for about 2 minutes or until the coating is golden.

4 As they are cooked, remove the banana fritters from the oil with a slotted spoon and place on kitchen paper to drain. Cook the rest of the battered bananas in the same way.

SERVES FOUR

INGREDIENTS
 4 firm bananas
 75g/3oz/¾ cup plain flour
 50g/2oz/½ cup cornflour
 10ml/2 tsp baking powder
 175ml/6fl oz/¾ cup water
 5ml/1 tsp sesame oil
 groundnut, sunflower or corn oil, for
  deep frying
For the caramel
 225g/8oz/1 cup granulated sugar
 30ml/2 tbsp sesame seeds
 60ml/4 tbsp water

1 Peel the bananas, then cut them diagonally into thick slices. Sift the flours and baking powder into a large bowl. Quickly beat in the water and sesame oil, taking care not to overmix. Stir in the bananas until coated.

5 When all the banana pieces have been fried, make the caramel. Mix the sugar, sesame seeds and water in a pan. Heat gently, stirring occasionally, until the sugar has dissolved. Raise the heat slightly and continue cooking, without stirring, until the syrup becomes a light caramel. Remove from the heat.

6 Have ready a bowl of iced water. Working quickly, drop one fritter at a time into the hot caramel. Flip over with a fork, remove immediately and plunge the piece into the iced water. Remove from the water quickly (using your fingers for speed, but taking care) and drain on a wire rack while coating the rest. Serve immediately.

HOT DATE PUDDINGS <u>WITH</u> TOFFEE SAUCE

FRESH DATES MAKE THIS PUDDING LESS RICH THAN THE CONVENTIONAL DRIED DATE VERSION, BUT IT IS STILL A BIT OF AN INDULGENCE! IT IS PREFERABLE TO PEEL THE DATES AS THE SKINS CAN BE TOUGH: SIMPLY SQUEEZE THEM BETWEEN YOUR THUMB AND FOREFINGER AND THE SKINS WILL POP OFF.

<u>SERVES SIX</u>

INGREDIENTS
  50g/2oz/¼ cup butter, softened
  75g/3oz/½ cup light muscovado sugar
  2 eggs, beaten
  115g/4oz/1 cup self-raising flour
  2.5ml/½ tsp bicarbonate of soda
  175g/6oz/1 cup fresh dates, peeled,
    stoned and chopped
  75ml/5 tbsp boiling water
  10ml/2 tsp coffee and chicory
    essence
For the toffee sauce
  75g/3oz/½ cup light muscovado sugar
  50g/2oz/¼ cup butter
  60ml/4 tbsp double cream
  30ml/2 tbsp brandy

1 Preheat the oven to 180°C/350°F/ Gas 4. Place a baking sheet in the oven to heat up. Grease six individual pudding moulds or tins. Cream the butter and sugar in a mixing bowl until pale and fluffy. Gradually add the eggs, beating well after each addition.

2 Sift the flour and bicarbonate of soda together and fold into the creamed mixture. Put the dates in a heatproof bowl, pour over the boiling water and mash with a potato masher. Add the coffee and chicory essence, then stir the paste into the creamed mixture.

3 Spoon the mixture into the prepared moulds or tins. Place on the hot baking sheet and bake for 20 minutes.

4 Meanwhile, make the toffee sauce. Put all the ingredients in a pan and heat very gently, stirring occasionally, until the mixture is smooth. Increase the heat and boil for 1 minute.

5 Turn the warm puddings out on to individual dessert plates. Spoon a generous amount of sauce over each portion and serve at once.

COOK'S TIP
The sauce is a great standby. Try it on poached apple or pear slices, over ice cream or with a steamed pudding.

RUM AND BANANA WAFFLES

TO SAVE TIME, THESE SCRUMPTIOUS DESSERT WAFFLES CAN BE MADE IN ADVANCE, WRAPPED TIGHTLY, FROZEN, AND THEN WARMED THROUGH IN THE OVEN JUST BEFORE SERVING.

SERVES FOUR

INGREDIENTS

225g/8oz/2 cups plain flour
10ml/2 tsp baking powder
5ml/1 tsp bicarbonate of soda
15ml/1 tbsp caster sugar
2 eggs
50g/2oz/¼ cup butter, melted
175ml/6fl oz/¾ cup milk, plus extra
  if needed
300ml/½ pint/1¼ cups buttermilk
5ml/1 tsp pure vanilla essence
single cream, to serve
For the bananas
6 bananas, thickly sliced
115g/4oz/1 cup pecan nuts, broken
  into pieces
50g/2oz/⅓ cup demerara sugar
75ml/5 tbsp maple syrup
45ml/3 tbsp dark rum

2 Add the buttermilk and vanilla to the batter and whisk well. Cover and leave to stand for 30 minutes. Preheat the oven to 150°C/300°F/Gas 2.

3 Place a hand-held waffle iron over the heat. Stir the batter and add more milk if required (the consistency should be quite thick). Open the waffle iron and pour some batter over two-thirds of the surface. Close it and wipe off any excess batter.

4 Cook for 3–4 minutes, carefully turning the waffle iron over once during cooking. If using an electric waffle maker, follow the manufacturer's instructions for cooking.

5 When the batter stops steaming, open the iron and lift out the waffle with a fork. Put it on a heatproof plate and keep it hot in the oven. Repeat with the remaining batter to make eight waffles in all. Preheat the grill.

6 Cook the bananas. Spread them out on a large shallow baking tin and top with the nuts. Scatter over the demerara sugar. Mix the maple syrup and rum together and spoon over.

1 Sift the dry ingredients into a large mixing bowl. Make a well in the centre. Add the eggs, melted butter and milk. Whisk together, gradually incorporating the flour mixture, until smooth.

COOK'S TIP
If you don't own a waffle iron, prepare the batter as directed, but make small pancakes in a heavy-based frying pan. Alternatively, use ready-made waffles, which are available from most large supermarkets, and reheat as directed on the packet before serving with the hot banana topping.

VARIATIONS
Use other fruits for the waffle topping, if you like. Small chunks of fresh or drained, canned pineapple, thin wedges of peaches or nectarines or even orange slices would be delicious alternatives to the sliced banana.

7 Grill for 3–4 minutes or until the sugar begins to bubble. Serve on top of the waffles with single cream.

MANGO AND TAMARILLO PASTRIES

THESE FRUIT-TOPPED LITTLE PASTRIES GO DOWN A TREAT WITH A CUP OF AFTERNOON TEA.

MAKES EIGHT

INGREDIENTS
225g/8oz ready-rolled puff pastry
(30 × 25cm/12 × 10in rectangle)
1 egg yolk, lightly beaten
115g/4oz/½ cup white marzipan
40ml/8 tsp ginger or apricot conserve
1 mango, peeled and thinly sliced off
the stone
2 tamarillos, halved and sliced
caster sugar, for sprinkling

1 Preheat the oven to 200°C/400°F/
Gas 6. Unroll the pastry and cut it into
8 rectangles. Place on baking sheets.

VARIATION
Use apricot slices instead of tamarillos,
or a mix of plums and peaches.

2 Using a sharp knife, score the
surface of each piece of pastry into a
diamond pattern, then brush with the
egg yolk to glaze. Cut eight thin slices
of marzipan and lay one slice on each
pastry rectangle. Top each with a
teaspoon of the ginger or apricot
conserve and spread over evenly.

3 Top the pastry rectangles with
alternate slices of mango and tamarillo.
Sprinkle with some of the caster sugar,
then bake for 15–20 minutes until the
pastry is well puffed up and golden.
Remove the pastries to a wire rack to
cool. Sprinkle with more caster sugar
before serving.

EXOTIC FRUIT TRANCHE

THIS IS A GOOD WAY TO MAKE THE MOST OF A SMALL SELECTION OF EXOTIC FRUIT.

SERVES EIGHT

INGREDIENTS
175g/6oz/1½ cups plain flour
50g/2oz/¼ cup unsalted butter
25g/1oz/2 tbsp white vegetable fat
50g/2oz/¼ cup caster sugar
2 egg yolks
about 15ml/1 tbsp cold water
115g/4oz/scant ½ cup apricot
   conserve, sieved and warmed
For the filling
150ml/¼ pint/⅔ cup double cream,
   plus extra to serve
250g/9oz/generous 1 cup mascarpone
   cheese
25g/1oz/¼ cup icing sugar, sifted
grated rind of 1 orange
450g/1lb/3 cups mixed prepared
   fruits, such as mango, papaya, star
   fruit, kiwi fruit and blackberries
90ml/6 tbsp apricot conserve, sieved
15ml/1 tbsp white or coconut rum

1 Sift the flour into a bowl and rub in the butter and white vegetable fat until the mixture resembles fine breadcrumbs. Stir in the caster sugar. Add the egg yolks and enough cold water to make a soft dough. Thinly roll out the pastry between two sheets of clear film and use the pastry to line a 35 × 12cm/14 × 4½in fluted tranche tin. Allow the excess pastry to hang over the edge of the tin and chill for 30 minutes.

2 Preheat the oven to 200°C/400°F/ Gas 6. Prick the base of the pastry case and line with non-stick baking paper and baking beans. Bake for 10–12 minutes. Lift out the paper and beans and return the pastry case to the oven for 5 minutes. Trim off the excess pastry and brush the inside of the case with the warmed apricot conserve to form a seal. Leave to cool on a wire rack.

3 Make the filling. Whip the cream to soft peaks, then stir it into the mascarpone with the icing sugar and orange rind. Spread in the cooled pastry case and top with the prepared fruits. Warm the apricot conserve with the rum and drizzle or brush over the fruits to make a glaze. Serve with extra cream.

COOK'S TIP
If you don't have a tranche tin, line a 23cm/9in flan tin with the pastry.

MANGO PIE

THIS RECIPE COMES STRAIGHT FROM THE CARIBBEAN AND CAPTURES ALL THE SUNSHINE FLAVOURS OF THAT EXOTIC SETTING. FOR THE TASTIEST PIE, BE SURE THAT THE MANGOES ARE GOOD AND RIPE.

SERVES SIX

INGREDIENTS

175g/6oz/1½ cups plain flour
a pinch of salt
75g/3oz/⅓ cup unsalted butter,
    chilled and diced
25g/1oz/2 tbsp white vegetable fat,
    chilled and diced
15ml/1 tbsp caster sugar, plus extra
    for sprinkling
about 45ml/3 tbsp cold water
beaten egg, to glaze
vanilla ice cream, to serve
For the filling
2 ripe mangoes
45ml/3 tbsp fresh lime juice
115g/4oz/½ cup caster sugar
15ml/1 tbsp arrowroot mixed to a
    paste with 15ml/1 tbsp water

1 Sift the flour and salt into a large mixing bowl. Rub in the butter and white vegetable fat with your fingertips until the mixture resembles fine breadcrumbs, then stir in the caster sugar. Add just enough of the cold water to make a dough.

VARIATIONS
Make the pie using one mango and one papaya, peeled, seeded and sliced. Add a little ground cinnamon and some freshly grated nutmeg to the filling for a sweet spice flavour.

COOK'S TIP
If the top of the pie begins to brown too much during baking, simply cover it loosely with a piece of foil.

2 Knead lightly, then roll out two-thirds of the pastry and line a 18cm/7in pie dish. Wrap the remaining pastry in clear film and chill both the pastry and the pastry case for 30 minutes.

3 Meanwhile, make the filling. Peel the mangoes and slice the flesh off the stone. Reserve half the sliced mango, and coarsely chop the rest.

4 Place the chopped mango in a saucepan with the lime juice and caster sugar. Cover and cook for 10 minutes or until soft. Pour in the arrowroot paste and cook, stirring all the time, until thickened. Set the filling aside to cool.

5 Preheat the oven to 190°C/375°F/ Gas 5. Pour the cooled mango sauce into the chilled pastry case and top with the reserved mango slices. Roll out the remaining pastry to make a pie lid.

6 Dampen the rim of the pastry case and add the pastry lid. Crimp the edges to seal, then cut a cross in the centre to allow the steam to escape.

7 Glaze the pastry with the beaten egg and sprinkle lightly with caster sugar. Bake for 35–40 minutes until the pastry is golden brown. Cool slightly on a wire rack. Serve warm with vanilla ice cream.

BANANA AND PECAN BREAD

BANANAS AND PECAN NUTS JUST SEEM TO BELONG TOGETHER. THIS IS A REALLY MOIST AND DELICIOUS TEA BREAD. SPREAD IT WITH CREAM CHEESE OR JAM, OR SERVE AS A DESSERT WITH WHIPPED CREAM.

MAKES A 900G/2LB LOAF

INGREDIENTS
115g/4oz/½ cup butter, softened
175g/6oz/1 cup light muscovado
   sugar
2 large eggs, beaten
3 ripe bananas
75g/3oz/¾ cup pecan nuts,
   coarsely chopped
225g/8oz/2 cups self-raising flour
2.5ml/½ tsp ground mixed spice

1 Preheat the oven to 180°C/350°F/ Gas 4. Generously grease a 900g/2lb loaf tin and line it with non-stick baking paper. Cream the butter and muscovado sugar in a large mixing bowl until the mixture is light and fluffy. Gradually add the eggs, beating after each addition, until well combined.

2 Peel and then mash the bananas with a fork. Add them to the creamed mixture with the chopped pecan nuts. Beat until well combined.

COOK'S TIP
If the mixture shows signs of curdling when you add the eggs, stir in a little of the flour to stabilize it.

3 Sift the flour and mixed spice together and fold into the banana mixture. Spoon into the tin, level the surface and bake for 1–1¼ hours or until a skewer inserted into the centre of the loaf comes out clean. Cool for 10 minutes in the tin, then invert the tin on a wire rack. Lift off the tin, peel off the lining paper and cool completely.

DATE AND WALNUT BROWNIES

THESE RICH BROWNIES ARE GREAT FOR AFTERNOON TEA, BUT THEY ALSO MAKE A FANTASTIC DESSERT. REHEAT SLICES BRIEFLY IN THE MICROWAVE OVEN AND SERVE WITH CRÈME FRAÎCHE.

MAKES TWELVE

INGREDIENTS
350g/12oz plain chocolate, broken
   into squares
225g/8oz/1 cup butter, diced
3 large eggs
115g/4oz/½ cup caster sugar
5ml/1 tsp pure vanilla essence
75g/3oz/¾ cup plain flour, sifted
225g/8oz/1½ cups fresh dates,
   peeled, stoned and chopped
200g/7oz/1¾ cups walnut pieces
icing sugar, for dusting

COOK'S TIP
When melting the chocolate and butter, keep the water in the pan beneath hot, but do not let it approach boiling point. Chocolate is notoriously sensitive to heat; it is vital not to let it get too hot or it may stiffen into an unmanageable mass.

1 Preheat the oven to 190°C/375°F/ Gas 5. Generously grease a 30 × 20cm/ 12 × 8in baking tin and line with non-stick baking paper.

2 Put the chocolate and butter in a large heatproof bowl. Place the bowl over a pan of hot water and leave until both have melted. Stir until smooth, then lift the bowl out and cool slightly.

3 In a separate bowl, beat the eggs, sugar and vanilla. Then beat into the chocolate mixture and fold in the flour, dates and nuts. Pour into the tin.

4 Bake for 30–40 minutes, until firm and the mixture comes away from the sides of the tin. Cool in the tin, then turn out, remove the paper and dust with icing sugar.

MANGO CHUTNEY

THIS CLASSIC CHUTNEY IS CONVENTIONALLY SERVED WITH CURRIES AND INDIAN POPPADOMS, BUT IT IS ALSO DELICIOUS WITH BAKED HAM OR A TRADITIONAL CHEESE PLOUGHMAN'S LUNCH.

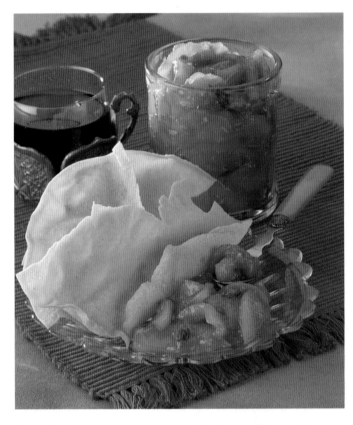

MAKES 450G/1LB

INGREDIENTS
  3 firm green mangoes
  150ml/¼ pint/⅔ cup cider vinegar
  130g/4½oz/⅔ cup light
    muscovado sugar
  1 small red finger chilli or jalapeño
    chilli, split
  2.5cm/1in piece of fresh root ginger,
    peeled and finely chopped
  1 garlic clove, finely chopped
  5 cardamom pods, bruised
  2.5ml/½ tsp coriander
    seeds, crushed
  1 bay leaf
  2.5ml/½ tsp salt

1 Peel the mangoes and cut the flesh off the stone. Slice the mango flesh lengthways, then cut across into small chunks or thin wedges.

2 Place these in a large saucepan, add the vinegar and cover. Cook over a low heat for 10 minutes.

3 Stir in the muscovado sugar, chilli, ginger, garlic, bruised cardamoms and coriander. Add the bay leaf and salt. Bring to the boil slowly, stirring often.

4 Lower the heat and then simmer, uncovered, for 30 minutes or until the mixture is thick and syrupy.

5 Ladle into hot sterilized jars, seal and label. Store for 1 week before eating. Keep chilled after opening.

PAPAYA AND LEMON RELISH

THIS CHUNKY RELISH IS BEST MADE WITH A FIRM, UNRIPE PAPAYA. IT SHOULD BE LEFT FOR A WEEK BEFORE EATING TO ALLOW ALL THE FLAVOURS TO MELLOW. STORE THE UNOPENED JARS IN A COOL PLACE, AWAY FROM SUNLIGHT. SERVE WITH ROAST MEATS OR WITH A ROBUST CHEESE AND CRACKERS.

MAKES 450G/1LB

INGREDIENTS

- 1 large unripe papaya
- 1 onion, thinly sliced
- 40g/1½oz/⅓ cup raisins
- 250ml/8fl oz/1 cup red wine vinegar
- juice of 2 lemons
- 150ml/¼ pint/⅔ cup elderflower cordial
- 165g/5½oz/¾ cup golden granulated sugar
- 1 cinnamon stick
- 1 fresh bay leaf
- 2.5ml/½ tsp hot paprika
- 2.5ml/½ tsp salt

1 Peel the papaya and cut it lengthways in half. Remove the seeds with a small spoon. Cut the flesh into small chunks and place in a large saucepan.

2 Add the onion slices and raisins to the papaya chunks, then stir in the vinegar. Bring to a boil, lower the heat and simmer for 10 minutes.

3 Add all the remaining ingredients and bring to the boil, stirring all the time. Check that all the sugar has dissolved, then lower the heat and simmer for 50–60 minutes or until the relish is thick and syrupy.

4 Ladle into hot sterilized jars. Seal and label and store for 1 week before using. Keep chilled after opening.

MELONS, GRAPES, FIGS AND RHUBARB

Some fruits are in a class of their own. Melons, grapes and figs have little in common, apart from the fact that they are all fruits, and rhubarb cannot even lay claim to that characteristic: it is technically a vegetable. Without these treasures, however, the food world would be a poorer place. Melons are the cool fruits, grapes the sybarites' choice, figs the sweetest treats and rhubarb the perfect excuse for custard!

MELONS

Sweet melons are members of a large family of fruits and vegetables which grow on trailing vines and include cucumbers, squashes and marrows. They come in a huge number of varieties (possibly thousands) and range in size from a single portion to melons which are large enough to provide a dozen servings. They have a hard, often beautifully patterned rind and very juicy, refreshing flesh enclosing a central cavity filled with a large number of pale, pointed, edible seeds.

History

Melons originated in Africa or Asia and have been known in China for at least 3,000 years. These early melons were bitter, rather like cucumbers, and could not be eaten raw. Hybridization resulted in sweeter fruits, which the Moors brought to Spain from Persia or Africa. They were taken to Italy, and by the fifteenth century reached France, where they were propagated enthusiastically by the Avignon popes. Christopher Columbus took melons to the New World; when his men had eaten the fruit, they discarded the seeds, which produced large melon crops. These popular fruits are now grown in most warm parts of the world.

Varieties

Melons fall into two main categories – summer fruit, which includes all those varieties with cross-hatched skin that looks like brown netting, and winter melons, which have smooth or finely ridged pale or bright yellow rind and delicate, pale flesh, which can be rather lacking in taste.

Summer melons

Cantaloupe This summer melon takes its name from the Italian town of Cantalupo near Rome, where the fruits were grown in profusion on the papal estate. Most cantaloupes are slightly elongated with craggy pale green or golden rinds, marked into segments, and have aromatic orangey-yellow flesh.

Charentais Charentais have smooth, grey-green rinds and very fragrant orange flesh. A ripe charentais gives off a heady, delicious aroma. Most of the charentais melons are grown around Cavaillon in France, and are sometimes sold under this name. The French writer Alexandre Dumas so loved these melons that he offered the municipality of Cavaillon all his published and future works in exchange for a life annuity of twelve melons a year.

Galia A relative of the Ogen, Galia is a round melon with a raised pattern of fine netting on the skin. The skin turns from green to golden as it ripens, and the fragrant flesh is green and juicy.

Musk melons These summer melons, also known as "nutmeg" melons, are round or oval, with a raised pattern of lacy netting on the rind. The skins can be green or orange, and the sweet, highly aromatic flesh ranges from orangey-pink to pale green. They take their name from the Romans' habit of sprinkling the fruit with powdered musk to accentuate the flavour. Musk melons are often grown in hothouses.

Ogen A hybrid developed in Israel, this Cantaloupe melon has a smooth pale green skin, marked with green or orange lines, which turns golden when the fruit is ripe. The juicy flesh is sweet and aromatic.

Pineapple or **Khoob melons** These large oval melons have orangey-yellow netted skin and beautiful, juicy orange flesh, which has the aroma and faint flavour of pineapple.

Above: Ein d'Or, one of the winter melons, has golden skin and delicately flavoured flesh.

Winter melons

In addition to the winter melons listed below, there are the golden **Ein d'Or** and the **Piel de Sapo**, with rough-ridged, dark green skin and green-to-orange flesh. Its name means "toad's skin".

Casaba is a walnut-shaped melon with ridged, deep yellow skin and pale creamy flesh.

Crenshaws are pointed at the stem end and have smooth golden skins. They have the best flavour of all winter melons, with sweet juicy salmon-pink flesh and a pleasantly scented aroma.

Honeydew is the most common winter melon. Sadly, its name is often more flavoursome than its taste.

Watermelons See page 231.

Nutrition

Melons have a very high water content, so are low in calories (30 kilocalories per 100g/3¾oz). The more orange the flesh, the more beneficial carotenes it contains.

Left: The aromatic orangey-yellow flesh of Cantaloupes is delicious served with cured meats.

Buying and Storing

Melons should feel heavy for their size and give off a pleasant, sweet aroma; they should not smell too musky, as this is a sign that they are overripe. Gently press the stalk end with your thumb; it should "give" slightly, but check that the fruit has not started to rot. The rind should be thick and unblemished with a good colour for its type.

To ripen a melon, keep it at room temperature. Ripe melons are best kept in a cool, airy place. The fridge is fine, but wrap the melon in clear film or a polythene bag first, or the smell will permeate other foods. Melon balls or cubes can be frozen in rigid containers for up to three months, either as they are or in a light syrup.

Preparing and Serving

Aromatic ripe melons are best eaten raw, on their own, in a fruit salad (use the melon shell as a container) or as an hors d'oeuvre with Parma ham or salami. Melons can be served in long slices, balls or cubes. They should always be chilled. A sprinkling of salt and pepper or ground ginger enhances the flavour. Small round varieties can be halved horizontally, seeded and served as they are or with a filling such as raspberry coulis or ice cream. They can also be filled with port, although purists frown on this practice. For single-portion melons, cut off a lid and scoop out the seeds. Always scoop out melons into a sieve set over a bowl to catch all the juice. The seeds can be dried and roasted in the oven to make a delicious snack.

Melon goes well with sweet or savoury ingredients. It makes a refreshing salad if mixed with cucumber and tossed in lemon juice, a light cream cheese or

Above: Piel de Sapo whose name means "toad's skin".

VEGETABLES

DISCOVERING VEGETABLES

AS A CHILD, there were two basic types of vegetables for me: the ones my mother cooked and the ones given to us at school. My mother only ever bought fresh vegetables and she knew how to cook them, so they were simple but good. Vegetables at school were overcooked and invariably tasteless. Travel then broadened my outlook.

From my first teenage sojourns around Europe, I recall, even now, the vegetable stalls in a Barcelona market, piled high with tomatoes, peppers and aubergines. The exotic-looking produce of the Orient, Asia and Caribbean countries cannot fail to spark off an inquisitive and creative enthusiasm in those who are unfamiliar with them and even basic ingredients – potatoes, onions and carrots – do not look like sorry, everyday necessities when they are displayed with pride.

History

Vegetables, whether the root, stems, seeds or fruit, have been an essential part of our diet since the early existence of mankind, and many of our familiar vegetables were cultivated in prehistoric times. The Egyptians grew onions, garlic, radishes, lettuce and broad beans; and later the Greeks and Romans grew artichokes and fennel. By the Middle Ages a wealth of

vegetables was available, with recipes for them recorded in the first cookery books.

Early explorers returned with exotic ingredients, the spoils of their travels, to their native countries and created a huge appetite for new tastes among the wealthy classes of Europe. Marco Polo travelled to China and carried aromatic spices on his return to Europe. Christopher Columbus and subsequent explorers found potatoes, tomatoes, peppers, squashes and maize. Today we have the option of buying exactly what we want, when we want it. It's a luxury we pay for but one that means you are never stuck for an ingredient whatever the time of year. On the other hand there's much to be said for enjoying vegetables in their season. Vegetables from local growers will be the freshest you can buy and gardeners love the way their produce

Above: Roast Asparagus Crêpes with a cheese sauce

Right: Rocket

traces the seasons, never minding that it means gluts at some times of the year and only cabbages and roots at other times.

Nutrition

Vegetables are really good for you – all nutritionists agree. Vegetables protect against disease, they are an important source of many vitamins and minerals, and we should eat more. The nutritional value of vegetables varies according to type, freshness, preparation and cooking method. In general it can be said that along with fruit they are the main source of vitamin C. Some of the B-group vitamins are also found in

Right: Green, red, orange and yellow peppers

vegetables, particularly in green vegetables and pulses. Carrots and the dark green vegetables also include carotene which is used by the body to manufacture vitamin A. Vegetable oils are a useful source of vitamin E.

Vegetables can also contain calcium, iron, potassium and magnesium, as well as some trace elements which are also required in small quantities.

Starchy vegetables are an important

Above: Cherry tomatoes

Below: Tomato and Basil Tart

source of energy-giving carbohydrate and they may include useful quantities of fibre.

Freshly picked vegetables have the highest nutritional content, but this diminishes with staleness and exposure to sunlight. Use fresh vegetables as soon as possible after purchase and always avoid stale limp specimens. The peel and the layer directly beneath it contain the highest concentration of nutrients, so it is best to avoid

Right: Swiss chard is striking to look at as well as being delicious to eat.

peeling your vegetables or to remove the thinnest layer for maximum nutrient retention. Minerals and vitamins C and B are water soluble and they are lost by seepage into cooking water or the liquid over which vegetables are steamed. To minimize loss of nutrients, do not cut up vegetables finely as this creates a greater surface area for seepage. Vitamin C is also destroyed by long cooking and by exposure to alkalines. Raw and lightly cooked vegetables provide the best nutritional value and source of fibre. Any cooking liquid should, whenever possible, be used in stocks, gravies or sauces.

Vegetables can play a starring role in a recipe or they may be combined with other ingredients in a harmony of flavours. Over the following pages you will find an eclectic mix of classic dishes from around the world, some family favourites that have stood the test of time and others that I have devised over years of cooking. All the recipes make the most of each vegetable, so that their particular virtues can be appreciated to the full. The recipes are not designed for vegetarians although there are plenty of recipes which are vegetarian. In many instances, simply substituting vegetable stock for chicken stock will ensure that the recipe is acceptable. The great thing about cooking with vegetables is, however, that once you have got the hang of using them, a recipe really becomes unnecessary. You will discover how you most enjoy carrots, asparagus or less-common vegetables and this in turn will inspire you to experiment with vegetables you have not used before.

ONIONS AND LEEKS

Where would we be without the onion family?
Whether it's the merest hint of chives in a dressing, leeks in a
sauce, garlic adding its unmistakable tang or full-bodied onion
soup, this is the vegetable family that gives so much flavour to
our savoury dishes.

GARLIC

Garlic is an ingredient that almost anyone who does any cooking at all, and absolutely everyone who enjoys cooking, would not be without.

History

Garlic is known to have been first grown in around 3200 BC. Inscriptions and models of garlic found in the pyramids of Ancient Egypt show that garlic was not only an important foodstuff but that it had ceremonial significance as well. The Greeks and Romans likewise believed garlic to have magical qualities. Warriors would eat it for strength before going into battle, gods were appeased with gifts of garlic, and cloves of garlic were fastened round the necks of babies to ward off evil. So, vampire mythology has ancient precedents.

The Greeks and Romans also used garlic for its therapeutic qualities. Not only was it thought to be an aphrodisiac but also it was believed to be good for eczema, toothache and snake bites.

Although garlic found its way all over Europe – vats of butter, very strongly flavoured with garlic, have been found by archaeologists working in Ireland which date back 200-300 years – basically, its popularity today derives from our liking for Mediterranean, Indian and Asian food, where garlic plays a very important part in many dishes.

Nutrition

As is often the case, what was once dismissed as an old wives' tale is, after thorough scientific inquiry, found to be true. Garlic is a case in point; most authorities accept that it has many therapeutic properties. The most significant of these is that it lowers blood cholesterol, thus helping prevent heart disease. Also, raw garlic contains a powerful antibiotic and there is evidence that it has a beneficial effect against cancer and strokes, and increases the absorption of vitamins. Many garlic enthusiasts take their garlic in tablet form, but true devotees prefer to take it as it comes.

Right: A string of pink-skinned garlic

Varieties

There are numerous varieties of garlic, from the large "elephant" garlic, to small tight bulbs. Their papery skin can be white, pink or purple. Colour makes no difference to taste but the particular attraction of the large purple bulbs is that they make a beautiful display in the kitchen.

As a general rule, the smaller the garlic bulb, the stronger it is likely to be. However, most garlic sold in shops is not classified in either shape or form (unless it is elephant garlic) and in practice you will simply pick up whatever you need, either loose, in bunches or on strings.

Garlic grown in a hot climate is likely to be the most pungent, and fresh new season's garlic has a subtle, mild flavour that is particularly good if it is to be used raw, for example, in salads and for dressings.

Above: Elephant garlic is shown beside normal-size bulbs.

Buying and Storing

Garlic bulbs should be firm and round with clear, papery skins. Avoid any that are beginning to sprout. Garlic bulbs keep well stored in a cool, dry place; if the air is damp they will sprout and if it is too warm the cloves will eventually turn to grey powder.

Preparing and Cooking

First break the garlic bulb into cloves and then remove the papery skin. You can blanch this off with hot water but using a fingernail or knife is just as effective. When a garlic clove is split lengthways a shoot is revealed in the centre, which is occasionally green, and some people remove this whatever the colour. Cloves are the little segments which make up the bulb and most recipes call for one or more cloves of garlic. (Don't use a bulb when the recipe just calls for a clove!)

Crush cloves either with the blade of a knife or use a garlic crusher. Crushed garlic cooks more evenly and distributes its flavour in food better than when it is used sliced or finely chopped (stir-fries are the exception). Prepare the garlic according to the strength of flavour required: thinly sliced garlic is milder than chopped, which in turn is milder than crushed garlic and, of course, cooking mutes the pungency.

Garlic Breath

The taste and smell of garlic tends to linger on the breath and can be a problem to get rid of. Chewing parsley is a well-known remedy but is only moderately successful. Chewing the seeds of cardamom pods is also said to work but is rather unpleasant. The best suggestion is to eat garlic with your friends so that nobody notices!

CHICKEN WITH SHALLOTS

SERVES FOUR

INGREDIENTS
    1 small chicken, about 1.3kg/3lb,
        or 4 chicken pieces
    seasoned plain flour, for coating
    30ml/2 tbsp sunflower oil
    25g/1oz butter
    115g/4oz unsmoked streaky
        bacon, chopped
    2 garlic cloves
    450ml/¾ pint/1¾ cups red wine
    1 bay leaf
    2 thyme sprigs
    250g/9oz shallots
    115g/4oz/1½ cups button mushrooms,
        halved if large
    10ml/2 tsp plain flour
    salt and freshly ground black pepper

1 Preheat the oven to 180°C/350°F/
Gas 4. Remove any excess skin or fat
from the chicken and cut into four or
eight pieces. Place a little seasoned flour
in a large plastic bag, add the chicken
pieces and shake to coat evenly.

2 Heat half the oil and half the butter in
a large flameproof casserole and fry the
bacon and garlic for 3–4 minutes. Add
the chicken pieces and fry until lightly
browned. Add the wine, bay leaf and
thyme and bring to the boil. Cover and
cook in the oven for 1 hour.

3 Peel the shallots and boil them in
salted water for 10 minutes. Heat the
remaining oil in a small frying pan and
fry the shallots for 3–4 minutes until
beginning to brown. Add the mushrooms
and fry for a further 2–3 minutes.

4 Stir the shallots and mushrooms into
the casserole with the chicken and cook
for a further 8–10 minutes. Using a fork,
blend the flour with the remaining butter
to make a thick paste.

5 Transfer the chicken pieces, shallots
and mushrooms to a serving dish and
keep warm. Bring the liquid to the boil
and then add small pieces of the flour
paste, stirring vigorously after each
addition. When all the paste has been
added and the sauce is thick, either pour
over the chicken pieces or return the
chicken to the casserole and serve.

GLAZED SHALLOTS

SERVES FOUR

INGREDIENTS
    350–400g/12–14oz shallots
    15ml/1 tbsp olive oil
    25g/1oz butter
    15ml/1 tbsp sugar
    about 175ml/6fl oz/¾ cup water
    salt and freshly ground black pepper

1 Peel the shallots and break in two if
the bulbs are joined. Heat the oil and
butter in a heavy-based saucepan and
gently fry the shallots over a moderate
heat for 5–6 minutes until patches of
brown begin to appear. Stir occasionally.

2 Sprinkle the shallots with the sugar
and cook, stirring, for 1 minute.

3 Add enough water to just cover the
shallots and then cover and simmer over
a low heat for about 25–35 minutes until
completely tender, adding a little extra
water if necessary, then remove the lid
and continue simmering gently until the
liquid has reduced to a thin syrup. Stir
occasionally. Season with salt, if liked.

4 Spoon the shallots into a serving dish
and pour over the syrup. Sprinkle with
black pepper. Serve with roast meat or a
baked vegetable dish.

SHOOTS
AND STEMS

Here are some of Nature's most tender vegetables. Asparagus, fennel, samphire and the American fiddlehead fern have the taste of early summer, while the globe artichoke arrives later but is no less delicious for its tardiness. Celery and beansprouts are available all year round and, like other shoots and stems, add a fresh taste to a meal.

ASPARAGUS

Asparagus is most definitely a luxury vegetable. Its price, even in season, sets it apart from cabbages and cauliflowers, and it has a taste of luxury too. The spears, especially the thick green spears, at their best in early summer, have an intense, rich flavour that is impossible to describe but easy to remember. If the gods eat, they will eat asparagus – served simply with a good hollandaise sauce!

History

The ancient Greeks enjoyed eating wild asparagus but it was not until the Roman period that we know it was cultivated. Even then asparagus was highly thought of; it is recorded that Julius Caesar liked to eat it with melted butter. There is little mention of asparagus being eaten in England until the seventeenth century. Mrs Beeton has 14 recipes for asparagus and from the prices quoted in her cookbook it is apparent that it was expensive even in Victorian times.

Nutrition

Asparagus provides vitamins A, B2 and C and is also a very good source of potassium, iron and calcium. It is a well-known diuretic.

Varieties

There are many varieties of asparagus and many different ways of raising it too. Spanish and some Dutch asparagus is white with ivory tips; it is grown under mounds of soil and cut just as the tips begin to show. The purple variety is mostly grown in France, where the spears are cut once the tips are about 4cm/1$\frac{1}{2}$in above the ground. As a consequence, the stalks are white and the tops tinged with green or purple. In contrast, both English and American asparagus grow above the ground and the spears are entirely green. Arguments continue over which has the better flavour, with most growers expressing a preference for their own asparagus!

Thin, short asparagus are called sprue and are excellent when briefly steamed or stir-fried and added to salads. In Italy, they are served by themselves, scattered with grated Parmesan cheese.

Buying and Storing

Asparagus has a relatively short growing season from late spring to early summer. Nowadays, it is available in the shops almost all year round but outside the season it will have been imported. It is still good, but it is expensive and will not have the flavour of home-produced asparagus, because it starts to lose its flavour once it is cut.

When buying asparagus, the tips should be tightly furled and fresh looking, and the stalks fresh and straight. If the stalks are badly scarred or droopy, it indicates that they have been hanging around for too long and it is not worth buying. Asparagus will keep for several days if necessary. Untie the bundles and store in the salad drawer of the fridge.

Left: Asparagus
Above: White asparagus

Preparing

The bottom of the asparagus stalk is usually hard and woody, so will probably need cutting off. If the bottom parts of the stem also feel hard, pare them away with a potato peeler *(see below)*. However, if the asparagus is very fresh this will not be necessary, and sprue rarely needs trimming at all.

Cooking

The problem when cooking asparagus is that the stalks take longer to cook than the tender tips, which need to be only briefly steamed. Ideally, use an asparagus kettle. Place the asparagus spears with the tips upwards in the wire basket and then lower into a little boiling salted water in the kettle. Cover and cook until the stems are tender.

Alternatively, if you do not have an asparagus kettle, place the bundle upright in a deep saucepan of boiling salted water. (The bundle can be wedged into place with potatoes.) Cover with a dome of foil and cook for 5–10 minutes or until the spears are tender. The cooking time depends largely on the thickness of the spears but take care not to overcook; the spears should still have a "bite" to them.

Asparagus can also be roasted in a little olive oil. This cooking method intensifies the flavour and is gratifyingly simple. Serve with just a sprinkling of sea salt – it's quite delicious! If you are steaming asparagus, serve simply with melted butter, which perfectly complements the luxury of the vegetable.

FENNEL

The vegetable fennel is closely related to the herb and spice of the same name. It is called variously Florence fennel, sweet fennel, *finocchio dulce* or Italian fennel.

Like the herb, Florence fennel has the distinct flavour of anise, a taste that seems to go particularly well with fish, so the vegetable is often served with fish dishes while the herb or spice is commonly used in fish stocks, sauces or soups. The leaves are edible and can be used in soups and stocks as well as for garnishing.

History

Florence fennel has only been popular in Britain for the last 20 years, although it has a long history of cultivation, having been eaten by the Ancient Egyptians, Greeks and Romans. In Italy, fennel has been eaten for several centuries: many of the best fennel recipes come from Italy and also from other parts of the Mediterranean.

Buying and Storing

If possible, buy small tender bulbs. The bulbs should be clean and white with no bruises or blemishes and the feathery leaves should be green and lively. Fennel will keep for a day or two in the salad drawer of the fridge.

Preparing

Unless the bulbs are very young and tender, remove the first layer of skin, as it is likely to be tough (this can be used for a stock). Fennel can then be sliced into slivers by cutting downwards or into rings by cutting across the bulb. When used raw in salads, it needs to be cut into smaller pieces.

Cooking and Serving

Fennel can be served raw if it is thinly sliced and then dressed with a light vinaigrette. In salads, its flavour contrasts well with apple, celery and other crunchy ingredients. Fennel is also excellent braised with onions, tomatoes and garlic.

Right: Florence fennel
Opposite: Marsh samphire

SAMPHIRE

There are two types of samphire. Marsh samphire grows in estuaries and salt marshes while rock samphire, sometimes called sea fennel, grows on rocky shores. The two are understandably confused since they are both connected with the sea, yet they are completely different plants.

The type likely to be sold by a fishmonger is marsh samphire. It is also known as glasswort and is sometimes called sea asparagus, as its shoots are similar to sprue, small asparagus shoots.

Although marsh samphire grows easily and is commonly found all over Europe and North America, it is not cultivated and is only available for a short time while it is in season, normally in late summer and early autumn.

Samphire has a distinctly salty, iodine flavour and a pleasant crisp texture. The flavour is reminiscent of the sea and goes particularly well with fish and seafood. However, samphire can be enjoyed simply steamed and dipped into melted butter.

Buying and Storing

When in season, good fishmongers get regular stocks of marsh samphire, and it should look bright and fresh. Buy it when you need it, as it will not keep long.

Preparing and Cooking

If necessary, wash marsh samphire under cold running water. It is best steamed over a pan of boiling water for no more than 3 minutes. Otherwise, blanch in boiling water for 3–5 minutes and then drain. Samphire can be eaten raw but blanching it removes some of the saltiness.

To eat samphire, draw the shoots through the teeth to peel the succulent part from the thin central core.

SHOOT AND STEM RECIPES

If the season's right, you owe it yourself — and your guests — to make the most of shoots and stems. What could be a more perfect way to start a meal than with fresh Asparagus with Tarragon Hollandaise? Alternatively roast asparagus, French-style, for Roast Asparagus Crêpes. Other favourites include Celery, Avocado and Walnut Salad and Fennel and Mussel Provençal, while for something new, try Samphire with Chilled Fish Curry or Celeriac and Blue Cheese Roulade.

ASPARAGUS SOUP

HOME-MADE ASPARAGUS SOUP HAS A DELICATE FLAVOUR, QUITE UNLIKE THAT FROM A CAN. THIS SOUP IS BEST MADE WITH YOUNG ASPARAGUS, EARLY IN THE SEASON, WHICH IS TENDER AND BLENDS WELL. SERVE IT WITH WAFER-THIN SLICES OF BREAD.

SERVES FOUR

INGREDIENTS
    450g/1lb young asparagus
    40g/1½ oz/3 tbsp butter
    6 shallots, sliced
    15g/½ oz/2 tbsp plain flour
    600ml/1 pint/2½ cups vegetable
       stock or water
    15ml/1 tbsp lemon juice
    250ml/8fl oz/1 cup milk
    120ml/4fl oz/½ cup single cream
    10ml/2 tsp chopped fresh chervil
    salt and freshly ground black pepper

1 Trim the stalks of the asparagus if necessary. Cut 4cm/1½in off the tops of half the asparagus and set aside for a garnish. Slice the remaining asparagus.

2 Melt 25g/1oz/2 tbsp of the butter in a large saucepan and gently fry the sliced shallots for 2–3 minutes until soft but not brown, stirring occasionally.

3 Add the sliced asparagus and fry over a gentle heat for about 1 minute. Stir in the flour and cook for 1 minute. Stir in the stock or water and lemon juice, and season to taste. Bring to the boil and then simmer, partially covered, for 15–20 minutes until the asparagus is very tender.

4 Cool slightly and then process the soup in a food processor or blender until smooth. Then press the purée through a sieve placed over a clean saucepan. Add the milk by pouring and stirring it through the sieve with the asparagus so as to extract the maximum amount of asparagus purée.

5 Melt the remaining butter and fry the reserved asparagus tips gently for about 3–4 minutes to soften.

6 Heat the soup gently for 3–4 minutes. Stir in the cream and the asparagus tips. Continue to heat gently and serve sprinkled with the chopped fresh chervil.

ROAST ASPARAGUS CRÊPES

ROAST ASPARAGUS IS DELICIOUS AND GOOD ENOUGH TO EAT JUST AS IT COMES. HOWEVER, FOR A REALLY SPLENDID STARTER, TRY THIS SIMPLE RECIPE. EITHER MAKE SIX LARGE OR TWELVE COCKTAIL-SIZE PANCAKES TO USE WITH SMALLER STEMS OF ASPARAGUS.

<u>SERVES SIX</u>

INGREDIENTS
    90–120ml/6–8 tbsp olive oil
    450g/1lb fresh asparagus
    175g/6oz/¾ cup mascarpone cheese
    60ml/4 tbsp single cream
    25g/1oz Parmesan cheese, grated
    sea salt
For the pancakes
    175g/6oz 1½ cup plain flour
    2 eggs
    350ml/12fl oz/1½ cups milk
    vegetable oil, for frying
    a pinch of salt

1 To make the pancake batter, mix the flour with the salt in a large bowl, food processor or blender, then add the eggs and milk and beat or process to make a smooth, fairly thin batter.

2 Heat a little oil in a large frying pan and add a small amount of batter, swirling the pan to coat the base evenly. Cook over a moderate heat for about 1 minute, then flip over and cook the other side until golden. Set aside and cook the rest of the pancakes in the same way; the mixture makes about six large or 12 smaller pancakes.

3 Preheat the oven to 180°C/350°F/ Gas 4 and lightly grease a large shallow ovenproof dish or roasting tin with some of the olive oil.

4 Trim the asparagus by placing on a board and cutting off the bases. Using a small sharp knife, peel away the woody ends, if necessary.

5 Arrange the asparagus in a single layer in the dish or tin, trickle over the remaining olive oil, rolling the asparagus to coat each one thoroughly. Sprinkle with salt and then roast in the oven for 8–12 minutes until tender (the cooking time depends on the stem thickness).

6 Blend the mascarpone cheese with the cream and Parmesan cheese and spread a generous tablespoonful over each of the pancakes, leaving a little extra for the topping. Preheat the grill.

7 Divide the asparagus spears among the pancakes, roll up and arrange in a single layer in an ovenproof dish. Spoon over the remaining cheese mixture and then place under a moderate grill for 4–5 minutes, until heated through and golden brown. Serve at once.

ROOTS

Roots are the mainstays of our winter meals. Parsnips, turnips, swedes and potatoes combine to make wonderful warming stews. Jerusalem artichokes are another winter favourite and, as winter turns to spring, young carrots and Jersey Royal potatoes appear. Exotic roots such as sweet potatoes and yams are available almost all year round, and look out too for salsify — a root vegetable that can be enjoyed whatever the season.

Pentland Dell: A long, oval-shaped potato with a floury texture that does tend to disintegrate when boiled. It is popular for roasting as the outside becomes soft when par-boiled and then crisps up with the fat during roasting.

Romano: The Romano has a distinctive red skin with creamy flesh and is a good all-rounder, similar to Desirée.

Wilja: Introduced from Holland, this is a pale, yellow-fleshed potato with a good, sweet flavour and waxy texture.

Other Varieties

Although most of these varieties are also main crop, they are less widely available than those listed above but they are increasingly sold in supermarkets. They are recommended for salads but are also excellent sautéed or simply boiled.

Cara: A large main crop potato, which is excellent baked or boiled but is a good all-rounder.

Finger Potatoes: Thumb-size, long baby potatoes are sometimes called finger potatoes or fingerlings. Among the many varieties are the German Lady's Finger. Since they are new crop potatoes, they need simply be boiled and then served either in salads or with a little butter and a sprinkling of parsley.

La Ratte: A French potato with a smooth skin and waxy yellow flesh. It has a chestnut flavour and is good in salads.

Linzer Delikatess: These small, kidney-shaped potatoes look a little like Jersey Royals but have a pale smooth skin. They do not have much taste and are best in salads where their flavour can be enhanced with other ingredients.

Pink Fir Apple: This is an old English variety, with pink skin and smooth yellow flesh. It is becoming increasingly popular and has a distinctive flavour.

Opposite above: Cara (left) and Estima (right) potatoes
Opposite below: Linzer Delikatess potatoes
Above: Desirée (left) and King Edward (right) potatoes
Right: Finger potatoes

CARROTS

After potatoes, carrots are without doubt
our best-known and best-loved root
vegetable. In the days when vegetables
were served merely as an accessory to
meat, carrots always made an
appearance – often overcooked but still
eaten up because, we were told, they
helped you to see in the dark.

Carrots have many different flavours,
depending on how they are cooked.
Young, new season carrots braised in
butter and a splash of water are intensely
flavoured and sweet; when steamed,
they are tender and melting. Carrots
grated into salads are fresh and clean
tasting, while in casseroles they are
savoury with the characteristic "carrot"
flavour. In soups they are fragrant and
mild, and in cakes their flavour can
hardly be detected, yet their sweetness
adds richness.

History

Until the Middle Ages, carrots were
purple. The orange carrots came from
Holland, from where they were exported
during the seventeenth and eighteenth
centuries. Although purple and white
carrots continued to be eaten in France,
nowadays they are something of a rarity.

Nutrition

The carrot contains large amounts of
carotene and vitamin A, along with
useful amounts of vitamins B3, C and E.
When eaten raw, they also provide good
quantities of potassium, calcium, iron
and zinc, but these are reduced when
carrots are boiled.

The idea that carrots are good for your
night sight originated in the Second
World War. Early radar stations were
established along the south and east
coasts of England in 1939 to detect
aggressors in the air or at sea. The
Germans attributed this sudden
remarkable night vision to the British
habit of eating carrots. Indeed, the
vitamin A in carrots forms retinol, a lack
of which brings on night blindness.

Buying and Storing

Home-grown carrots are so much nicer than the shop-bought ones. Almost all vegetables have a better flavour if grown organically, but this is particularly true of carrots.

When buying carrots, look out for the very young, pencil-thin ones, which are beautifully tender either eaten raw or steamed for just a few minutes. Young carrots are commonly sold with their feathery tops intact, which should be fresh and green. Older carrots should be firm and unblemished. Avoid tired-looking carrots as they will have little nutritional value.

Carrots should not be stored for too long. They will keep for several days if stored in a cool, airy place or in the salad drawer of the fridge.

Preparing

Preparation depends on the age of the carrots. The valuable nutrients lie either in or just beneath the skin, so if the carrots are young, simply wash them under cold running water. Medium-size carrots may need to be scraped and large carrots will need either scraping or peeling.

Cooking

Carrots are excellent cooked or raw. Children often like raw carrots as they have a very sweet flavour. They can be cut into julienne strips, with a dressing added, or grated into salads and coleslaw – their juices run and blend wonderfully with the dressing. Carrots can be cooked in almost any way you choose. As an accompaniment, cut them into julienne strips and braise in butter and cider, or cook in the minimum of stock and toss in butter and a sprinkling of caraway seeds.

Roasted carrots are delicious, with a melt-in-the-mouth sweetness. Par-boil large ones first, but younger carrots can be quickly blanched or added direct to the roasting tin with a joint of meat.

HORSERADISH

Horseradish is grown for its pungent root, which is normally grated and mixed with cream or oil and vinegar and served with roast beef. Fresh horseradish is available in many supermarkets in the spring, and you can make your own horseradish sauce by simply peeling the root and then mixing 45ml/3 tbsp grated horseradish with 150ml/¼ pint/⅔ cup whipping cream and adding a little Dijon mustard, vinegar and sugar to taste. As well as being excellent with hot or cold beef, horseradish sauce is delicious with smoked trout or mackerel or spread thinly on sandwiches with a fine pâté.

Left: Carrots
Right: Horseradish

ROOTS
RECIPES

*For tasty, nourishing meals, you don't need to look
further than roots, whether it is carrots, beetroot or
the ever popular potato. Potatoes Dauphinois or
Artichoke Rösti are the stuff of winter evenings —
warm and filling, simple to make, great to eat. For
something with a more exotic flavour, try Yam
Fritters or Mediterranean Chicken with Turnips.*

CARROT AND CORIANDER SOUP

NEARLY ALL ROOT VEGETABLES MAKE EXCELLENT SOUPS AS THEY PURÉE WELL AND HAVE AN EARTHY FLAVOUR WHICH COMPLEMENTS THE SHARPER FLAVOURS OF HERBS AND SPICES. CARROTS ARE PARTICULARLY VERSATILE AND THIS SIMPLE SOUP IS ELEGANT IN BOTH FLAVOUR AND APPEARANCE.

SERVES FOUR TO SIX

INGREDIENTS
450g/1lb carrots, preferably young
  and tender
15ml/1 tbsp sunflower oil
40g/1½oz/3 tbsp butter
1 onion, chopped
1 celery stalk, sliced plus 2–3 pale
  leafy celery tops
2 small potatoes, chopped
1 litre/1¾ pints/4 cups chicken stock
10–15ml/2–3 tsp ground coriander
15ml/1 tbsp chopped fresh coriander
200ml/7fl oz/⅞ cup milk
salt and freshly ground black pepper

1 Trim the carrots, peel if necessary and cut into chunks. Heat the oil and 25g/1oz/2 tbsp of the butter in a large flameproof casserole or heavy-based saucepan and fry the onion over a gentle heat for 3–4 minutes until they are slightly softened but not browned.

2 Cut the celery stalk into slices. Add the celery and potatoes to the onion in the pan, cook for a few minutes and then add the carrots. Fry over a gentle heat for 3–4 minutes, stirring frequently, and then cover. Reduce the heat even further and sweat for about 10 minutes. Shake the pan or stir occasionally so the vegetables do not stick to the base.

3 Add the stock, bring to the boil and then partially cover and simmer for a further 8–10 minutes until the carrots and potatoes are tender.

4 Remove 6–8 tiny celery leaves for garnish and finely chop the remaining celery tops (about 15ml/1 tbsp once chopped). Melt the remaining butter in a small saucepan and fry the ground coriander for about 1 minute, stirring all the time.

5 Reduce the heat and then add the chopped celery and fresh coriander and fry for about 1 minute. Set aside.

6 Purée the soup in a food processor or blender and pour into a clean saucepan. Stir in the milk, coriander mixture and seasoning. Heat gently, taste and adjust the seasoning. Serve garnished with the reserved celery.

COOK'S TIP
For a more piquant flavour, add a little lemon juice just before serving.

PAN-FRIED SWEET POTATOES WITH BACON

THIS IS A COMFORTING DISH TO EAT ON A COLD WINTER'S EVENING. BACON AND ONION COUNTERACT THE SWEETNESS OF THE POTATO, AND THE CAYENNE PEPPER GIVES THE NECESSARY EXTRA "KICK".

SERVES FOUR

INGREDIENTS
675–900g/1½–2lb sweet potatoes
juice of 1 lemon
15ml/1 tbsp plain flour
a good pinch of cayenne pepper
about 45ml/3 tbsp sunflower oil
1 large onion, chopped
115g/4oz streaky bacon, chopped
50g/2oz/1 cup fresh brown or
    white breadcrumbs
salt

1 Peel the sweet potatoes and cut into chunks about 4cm/1½in square. Place in a pan of boiling water with the lemon juice and a little salt, and simmer for 8–10 minutes until cooked but not soft.

2 Mix together the flour, cayenne pepper and a pinch of salt. Drain the potatoes and then dust with the seasoned flour, coating the pieces well.

3 Heat 15ml/1tbsp of the oil in a large frying pan and fry the onion for about 2 minutes. Add the bacon and fry over a gentle heat for 6–8 minutes until the onion and bacon are golden. Transfer to a plate using a slotted spoon.

4 Add the breadcrumbs and fry, stirring, for about 1–2 minutes until golden. Add to the plate with the bacon.

5 Heat the remaining oil in the pan and fry the potatoes for 5–6 minutes, turning occasionally, until evenly browned. Stir in the breadcrumb and bacon mixture and cook for 1 minute. Serve at once.

YAM FRITTERS

YAMS HAVE A SLIGHTLY DRIER FLAVOUR THAN POTATOES AND ARE PARTICULARLY GOOD WHEN MIXED WITH SPICES AND THEN FRIED. THE FRITTERS CAN ALSO BE MOULDED INTO SMALL BALLS AND DEEP FRIED. THIS IS A FAVOURITE AFRICAN WAY OF SERVING YAMS.

MAKES ABOUT 18–20

INGREDIENTS
  675g/1½lb yams
  milk, for mashing
  2 small eggs, beaten
  45ml/3 tbsp chopped tomato flesh
  45ml/3 tbsp finely chopped
    spring onions
  1 green chilli, seeded and
    finely sliced
  flour, for shaping
  40g/1½oz/¾ cup white breadcrumbs
  vegetable oil, for shallow frying
  salt and freshly ground black pepper

1 Peel the yams and cut into chunks. Place in a saucepan of salted water and boil for 20–30 minutes until tender. Drain and mash with a little milk and about 45ml/3 tbsp of the beaten eggs.

2 Add the chopped tomato, spring onions, chilli and seasoning and stir well to mix thoroughly.

3 Using floured hands, shape the yam and vegetable mixture into round fritters, about 7.5cm/3in in diameter.

4 Dip each in the remaining egg and then coat evenly with the breadcrumbs. Heat a little oil in a large frying pan and fry the fritters for about 4–5 minutes until golden brown. Turn the fritters over once during cooking. Drain well on kitchen paper and serve.

EDDO, CARROT AND PARSNIP MEDLEY

EDDO (TARO), LIKE YAMS, IS WIDELY EATEN IN AFRICA AND THE CARIBBEAN, OFTEN AS A PURÉE. HERE, IT IS ROASTED AND COMBINED WITH MORE COMMON ROOT VEGETABLES TO MAKE A COLOURFUL DISPLAY.

SERVES FOUR TO SIX

INGREDIENTS
  450g/1lb eddoes (taros)
  350g/12oz parsnips
  450g/1lb carrots
  25g/1oz/2 tbsp butter
  45ml/3 tbsp sunflower oil
For the dressing
  30ml/2 tbsp fresh orange juice
  30ml/2 tbsp demerara sugar
  10ml/2 tsp soft green peppercorns
  salt
  fresh parsley, to garnish

1 Preheat the oven to 200°C/400°F/ Gas 6. Thickly peel the eddoes, making sure to remove all the skin as this can be an irritant. Cut into pieces about 5 x 2cm/2 x ¾in by 2cm/¾in, and place in a large bowl.

2 Peel the parsnips, halve lengthways and remove the inner core if necessary. Cut into the same size pieces as the eddo and add to the bowl. Blanch in boiling water for 2 minutes and then drain. Peel or scrub the carrots, and halve or quarter them according to their size.

3 Place the butter and sunflower oil in a roasting tin and heat in the oven for 3–4 minutes. Add the vegetables, turning them in the oil to coat evenly. Roast in the oven for 30 minutes.

4 Meanwhile, blend the orange juice, sugar and soft green peppercorns in a small bowl. Remove the roasting tin from the oven and allow to cool for a minute or so and then carefully pour the mixture over the vegetables, stirring to coat them all. (If the liquid is poured on too soon the hot oil will spit.)

5 Return the tin to the oven and cook for a further 20 minutes or until the vegetables are crisp and golden. Then transfer to a warmed serving plate and sprinkle with a little salt. Garnish with fresh parsley to serve.

GREENS

Whatever the season, there is something for everyone when it

comes to greens. Cauliflowers, kale, broccoli and Brussels

sprouts are all members of the cabbage family and like the

cabbage itself are among the most nutritious of all vegetables.

Spinach too is full of vitamins and minerals and is wonderfully

versatile, and if you want to ring the changes, Oriental

cabbages, such as Chinese leaves or pak choi are widely available

and quite delicious.

SPROUTING BROCCOLI AND CALABRESE

Varieties

Calabrese broccoli: This is the vegetable that today we commonly call broccoli, with large beautiful, blue-green heads on succulent stalks. It is named after the Italian province of Calabria where this variety was first developed.

Purple sprouting broccoli: The original variety – it has long thin stalks with small flowerheads that are normally purple but can be white or green. Heads, stalks and tender leaves are all edible. The purple heads turn green when cooked but the others keep their colour. This variety is more seasonal than the readily available calabrese; it is usually available from late winter onwards.

Buying and Storing

If possible, buy loose broccoli rather than the pre-wrapped bundles, because it is easier to check that it is fresh and also because wrapped vegetables tend to deteriorate more quickly.

Purple sprouting broccoli can also be - sold loose or prepacked. Check that the stalk, flowerhead and leaves all look fresh and that the flowerlets are tightly closed and bright green. Neither type will keep for long.

Broccoli or calabrese is a relatively modern vegetable and is one of the most popular. It is quick and easy to prepare with little or no waste and similarly easy to cook. It is attractive, whether served raw or cooked, and you can buy it in the quantity you require, unlike cauliflower or cabbage.

History

Before calabrese came into our shops, people bought and ate purple sprouting broccoli. This is basically an "untidy" version of calabrese, with long shoots and clusters of flowerheads at the end – the broccoli we know today has neat tidy heads. The stalks of purple sprouting broccoli have a faint asparagus flavour.

The Romans cooked purple sprouting broccoli in wine or served it with sauces and it is still a popular vegetable today in Italy, cooked in the oven with anchovies and onions or served with pasta in a garlic and tomato sauce.

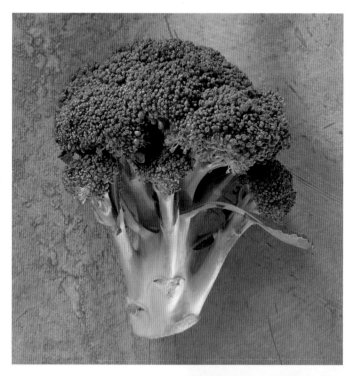

Preparing and Cooking

Trim the ends of the stalks and pull off any discoloured leaves.

Calabrese broccoli: Break into even-size pieces, dividing the stem and flowerhead lengthways if they are thick. Cook in a little boiling water for 4–5 minutes until just tender and then drain. Do not steam this variety of broccoli as its vibrant green colour tends to turn grey.

Purple sprouting broccoli: Either steam in long, even-size lengths in a steamer or, if you have an asparagus kettle, cook as you would asparagus. Alternatively, tie the stems loosely together and stand in a little water – if necessary, wedge it in with a potato or rolled up piece of foil. Cover with a dome of foil and steam for about 4–5 minutes until tender.

Serving

Serve both varieties simply with butter and lemon juice or with a hollandaise or Béarnaise sauce as an accompaniment. They are also excellent stir-fried.

Opposite above: Purple cauliflower
Opposite below: Purple sprouting broccoli
Left: Calabrese broccoli
Below: Turnip tops

TURNIP TOPS

Turnip tops, like beet greens, are both delicious and nutritious. They are not widely available but if you are able to buy some or if you grow your own, slice them (see below), boil or steam for a few minutes, drain and serve with butter.

CABBAGE

Cabbage, sliced and cooked, can be one of two things: deliciously crisp, with a mild pleasant flavour – or overcooked and truly horrible! Cabbage and other brassicas contain the chemical hydrogen sulphide, which is activated during cooking at about the point the vegetable starts to soften. It eventually disappears, but during the in-between time, cabbage will acquire its characteristic rank smell and flavour. So, either cook cabbage briefly, or cook it long and slowly, preferably with other ingredients so that flavours can mingle.

History

Cabbage has a long and varied history. However, because there are so many varieties of cabbage under the general heading of "brassica", it is difficult to be sure whether the variety the Greeks and Romans enjoyed is the same as today's round cabbage, or something more akin to kale or even Chinese cabbage.

The round cabbages we know today were an important food during the Dark Ages, and by the Middle Ages they were in abundance, as you will see if you study the paintings of that period. They often show kitchen tables or baskets at market positively groaning with fruit and vegetables, and cabbages in all their shapes and sizes were usually featured.

Medieval recipes suggest cooking the cabbage with leeks, onions and herbs. In the days when all except the very wealthy cooked everything in one pot, it is fair to assume that cabbages were cooked long and slowly until fairly recently.

Varieties

Savoy cabbage: This is a variety of green cabbage with crimped or curly leaves. It has a mild flavour and is particularly tender, thus needing less cooking than other varieties.
Spring greens: These have fresh loose heads with a pale yellow-green heart. Available in spring, they are delicious sliced, steamed and simply served with butter.

Right: Savoy cabbage
Opposite above: Green cabbage
Opposite below: Spring greens

GREENS RECIPES

*Greens are so good for you we really should eat lots
more. They're also versatile and quite delicious, so
there's no excuse either! Broccoli Crumble and
Balti-style Cauliflower with Tomatoes are quick
and easy dishes, or try Broccoli and Chicken
Lasagne or Spinach in Filo with Three Cheeses for
great family eating. Stir-fried Brussels Sprouts
presents sprouts in whole new and delicious light,
while the traditional Greek dish, Dolmades, is
surprisingly simple to prepare.*

STIR-FRIED BRUSSELS SPROUTS

SERVES FOUR

INGREDIENTS
    450g/1lb Brussels sprouts
    15ml/1 tbsp sunflower oil
    6–8 spring onions, cut into 2.5cm/
        1in lengths
    2 slices fresh root ginger
    40g/1½oz/¼ cup flaked almonds
    150–175ml/5–6fl oz/⅔–¾ cup
        vegetable or chicken stock
    salt

1 Trim the bases of the Brussels sprouts and remove any large outer leaves. Cut into slices about 7mm/⅓in thick.

2 Heat the oil in a wok or heavy-based frying pan and fry the spring onions and the ginger for about 2–3 minutes, stirring frequently. Add the almonds and stir-fry over a moderate heat until both the onions and almonds begin to brown.

3 Remove and discard the ginger, reduce the heat and stir in the Brussels sprouts. Stir-fry for a few minutes and then pour in the stock and cook over a gentle heat for 5–6 minutes or until the sprouts are nearly tender.

4 Add a little salt, if necessary, and then increase the heat to boil off the excess liquid. Spoon into a warmed serving dish and serve immediately.

BRUSSELS SPROUTS GRATIN

SERVES FOUR

INGREDIENTS
    15g/½oz/1 tbsp butter
    150ml/¼ pint/⅔ cup whipping cream
    150ml/¼ pint/⅔ cup milk
    25g/1oz Parmesan cheese, grated
    675g/1½lb Brussels sprouts,
        thinly sliced
    2 garlic cloves, finely chopped
    salt and freshly ground black pepper

1 Preheat the oven to 150°C/300°F/ Gas 2 and butter a shallow ovenproof dish. Blend together the cream, milk, Parmesan cheese and seasoning.

2 Put a layer of Brussels sprouts in the base of the prepared dish, sprinkle with a little garlic and pour over about a quarter of the cream mixture. Add another layer of sprouts and continue building layers in this way, ending with the remaining cream and milk.

3 Cover loosely with greaseproof paper and then bake for 1–1¼ hours. Halfway through cooking, remove the paper and press the sprouts under the liquid in the dish. Return to the oven to brown.

BEANS, PEAS AND SEEDS

Sweet and succulent, beans and peas are the vegetables we first

turn to when we need a tasty accompaniment. Okra, like

mangetouts and most fresh beans come complete with pods.

Podded peas are best when absolutely fresh, dried beans

give us another huge dimension of vegetable dishes, while

sweetcorn is a delight, whether kept on the cob or

served as kernels on the side.

BROAD BEANS

One of the delights of having a garden is discovering how truly delicious some vegetables are when garden fresh. This seems particularly true of broad beans, which have a superb sweet flavour that sadly can never be reproduced in the frozen product. If you're lucky enough to grow or be given fresh broad beans, don't worry about recipes; just cook them until tender and serve with butter. It will be a revelation! However, if you're not one of those lucky few, don't dismiss broad beans, as they are still a really versatile vegetable. They can be used in soups or casseroles, and, since they have a mealy texture, they also purée very well.

History

People have been eating broad beans almost since time began. A variety of wild broad bean grew all over southern Europe, north Africa and Asia, and they would have been a useful food for early man. There is archaeological evidence that by Neolithic times broad beans were being farmed, making them one of the first foods to be cultivated.

Broad beans will grow in most climates and most soils. They were a staple food for people throughout the Dark Ages and the Middle Ages, and were grown for feeding people and livestock until the potato replaced them in the seventeenth and eighteenth centuries. Broad beans were an important source of protein for the poor, and dried they would have provided nourishing meals for families until the next growing season.

Nutrition

Beans are high in both protein and carbohydrates and are also a good source of vitamins A, B1 and B2. They also provide potassium and iron as well as several other minerals.

Buying and Storing

Buy the beans as fresh as possible. The pods should preferably be small and tender. Use as soon as possible.

Preparing

Very young beans in tender pods, no more than 7.5cm/3in in length, can be

eaten pod and all; top and tail, and then slice roughly. Usually, however, you will need to shell the beans. Elderly beans are often better skinned after they are cooked to rid them of the strong, bitter flavour that puts many people off this vegetable.

Cooking

Plunge shelled beans (or in their pods if very young) into rapidly boiling water and cook until just tender. They can also be par-boiled and then finished off braised in butter. For a simple purée, blend the cooked beans with garlic cooked in butter, cream and a pinch of fresh herbs, such as savory or thyme.

LIMA BEANS

These are popular in the US, named after the capital of Peru, and are sold mainly shelled. They are an essential ingredient in the Native-American dish *succotash*. Lima beans should be cooked in a little boiling water until tender. Elderly beans need skinning after they are cooked. The dried bean, also known as the butter bean, can be large or small. These large beans tend to become mushy when cooked so are best used in soups or purées.

Above: Broad beans
Below: Lima beans
Opposite: Runner beans

RUNNER BEANS

The runner bean is native to South America, where it has been cultivated for more than 2,000 years, and there is archaeological evidence of its existence much earlier than that.

It is a popular vegetable to grow. Most home vegetable gardeners have a patch of runner beans – they are easy to grow and, like all legumes, their roots contain bacteria that help renew the nitrogen supplies in the soil.

They have a more robust flavour and texture than French beans and also are distinct from green beans in several ways: They are generally much larger with long, flattened pods; their skin is rough textured, although in young beans this softens during cooking; and they have purple beans within the pods, unlike green beans whose beans are mostly white or pale green. Nevertheless, the runner bean belongs to the same family as all the green beans.

Buying and Storing

Always buy young beans as the pods of larger beans are likely to be tough. The pods should feel firm and fresh; if you can see the outline of the bean inside the pod it is likely to be fibrous – although you could leave the beans to dry out and use the dried beans later in the season. Ideally, the beans inside should be no larger than your small fingernail.

Use as soon as possible after buying; they do not store well.

Preparing

Runner beans need to be topped and tailed and they may also need stringing. Carefully put your knife through the top of the bean without cutting right through it, and then pull downwards; if a thick thread comes away, the beans need stringing, so do the same on the other side. The beans can then be sliced using either a sharp knife or a slicer. Slice through the beans lengthways, not diagonally, so that you will be able to serve them with just a little skin and lots of flesh.

Cooking

Plunge the beans into boiling salted water and cook until *al dente*.

PEAS

Fresh peas are wonderful – try tasting them raw, straight from their pod. Unfortunately, the season for garden peas is short, and frozen peas, which are the next best thing, never quite come up to the mark. If you grow your own peas, for three or four weeks in early summer, you can eat like kings; otherwise you can buy them from a good greengrocer, who may be able to keep you supplied all through the early summer.

History

Peas have an even longer history than broad beans, with the archaeological evidence showing they were cultivated as long ago as 5700 BC. High in protein and carbohydrate, they would have been another important staple food and were eaten fresh, or dried in soups or potage.

Pease porridge is mentioned in a Greek play written in 5 BC. Pease pudding, probably something similar, made with split peas with onion and herbs, is an old-fashioned but still very popular dish, especially in the north of England, and is traditionally eaten with pork.

But one of the first recipes for peas, comes from *Le Cuisinier Français*, which was translated into English in the middle of the seventeenth century. It gives a recipe for *petits pois à la française* (peas cooked with small hearted lettuces) – still a popular recipe today.

Varieties

Mangetouts: These are eaten whole and have a delicate flavour, providing they are not overcooked. Unfortunately, they are easy to overcook and the texture then becomes rather slippery. Alternatively, blanch or stir-fry them. They are also good served raw in salads.

Petits pois: These are not, as you might expect, immature peas but are a dwarf variety. Gardeners grow their own, but they are not available fresh in the shops as they are mainly grown commercially for canning or freezing.

Snow peas, Sugar peas, Sugar snaps: These have the distinct fresh flavour of raw peas and are more plump and have more snap than mangetouts.

Buying and Storing

Only buy fresh peas, and use them as soon as possible. It is wiser to buy frozen peas rather than old peas, which can be tough and dry. In top condition, the pods are bright green and lively looking; the more withered the pod, the longer they have been hanging around. It is possible to surreptitiously sample peas on occasions, to check if they are fresh (greengrocers don't seem to mind so long as you buy something).

Preparing

Shelling peas can be very relaxing. Press open the pods and use your thumb to push out the peas *(below)*. Mangetouts and sugar snaps just need to be topped and tailed *(below right)*.

Cooking

Cook peas with a sprig of mint in a pan of rapidly boiling water or in a covered steamer until tender. Alternatively, melt butter in a flameproof casserole, add the peas and then cover and sweat over a gentle heat for 4–5 minutes. Cook mangetouts and snow peas in any of these ways but for a shorter time.

Opposite: peas.
Above right: Sugar snap peas.

SWEETCORN

Fresh sweetcorn, eaten on the cob with salt and a little butter is deliciously sweet. Some gardeners who grow it have a pan ready on the boil, so that when they cut the corn it goes into the pan in only the time it takes to race up from the garden to the kitchen. Buying it from the supermarket is inevitably a bit risky, although if it is purchased in season, sweetcorn can be very good indeed.

History

In 1492, as Christopher Columbus disembarked on the island now called Cuba, he was met by Native Americans offering two gifts of hospitality – one was tobacco and the other something the Indians called *maïs*. The English word for staple food was then corn, so that when Columbus and his crew saw that maize was the staple food for the Indians, it was dubbed "Indian corn".

Corn originated in South America and had enormous significance to the Native Americans of the whole continent, who were said to have lived and died by corn. They referred to it as their "first mother and father, the source of life". By far their most important food, the corn plant was used for their shelters and for fences, and they also wore corn and decorated their bodies with it.

The Aztecs conducted corn planting ceremonies that including human sacrifices, and other tribes had similar customs to appease the god "corn". Countless myths and legends have been woven around corn, each tribe telling a slightly different story, but each on the same theme of planting and harvesting corn. For anthropologists and historians, they make compelling study.

Nutrition

Corn is a good carbohydrate food and is rich in vitamins A, B and C. It contains protein, but not as much as most other cereals. It's also a good source of potassium, magnesium, phosphorus and iron.

Varieties

There are five main varieties of corn – popcorn, sweetcorn, dent corn, flint corn and flour corn. Dent corn is the most commonly grown worldwide, for animal

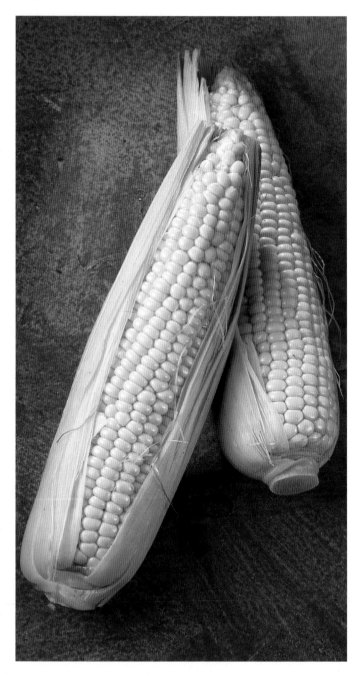

feeds and oil, and the corn we eat on the cobs is sweetcorn. Baby sweet cobs of corn are picked when immature and are cooked and eaten whole.

Buying and Storing

As soon as corn is picked, its sugar begins to turn to starch and therefore the sooner it goes into the pot, the better. Wherever possible, buy locally grown sweetcorn.

Look for husks that are clean and green and tassels which are golden, with no sign of matting. The corn itself should look plump and yellow. Avoid cobs with pale or white kernels or those with older shrivelled kernels which will undoubtedly be disappointing.

Preparing

Strip away the husks. To use the kernels for recipes, cut downwards using a sharp knife from top to bottom *(left)*.

Cooking

Cook corn-on-the-cob in plenty of boiling salted water until tender. Timing depends on the size of the cobs but 10–15 minutes will normally be enough. Serve them with sea salt and butter, but if the cobs are really sweet, leave out the butter. Stir-fry baby sweetcorn cobs briefly and serve in oriental dishes.

Opposite: Sweetcorn cobs
Below: Baby sweetcorn cobs

BEAN, PEA AND SEED RECIPES

Whether you're looking for classic side dishes, or for something more unusual, peas and beans are a great choice. Broad Beans à la Paysanne or Peas with Baby Onions and Cream are favourites everywhere; India-style Okra or Runner Beans with Garlic will please the more adventurous. Sweetcorn is particularly versatile; use it for snacks such as Sweetcorn and Cheese Pasties, or for a delicious main course soup, Sweetcorn and Scallop Chowder.

RUNNER BEANS WITH GARLIC

DELICATE AND FRESH-TASTING FLAGEOLET BEANS AND GARLIC ADD A DISTINCT FRENCH FLAVOUR TO THIS SIMPLE SIDE DISH. SERVE TO ACCOMPANY ROAST LAMB OR VEAL.

SERVES FOUR

INGREDIENTS

225g/8oz flageolet beans
15ml/1 tbsp olive oil
25g/1oz/2 tbsp butter
1 onion, finely chopped
1–2 garlic cloves, crushed
3–4 tomatoes, peeled and chopped
350g/12oz runner beans, prepared
    and sliced
150ml/¼ pint/⅔ cup white wine
150ml/¼ pint/⅔ cup vegetable stock
30ml/2 tbsp chopped fresh parsley
salt and freshly ground black pepper

1 Place the flageolet beans in a large saucepan of water, bring to the boil and simmer for ¾–1 hour until tender. Drain.

2 Heat the oil and butter in a large frying pan and sauté the onion and garlic for 3–4 minutes until soft. Then add the chopped tomatoes and continue cooking over a gentle heat until they are soft.

3 Stir the flageolet beans into the onion and tomato mixture, then add the runner beans, wine, stock and a little salt. Stir well. Cover and simmer for 5–10 minutes until the runner beans are tender.

4 Increase the heat to reduce the liquid, then stir in the parsley and season with a little more salt, if necessary, and pepper.

INDIAN–STYLE OKRA

WHEN OKRA IS SERVED IN INDIAN RESTAURANTS IT IS OFTEN FLAT AND SOGGY BECAUSE IT HAS BEEN OVERCOOKED OR LEFT STANDING. HOWEVER, WHEN YOU MAKE THIS DISH YOURSELF, YOU WILL REALIZE JUST HOW DELICIOUS OKRA CAN BE.

SERVES FOUR

INGREDIENTS
350g/12oz okra
2 small onions
2 garlic cloves, crushed
1cm/½in piece fresh root ginger
1 green chilli, seeded
10ml/2 tsp ground cumin
10ml/2 tsp ground coriander
30ml/2 tbsp vegetable oil
juice of 1 lemon

3 Reduce the heat and add the garlic and ginger mixture. Cook for about 2–3 minutes, stirring frequently, and then add the okra, lemon juice and 105ml/7 tbsp water. Stir well, cover tightly and simmer over a low heat for about 10 minutes until tender. Transfer to a serving dish, sprinkle with the fried onion rings and serve at once.

1 Trim the okra and cut into 1cm/½in lengths. Roughly chop one of the onions and place in a food processor or blender with the garlic, ginger, chilli and 90ml/ 6 tbsp water. Process to a paste. Add the cumin and coriander and blend again.

2 Thinly slice the remaining onion into half rings; fry in the oil for 6–8 minutes until golden brown. Transfer to a plate using a slotted spoon.

SQUASHES

*In their bright and beautiful colours, these are the vegetables that
say autumn. Locally grown courgettes are available from mid to
late summer, as are the pretty pattypans. Marrows follow in
late summer and then come the winter squashes — acorn squash,
kabocha, onion squash and pumpkins — just in time for
Hallowe'en and pumpkin pie.*

MARROWS AND SUMMER SQUASHES

Vegetable marrow is classified as a summer squash yet it is rather the poor relation of squashes. Most of the edible flesh is water and at best it is a rather bland vegetable, with a slightly sweet flavour. At worst, it is insipid and if cooked to a mush (which isn't unheard of), it is completely tasteless.

Marrows can be stuffed, although it involves a lot of energy expended for very little reward; but marrow cooked over a low heat in butter with no added water (so that it steams in its own juice) brings out the best in it.

History

Marrows, like all the summer and winter squashes, are native to America. Squashes were eaten by Native Americans, traditionally with corn and beans, and in an Iroquois myth the three

vegetables are represented as three inseparable sisters. Although the early explorers would almost certainly have come into contact with them, they were not brought back home, and the vegetable marrow was not known in England until the nineteenth century. Once introduced, however, it quickly became very popular. Mrs Beeton gives eight recipes for vegetable marrow and observes that "it is now extensively used". No mention at all is made of courgettes, which of course are simply immature marrows, as any gardener will know.

Varieties

The word "marrow" as a general term tends to refer to the summer squashes. At the end of summer and in the early autumn a good variety of the large summer squashes is available.

Vegetable marrows: This is the proper name for the large prize marrows, beloved of harvest festivals and country fairs. Buy small specimens whenever possible.

Spaghetti squashes/marrows: Long and pale yellow, like all marrows these squashes can grow to enormous sizes, but try to buy small specimens for convenience as well as flavour. They got their name from the resemblance of the cooked flesh to spaghetti.

To boil a spaghetti squash, first pierce the end, so that the heat can reach the middle, then cook for about 25 minutes or until the skin feels tender. Cut the squash in half lengthways, remove the seeds, and then fork the strands of flesh out on to a plate. It has a fragrant, almost honey and lemon flavour and tastes good with garlic butter or pesto.

Custard marrows: These are pretty, pale green squashes with scalloped edges and a similar flavour to courgettes. If possible, buy small specimens, about 10cm/4in across. Boil these whole until tender, then cut a slice off the tops, scoop out the seeds and serve with a knob of butter.

Buying and Storing

Buy vegetables that have clear, and unblemished flesh, and avoid any with soft or brown patches. Vegetable marrows and spaghetti squashes will keep for several months provided they are kept in a cool, dark place. Custard marrows will keep up to a week.

Preparing

Wash the skin. For sautéing or steaming, or if the skin is tough, peel it away. For braised marrow, cut into chunks and discard the seeds and pith (see right). For

stuffing, cut into slices or lengthways and discard the seeds and pith.

Cooking

Place chunks of marrow in a heavy-based pan with a little butter, cover and cook until tender. It can then be livened up with garlic, herbs or tomatoes. For stuffed marrow, blanch first, stuff, then cover or wrap it in foil to cook.

Opposite left: Spaghetti squashes
Opposite right: Custard marrows
Above: Vegetable marrows

SQUASH RECIPES

Pumpkins and squashes need long slow cooking, which is why these are the vegetables you need for warming dishes such as Pumpkin Soup, Onion Squash Risotto and Baked Marrow in Cream and Parsley. Courgettes on the other hand are best cooked quickly. Baked Courgettes, stuffed with goat's cheese, and Courgettes Italian-style, are cooked so that maximum flavour is retained, and the result is perfection.

ONION SQUASH RISOTTO

THIS RISOTTO PROVIDES A WARM AND COMFORTING MEAL AFTER A TIRING DAY. FOR A VEGETARIAN
ALTERNATIVE SIMPLY OMIT THE BACON AND USE VEGETABLE STOCK.

SERVES FOUR

INGREDIENTS

   1 onion squash or pumpkin, about
     900g–1kg/2–2¼lb
   30ml/2 tbsp olive oil
   1 onion, chopped
   1–2 garlic cloves, crushed
   115g/4oz streaky bacon, chopped
   115g/4oz/generous ½ cup arborio rice
   600–750ml/1–1¼ pints/2½–3 cups
     chicken stock
   40g/1½oz Parmesan cheese, grated
   15ml/1 tbsp chopped fresh parsley
   salt and freshly ground black pepper

1 Halve or quarter the onion squash or
pumpkin, remove the seeds and skin,
and then cut into chunks about 1–2cm/
½–¾in in size.

2 Heat the oil in a flameproof casserole
and fry the onion and garlic for about
3–4 minutes, stirring frequently. Add the
bacon and continue frying until both the
onion and bacon are lightly golden.

3 Add the squash or pumpkin, stir-fry
for a few minutes. Add the rice and cook
for about 2 minutes, stirring all the time.

4 Pour in about half of the stock and
season. Stir well and then half cover and
simmer gently for about 20 minutes,
stirring occasionally. As the liquid is
absorbed, add more stock and stir to
prevent the mixture sticking to the base.

5 When the squash and rice are nearly
tender, add a little more stock. Cook,
uncovered for 5–10 minutes. Stir in the
Parmesan cheese and parsley and serve.

PUMPKIN SOUP

THE SWEET FLAVOUR OF PUMPKIN IS GOOD IN SOUPS, TEAMING WELL WITH OTHER MORE SAVOURY
INGREDIENTS SUCH AS ONIONS AND POTATOES TO MAKE A MILD AND SOOTHING DISH.

SERVES FOUR TO SIX

INGREDIENTS

   15ml/1 tbsp sunflower oil
   25g/1oz/2 tbsp butter
   1 large onion, sliced
   675g/1½lb pumpkin, cut into
     large chunks
   450g/1lb potatoes, sliced
   600ml/1 pint/2½ cups vegetable stock
   a good pinch of nutmeg
   5ml/1 tsp chopped fresh tarragon
   600ml/1 pint/2½ cups milk
   about 5–10ml/1–2 tsp lemon juice
   salt and freshly ground black pepper

1 Heat the oil and butter in a heavy-
based saucepan and fry the onion for
4–5 minutes over a gentle heat until soft
but not browned, stirring frequently.

2 Add the pumpkin and potato, stir well
and then cover and sweat over a low heat
for about 10 minutes until the vegetables
are almost tender, stirring occasionally to
prevent them from sticking to the pan.

3 Stir in the stock, nutmeg, tarragon
and seasoning. Bring to the boil and then
simmer for about 10 minutes until the
vegetables are completely tender.

4 Allow to cool slightly, then pour into a
food processor or blender and pureé
until smooth. Pour back into a clean
saucepan and add the milk. Heat gently
and then taste, adding the lemon juice
and extra seasoning if necessary. Serve
piping hot with crusty brown bread.

CHOCOLATE COURGETTE CAKE

THE RECIPE FOR THIS MOIST CHOCOLATE CAKE FLAVOURED WITH COURGETTES OR ZUCCHINI, COMES FROM AMERICA. ALTHOUGH AN UNLIKELY COMBINATION, IT IS A DELICIOUS VARIATION WELL WORTH TRYING.

SERVES FOUR TO SIX

INGREDIENTS
    115g/4oz/½ cup margarine
    130ml/4½fl oz/½ cup sunflower oil
    115g/4oz/generous ½ cup caster sugar
    225g/8oz/1⅓ cups soft brown sugar
    3 eggs, beaten
    130ml/4½fl oz/½ cup milk
    350g/12oz/3 cups plain flour
    10ml/2 tsp baking powder
    60ml/4 tbsp cocoa powder
    2.5ml/½ tsp ground allspice
    450g/1lb courgettes, peeled
      and grated
    5ml/1 tsp vanilla essence
    225g/8oz plain chocolate dots

1 Preheat the oven to 190°C/375°F/ Gas 5 and line a 23 x 33cm/9 x13in baking tin with non-stick baking paper.

2 Cream the margarine, oil and sugars together until light and fluffy, then gradually beat in the eggs and milk.

3 Sift the flour, baking powder, cocoa powder and ground allspice together and fold gently into the mixture.

4 Stir in the grated courgettes and vanilla essence and spoon the mixture into the prepared tin. Smooth the top using a palette knife and sprinkle the chocolate dots over the top.

5 Bake in the oven for 35–45 minutes until the cake is firm and a knife comes out clean. Cut into squares while still warm and then leave to cool.

PUMPKIN AND HAM FRITTATA

A FRITTATA IS AN ITALIAN VERSION OF THE SPANISH TORTILLA, A SUBSTANTIAL OMELETTE MADE OF EGGS AND VEGETABLES. ALTHOUGH FRITTATAS ARE SOMETIMES EATEN COLD, THIS ONE TASTES BETTER WARM OR HOT, SERVED WITH CRUSTY BREAD.

SERVES FOUR

INGREDIENTS
30ml/2 tbsp sunflower oil
1 large onion, chopped
450g/1lb pumpkin, chopped into
   bite-size pieces
200ml/7fl oz/scant 1 cup
   chicken stock
115g/4oz smoked ham, chopped
6 eggs
10ml/2 tsp chopped fresh marjoram
salt and freshly ground black pepper

1 Preheat the oven to 190°C/375°F/Gas 5 and oil a large shallow ovenproof dish. Heat the oil in a large frying pan and fry the onion for 3–4 minutes until softened.

2 Add the pumpkin and fry over a brisk heat for 3–4 minutes, stirring frequently. Stir in the stock, cover and simmer over a gentle heat for 5–6 minutes until the pumpkin is slightly tender. Add the ham.

3 Pour the mixture into the prepared dish. Beat the eggs with the marjoram and a little seasoning. Pour into the dish and then bake for 20–25 minutes until the frittata is firm and lightly golden.

VEGETABLE FRUITS

What would we do without our fabulous range of vegetable

fruits? Here are the most colourful, and probably most versatile

of all our vegetables. Tomatoes and peppers are the basis of

countless dishes, with chillies adding their particular personality

to any dish where a little extra something is required.

Aubergines too are wonderfully versatile and for a Caribbean

flavour, there are plantains and green bananas.

opened, they can be kept for up to 4-6 weeks in the fridge.

Yellow tomatoes: These are exactly like red tomatoes – they may be round, plum or cherry-size – except they are yellow.

Buying and Storing

Ideally, tomatoes should be allowed to ripen slowly on the plant so that their flavour can develop. Consequently, home-grown tomatoes are best, followed by those grown and sold locally. When buying from a supermarket or your greengrocer, look at the leafy green tops; the fresher they look the better. Buy locally grown beefsteak or cherry tomatoes for salads; plum tomatoes for rich sauces. Paler tomatoes or those tinged with green will redden if kept in a brown paper bag or the salad drawer of the fridge, but if you intend to use tomatoes straight away, buy bright red specimens. Overripe tomatoes, where the skin has split and they seem to be bursting with juice, are excellent in soups. However, check for any sign of mould or decay, as this will spoil all your good efforts.

Preparing

Slice tomatoes across rather than downwards for salads and pizza toppings. For wedges, cut downwards into halves, quarters or eighths depending on the size of the tomato.

Cooking

Among the many classic tomato dishes is tomato soup, cooked to a delicate orange colour with stock or milk, or simmered with vegetables, garlic and basil. *Á la provençale* indicates that tomatoes are in the dish; in Provençal and Italian cooking, tomatoes are used with fish, meat and vegetables, in sauces and stuffings, with pasta and in superb salads. The Italian *tri colore salata* is a combination of large tomatoes, mozzarella and basil (the three colours of the Italian flag). The natural astringency of tomatoes means that, in salads, they need only be sprinkled with a fruity olive oil.

Chopped Tomatoes

Chopped tomatoes add a depth of flavour to all sorts of meat and vegetable dishes. Ideally, even in fairly rustic meals, the tomatoes should be peeled, since the skin can be irritating to eat once cooked. Some sauce recipes also recommend seeding tomatoes: cut the tomato into halves and scoop out the seeds before chopping (see above).

Skinning Tomatoes

Cut a cross in the tops of the tomatoes, then place in a bowl and pour over boiling water. Leave for a minute (see above), Use a sharp knife to peel away the skin, which should come away easily. Do a few at a time (five at most) otherwise they will begin to cook while soaking. Boil water for the next batch when you have finished peeling.

AUBERGINES

Many varieties of aubergines are grown and cooked all over the world. In Europe, Asia and America, they feature in a multitude of different dishes.

History

Although aubergines are a member of the nightshade family and thus related to potatoes, tomatoes and peppers, they were not discovered in the New World. The first mention of their cultivation is in China in 5 BC, and they are thought to have been eaten in India long before that. It was the Moors who introduced the aubergine to Spain some 1,200 years ago and it was grown in Andalucia. It is likely that they also introduced it to Italy, and possibly from there to other southern and eastern parts of Europe.

In spite of their popularity in Europe, aubergines did not become popular in Britain or the United States until very recently. Although previous generations of food writers knew about them, they gave only the occasional recipe for cooking with them.

Opposite: Plum tomatoes
Top: Aubergines
Above: Baby aubergines
Left: Japanese aubergines

VEGETABLE
FRUIT
RECIPES

Vegetable fruits are the perfect excuse for letting your cook's imagination run riot. Tomatoes, peppers, chillies and aubergines have a wonderful affinity, and by simply putting two or three of these ingredients together, almost by magic you have a superb summer supper. Whether it's Aubergine and Courgette Bake, Gazpacho, Spinach and Pepper Pizza or Eggs Flamenco, our favourite vegetable fruits play a starring role. And if you fancy sampling Caribbean cuisine, try Plantain Appetizer, served with piquant Guacamole.

AUBERGINE AND COURGETTE BAKE

*THIS IS A WONDERFULLY WARMING DISH FOR A WINTER'S DAY. USE
FRESH BASIL, IF AVAILABLE AS THE TASTE IS FAR SUPERIOR.*

SERVES FOUR TO SIX

INGREDIENTS

1 large aubergine
30ml/2 tbsp olive oil
1 large onion, chopped
1–2 garlic cloves, crushed
900g/2lb tomatoes, peeled
   and chopped
a handful of basil leaves, shredded
   or 5ml/1tsp dried basil
15ml/1 tbsp chopped fresh parsley
2 courgettes, sliced lengthways
plain flour, for coating
75–90ml/5–6 tbsp sunflower oil
350g/12oz mozzarella, sliced
25g/1oz Parmesan cheese, grated
salt and freshly ground black pepper

1 Slice the aubergine, sprinkle with salt
and set aside for 45–60 minutes. Heat
the olive oil in a large frying pan. Fry the
onion and garlic for 3–4 minutes until
softened. Stir in the tomatoes, half the
basil and parsley, and seasoning. Bring
to the boil. Reduce the heat and cook,
stirring, for 25–35 minutes, or until
thickened to a pulp.

2 Rinse and dry the aubergines. Dust
the aubergines and courgettes with flour.

3 Heat the sunflower oil in another
frying pan and fry the aubergine and
courgettes until golden brown. Set aside.

4 Preheat the oven to 180°C/350°F/
Gas 4. Butter an ovenproof dish. Put a
layer of aubergines and then courgettes
in the dish, pour over half the sauce and
scatter with half the mozzarella. Sprinkle
over most of the remaining basil and a
little parsley. Repeat the layers, ending
with mozzarella. Sprinkle the Parmesan
cheese and remaining herbs on top and
bake for 30–35 minutes. Serve at once.

AUBERGINES WITH TZATZIKI

SERVES FOUR

INGREDIENTS

2 aubergines
oil, for deep frying
salt
For the batter
75g/3oz/⅔ cup plain flour
a pinch of salt
1 egg
120–150ml/4–5fl oz/½–⅔ cup milk,
   or half milk, half water
pinch of salt
For the tzatziki
½ cucumber, peeled and diced
150ml/¼ pint/⅔ cup natural yogurt
1 garlic clove, crushed
15ml/1 tbsp chopped fresh mint

1 To make the tzatziki, place the
cucumber in a colander, sprinkle with
salt and leave for 30 minutes. Rinse,
drain well and pat dry on kitchen paper.
Mix the yogurt, garlic, fresh mint and
cucumber in a bowl. Cover and chill.
Slice the aubergine lengthways. Sprinkle
with salt. Leave for 1 hour.

2 To make the batter, sift the flour and
salt into a large bowl, add the egg and
liquid and beat until smooth.

3 Rinse the aubergines and then pat
dry. Heat 1cm/½in of oil in a large frying
pan. Dip the aubergine slices in the
batter and fry them for 3–4 minutes until
golden, turning once. Drain on kitchen
paper and serve with the tzatziki.

GAZPACHO

GAZPACHO IS A CLASSIC SPANISH SOUP. IT IS POPULAR ALL OVER SPAIN BUT NOWHERE MORE SO THAN IN ANDALUCIA, WHERE THERE ARE HUNDREDS OF VARIATIONS. IT IS A COLD SOUP OF TOMATOES, TOMATO JUICE, GREEN PEPPER AND GARLIC, WHICH IS SERVED WITH A SELECTION OF GARNISHES.

SERVES FOUR

INGREDIENTS

1.5kg/3–3½lb ripe tomatoes
1 green pepper, seeded and
  roughly chopped
2 garlic cloves, crushed
2 slices white bread, crusts removed
60ml/4 tbsp olive oil
60ml/4 tbsp tarragon wine vinegar
150ml/¼ pint/⅔ cup tomato juice
a good pinch of sugar
salt and freshly ground black pepper
ice cubes, to serve

For the garnishes

30ml/2 tbsp sunflower oil
2–3 slices white bread, diced
1 small cucumber, peeled and
  finely diced
1 small onion, finely chopped
1 red pepper, seeded and finely diced
1 green pepper, seeded and finely
  diced
2 hard-boiled eggs, chopped

1 Skin the tomatoes, then quarter them and remove the cores.

2 Place the pepper in a food processor and process for a few seconds. Add the tomatoes, garlic, bread, olive oil and vinegar and process again. Finally, add the tomato juice, sugar, seasoning and a little extra tomato juice or cold water and process. The consistency should be thick but not too stodgy.

3 Pour into a bowl and chill for at least 2 hours but no more than 12 hours, otherwise the textures deteriorate.

4 To prepare the bread cubes to use as a garnish, heat the oil in a frying pan and fry them over a moderate heat for about 4–5 minutes until golden brown. Drain well on kitchen paper.

5 Place each garnish in a separate small dish, or alternatively arrange them in rows on a large plate.

6 Just before serving, stir a few ice cubes into the soup and then spoon into serving bowls. Serve with the garnishes.

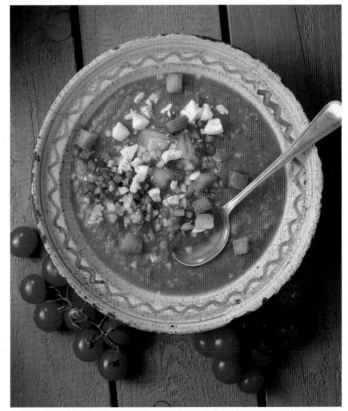

TOMATO AND BASIL TART

IN FRANCE, PÂTISSERIES DISPLAY MOUTH-WATERING SAVOURY TARTS IN THEIR WINDOWS. THIS IS A VERY
SIMPLE YET EXTREMELY TASTY TART MADE WITH RICH SHORTCRUST PASTRY, TOPPED WITH SLICES OF
MOZZARELLA CHEESE AND TOMATOES, AND ENRICHED WITH OLIVE OIL AND BASIL LEAVES.

SERVES FOUR

INGREDIENTS
    150g/5oz mozzarella,
        thinly sliced
    4 large tomatoes, thickly sliced
    about 10 basil leaves
    30ml/2 tbsp olive oil
    2 garlic cloves, thinly sliced
    sea salt and freshly ground
        black pepper
For the pastry
    115g/4oz/1 cup plain flour
    a pinch of salt
    50g/2oz/¼ cup butter or margarine
    1 egg yolk

1 To prepare the pastry, mix together
the flour and salt, then rub in the butter
and the egg yolk. Use cold water to make
a smooth dough; knead lightly on a
floured surface. Place in a polythene bag
and chill for about 1 hour.

2 Preheat the oven to 190°C/375°F/
Gas 5. Remove the pastry from the fridge
and allow about 10 minutes for it to
return to room temperature. Roll out into
a 20cm/8in round. Press into the base of
a 20cm/8in flan dish or tin. Prick all over
with a fork and then bake in the oven for
about 10 minutes until firm but not
brown. Allow to cool slightly on a wire
rack. Reduce the oven temperature to
180°C/350°F/Gas 4.

3 Arrange the mozzarella slices over the
pastry base. On top, arrange a single
layer of the sliced tomatoes, overlapping
them slightly. Dip the basil leaves in olive
oil and arrange them on the tomatoes.

4 Scatter the garlic on top, drizzle with
the remaining olive oil and season with a
little salt and a good sprinkling of black
pepper. Bake for 40–45 minutes, until
the tomatoes are well cooked. Serve hot.

EGGS FLAMENCO

A VARIATION OF THE POPULAR BASQUE DISH PIPERADE, THE EGGS ARE COOKED WHOLE INSTEAD OF BEING BEATEN BEFORE THEY ARE ADDED TO THE PEPPER MIXTURE. THE RECIPE IS KNOWN AS CHAKCHOUKA IN NORTH AFRICA AND MAKES A GOOD LUNCH OR SUPPER DISH.

SERVES FOUR

INGREDIENTS

2 red peppers
1 green pepper
30ml/2 tbsp olive oil
1 large onion, finely sliced
2 garlic cloves, crushed
5–6 tomatoes, peeled and chopped
120ml/4fl oz/½ cup puréed canned
  tomatoes or tomato juice
a good pinch of dried basil
4 eggs
40ml/8 tsp single cream
a pinch of cayenne pepper (optional)
salt and freshly ground black pepper

1 Preheat the oven to 180°C/350°F/ Gas 4. Seed and thinly slice the peppers. Heat the olive oil in a large frying pan. Fry the onion and garlic gently for about 5 minutes, stirring, until softened.

2 Add the peppers to the onion and fry for 10 minutes. Stir in the tomatoes and puréed tomatoes or juice, the basil and seasoning. Cook gently for a further 10 minutes until the peppers are soft.

3 Spoon the mixture into four ovenproof dishes, preferably earthenware. Make a hole in the centre and break an egg into each. Spoon 10ml/2 tsp cream over the yolk of each egg and sprinkle with a little black pepper or cayenne, as preferred.

4 Bake in the oven for 12–15 minutes until the white of the egg is lightly set. Serve at once with chunks of crusty warm Spanish or French bread.

SPINACH <u>AND</u> PEPPER PIZZA

MAKES TWO 30cm/12in PIZZAS

INGREDIENTS
  450g/1lb fresh spinach
  60ml/4 tbsp single cream
  25g/1oz Parmesan cheese, grated
  15ml/1 tbsp olive oil
  1 large onion, chopped
  1 garlic clove, crushed
  ½ green pepper, seeded and
    thinly sliced
  ½ red pepper, seeded and thinly sliced
  175–250ml/6–8fl oz/¾–1 cup passata
    or puréed tomatoes
  50g/2oz black olives, stoned
    and chopped
  15ml/1 tbsp chopped fresh basil
  175g/6oz mozzarella, grated
  175g/6oz Cheddar cheese, grated
  salt
For the dough
  25g/1oz fresh yeast or 15ml/1 tbsp
    dried yeast and 5ml/1 tsp sugar
  about 225ml/7fl oz/⅞ cup warm water
  350g/12oz/3 cups strong white flour
  30ml/2 tbsp olive oil
  5ml/1 tsp salt

1 To make the dough, cream together the fresh yeast and 150ml/¼ pint/⅔ cup of the water and set aside until frothy. If using dried yeast, stir the sugar into 225ml/7fl oz/⅞ cup water, sprinkle over the yeast and leave until frothy.

2 Place the flour and salt in a large bowl, make a well in the centre and pour in the oil and yeast mixture. Add the remaining water, if using fresh yeast, mix to make a stiff but pliable dough. Knead on a lightly floured surface for about 10 minutes until smooth and elastic.

3 Shape the dough into a ball and place in a lightly oiled bowl, cover with oiled clear film and leave in a warm place for about 1 hour until it has doubled in size.

4 To prepare the topping, cook the spinach over a moderate heat for 4–5 minutes until the leaves have wilted. Strain and press out the excess liquid. Place in a bowl and mix with the cream, Parmesan cheese and salt to taste.

5 Heat the oil in a frying pan and fry the onion and garlic over a moderate heat for 3–4 minutes until the onion has slightly softened. Add the peppers and continue cooking until the onion is lightly golden, stirring regularly.

6 Preheat the oven to 220°C/425°F/ Gas 7. Knead the dough briefly on a lightly floured surface. Divide the dough and roll out into two 30cm/12in rounds.

7 Spread each base with the passata sauce or puréed tomatoes. Add the onions and peppers and then spread over the spinach mixture. Scatter the olives and basil leaves and sprinkle with the mozzarella and Cheddar cheese.

8 Bake in the oven for 15–20 minutes, or until the crust is lightly browned and the top is beginning to turn golden. Allow to cool slightly before serving.

SALAD
VEGETABLES

*Colour is the name of the game these days when it comes to
salads. No longer do we have to suffer the limp green salads of
old. The choice of radicchio, lamb's lettuce, rocket and endive,
not to mention the many varieties of lettuce, means that today's
salads are bursting with different flavours and textures — a
treat for the eye and the palette.*

Nutrition

As well as containing vitamins A, C and E, lettuce provides potassium, iron and calcium, as well as traces of other minerals.

Buying and Storing

The best lettuce is the one fresh from the garden. The next best thing to do is to buy lettuce from a farm shop or pick-your-own (although if fertilizers and pesticides are used, their flavour will be disappointing compared to the organic product).

Today, lettuce is frequently sold ready shredded and packed with herbs and any other ingredients. Whether you buy lettuce pre-packed or from the shelf, it must be fresh. Soil and bugs can be washed off but those with limp or yellow leaves are of no use. Eat lettuce as soon as possible after purchasing; in the meantime keep it in a cool dark place, such as the bottom of the fridge.

Making Salads

Salads can be made by using only one lettuce or a mixture of many. There are no rules but choose leaves that give contrast in texture and colour as well as flavour. Fresh herbs, such as parsley, coriander and basil also add another interesting dimension.

Tear rather than cut the leaves of loose-leafed lettuce; icebergs and other large lettuces are commonly sliced or shredded. Eat salad as soon as possible after preparing.

Dressings should be well-flavoured with a hint of sharpness but must never be too astringent. Make them in a blender, a screw-top jar or in a large bowl so that the ingredients can be thoroughly blended. Always use the best possible oils and vinegars, in roughly the proportion of five oil to one vinegar or lemon juice. Use half good olive oil and half sunflower oil, or for a more fragrant dressing, a combination of walnut and sunflower oil. A pinch of salt and pepper is essential, English or French mustard is optional and the addition of a little sugar will blunt the flavour.

Add the dressing to the salad when ready to serve – never earlier.

ROCKET

Rocket has a wonderful peppery flavour and is excellent in a mixed green salad. It has small, bright green dandelion-shaped leaves. The Greeks and Romans commonly ate rocket (arugula) in mixed salads, apparently because it helped counterbalance the dampening effect lettuce had on the libido – rocket's aphrodisiac properties in antiquity are well catalogued. Seeds used to be sown around the statues of Priapus, the mythological Greek god of fertility and protector of gardens and herbs and son of Aphrodite and Dionysus.

Buying and Storing

Rocket is to be found either among the salads or fresh herbs in supermarkets. Buy fresh green leaves and use soon after purchasing. The leaves can be kept immersed in cold water.

Preparing and Serving

Discard any discoloured leaves. Add rocket to plain green salads, or grind with garlic, pine nuts and olive oil for a dressing for pasta.

Since it has such a striking flavour, a little rocket goes a long way, making it an excellent leaf for garnishing. It tastes superb contrasted with grilled goat's cheese, or one or two leaves can be added to sandwiches, or loosely packed into pitta bread pockets together with tomatoes, avocado, peanuts and bean sprouts, for example.

Opposite above: Oak leaf lettuce
Opposite below: curly endive
Below: Rocket

CHINESE LEAVES AND MOOLI WITH SCALLOPS

HERE'S A SPEEDY STIR-FRY MADE USING CHINESE CABBAGE, MOOLI AND SCALLOPS. BOTH THE MOOLI AND CHINESE LEAVES HAVE A PLEASANT CRUNCHY "BITE". YOU NEED TO WORK QUICKLY, SO HAVE EVERYTHING PREPARED BEFORE YOU START COOKING.

SERVES FOUR

INGREDIENTS
    10 prepared scallops
    75ml/5 tbsp vegetable oil
    3 garlic cloves, finely chopped
    1cm/½in piece fresh root ginger,
      finely sliced
    4–5 spring onions, cut lengthways
      into 2.5cm/1in pieces
    30ml/2 tbsp medium dry sherry
    ½ mooli (daikon), cut into
      1cm/½in slices
    1 Chinese cabbage, chopped
      lengthways into thin strips
For the marinade
    5ml/1 tsp cornflour
    1 egg white, lightly beaten
    a pinch of white pepper
For the sauce
    5ml/1 tsp cornflour
    45ml/3 tbsp oyster sauce

1 Rinse the scallops and separate the corals from the white meat. Cut each scallop into 2–3 pieces and slice the corals. Place them on two dishes.

2 For the marinade, blend together the cornflour, egg white and white pepper. Pour half over the scallops and the rest over the corals. Leave for 10 minutes.

3 To make the sauce, blend the cornflour with 60ml/4 tbsp water and the oyster sauce and set aside.

4 Heat about 30ml/2 tbsp of the oil in a wok, add half of the garlic and let it sizzle, and then add half the ginger and half of the spring onions. Stir-fry for about 30 seconds and then stir in the scallops (not the corals).

5 Stir-fry for 30–60 seconds until the scallops start to become opaque, then reduce the heat and add 15ml/1 tbsp of the sherry. Cook briefly and then spoon the scallops and the cooking liquid into a bowl and set aside.

6 Heat another 30ml/2 tbsp of oil in the wok, add the remaining garlic, ginger and spring onions and then stir-fry for 1 minute. Add the corals, stir-fry briefly and transfer to a dish.

7 Heat the remaining oil and add the mooli. Stir-fry for about 30 seconds and then stir in the cabbage. Stir-fry for about 30 seconds more then add the oyster sauce mixture and about 60ml/4 tbsp water. Allow the cabbage to simmer briefly and then stir in the scallops and corals, together with all their liquid, and cook briefly to heat through.

RADISH, MANGO <u>AND</u> APPLE SALAD

RADISH IS A YEAR-ROUND VEGETABLE AND THIS SALAD CAN BE SERVED AT ANY TIME OF YEAR, WITH ITS CLEAN, CRISP TASTES AND MELLOW FLAVOURS. SERVE WITH SMOKED FISH, SUCH AS ROLLS OF SMOKED SALMON, OR WITH CONTINENTAL HAM OR SALAMI.

SERVES FOUR

INGREDIENTS
 10–15 radishes
 1 apple, peeled cored and
  thinly sliced
 2 celery stalks, thinly sliced
 1 small ripe mango
 salt and freshly ground black pepper
 sprigs of dill, to garnish
For the dressing
 120ml/4fl oz/½ cup soured cream
 10ml/2 tsp creamed horseradish
 15ml/1 tbsp chopped fresh dill

3 Cut through the mango lengthways either side of the stone and make even criss-cross cuts through each side section. Bend each section back to separate the cubes, remove them with a small knife and add to the bowl. Pour the dressing over the vegetables and fruit and stir gently so that all the ingredients are coated in the dressing. When ready to serve, spoon the salad into an attractive salad bowl and garnish with sprigs of dill.

1 To prepare the dressing, blend together the soured cream, horseradish and dill in a small jug or bowl and season with a little salt and pepper.

2 Top and tail the radishes and then slice them thinly. Add to a bowl together with the thinly sliced apple and celery.

WATERCRESS SOUP

SERVES FOUR

INGREDIENTS
  15ml/1 tbsp sunflower oil
  15g/½oz/1 tbsp butter
  1 onion, finely chopped
  1 potato, diced
  about 175g/6oz watercress
  400ml/14fl oz/1⅔ cups chicken
    or vegetable stock
  400ml/14fl oz/1⅔ cups milk
  lemon juice
  salt and freshly ground black pepper
  soured cream, to serve (optional)

1 Heat the oil and butter in a large
saucepan and fry the onion over a gentle
heat until soft but not browned. Add the
potato, fry gently for 2–3 minutes and
then cover and sweat for 5 minutes over
a gentle heat, stirring occasionally.

2 Strip the watercress leaves from the
stalks and roughly chop the stalks.

3 Add the stock and milk to the pan, stir
in the chopped stalks and season with
salt and pepper. Bring to the boil and then
simmer gently, partially covered, for
10–12 minutes until the potatoes are
tender. Add all but a few of the watercress
leaves and simmer for 2 minutes.

4 Process the soup in a food processor
or blender, and then pour into a clean
saucepan and heat gently with the
reserved watercress leaves. Taste when
hot and add a little lemon juice and
adjust the seasoning.

5 Pour the soup into warmed soup
dishes and swirl in a little soured cream,
if using, just before serving.

COOK'S TIP
Provided you leave out the cream, this is
a low calorie but nutritious soup, which,
served with crusty bread, makes a very
satisfying meal.

WATERCRESS AND TWO-FISH TERRINE

*THIS IS A PRETTY, DELICATE DISH, IDEAL FOR A SUMMER BUFFET PARTY OR PICNIC. SERVE WITH LEMON
MAYONNAISE OR SOURED CREAM, AND A WATERCRESS AND GREEN SALAD.*

SERVES SIX TO EIGHT

INGREDIENTS
  350g/12oz monkfish, filleted
  175g/6oz lemon sole, filleted
  1 egg and 1 egg white
  45–60ml/3–4 tbsp lemon juice
  40–50g/1½–2o/1 cup fresh white
    breadcrumbs
  300ml/½ pint/1¼ cups whipping
    cream
  75g/3oz smoked salmon
  175g/6oz watercress, roughly chopped
  salt and freshly ground black pepper

1 Preheat the oven to 180°C/350°F/
Gas 4 and line a 1.5 litre/2½ pint/6¼ cup
loaf tin with non-stick baking paper.

2 Cut the fish into rough chunks,
discarding the skin and bones. Put the
fish into a food processor with a little salt
and pepper.

3 Process briefly and add the egg and
egg white, lemon juice, breadcrumbs
and cream. Process to a paste. Put the
mixture into a bowl. Take 75ml/5 tbsp of
the mixture and process with the smoked
salmon. Transfer to a separate bowl.
Take 75ml/5 tbsp of the white fish
mixture and process with the watercress.

4 Spoon half of the white fish mixture
into the base of the prepared loaf tin and
smooth the surface with a palette knife.

5 Spread over the watercress mixture,
then the smoked salmon mixture and
finally spread over the remaining white
fish mixture and smooth the top.

6 Lay a piece of buttered non-stick
baking paper on top of the mixture and
then cover with foil. Place the loaf tin in a
roasting tin, half-filled with boiling water
and cook in the oven for 1¼–1½ hours.
Towards the end of the cooking time the
terrine will begin to rise, which indicates
that it is ready.

7 Allow to cool in the tin and then turn
on to a serving plate and peel away the
baking paper. Chill for 1–2 hours.

MUSHROOMS

Delicious, succulent, soft, chewy — all sorts of adjectives can be used when describing mushrooms. There are now so many to choose from and each has its own particular flavour and character. From firm favourites such as button and field mushrooms, to ceps, morels and oyster mushrooms that grow in woodlands, these delicacies deserve a starring role in a multitude of dishes.

WOODLAND MUSHROOMS

Varieties

Ceps: Popular in France, where they are known as *cèpes* and in Italy where they are called *porcini*, these meaty, bun-shaped mushrooms have a fine almost suede-like texture and a good flavour. Instead of gills they have a spongy texture beneath the cap and unless they are very young it is best to scrape this away as it goes soggy when cooked. Ceps are excellent fried in oil or butter over a brisk heat to evaporate the liquid and then added to omelettes.

Alternatively, an Italian way of cooking is to remove the stalk and the spongy tubes, and brush the tops with olive oil. Grill for about 10 minutes under a moderate grill and then turn them over

and pour olive oil and a sprinkling of garlic into the centre. Grill for a further 5 minutes and then serve sprinkled with seasoning and parsley.

Chanterelles: Frilly, trumpet-shaped chanterelles are delicate mushrooms which range in colour from cream to a vivid yellow. Later, winter chanterelles, have greyish-lilac gills on the underside of their dark caps. Chanterelles have a delicate, slightly fruity flavour and a firm, almost rubbery texture. They are difficult to clean as their tiny gills tend to trap grit and earth. Rinse them gently under cold running water and then shake dry. Fry in butter over a gentle heat to start with so they exude their liquid and then increase the heat to boil it off. They are delicious

with scrambled eggs, or served alone with finely cut toast on the side.

Horns of Plenty/Black Trumpets: Named after its shape, this mushroom ranges in colour from mid-brown to black. As it is hollow, it will need to be brushed well to clean or, if a large specimen, sliced in half. This is a very versatile mushroom, and goes particularly well with fish.

Hedgehog Fungus: This mushroom is difficult to find either on sale or on the woodland floor, but it has great culinary value and is much sought after. Small, young specimens can be cooked whole or sliced, or even used raw in salads. More mature mushrooms may be bitter and are best cooked with butter and herbs. It goes well with both meat and fish.

Morels: These are the first mushroom of the year, appearing not in autumn but in spring. In Scandinavia they are called the "truffles of the north" and are considered among the great edible fungi. They are cone-shaped with a crinkled spongy cap but are hollow inside. You will need to wash them well under running water as insects tend to creep into their dark crevices. Morels need longer cooking than most fungi: sauté them in butter, add a squeeze of lemon and then cover and simmer for an hour until tender. The juices can then be thickened with cream or egg yolks.

Dried mushrooms: Most wild mushrooms are available dried. To reconstitute, soak in warm water for about 20–30 minutes; in the case of morels when they are to be added to stews, soak them for about 10 minutes. Dried mushrooms, particularly ceps, have an intense flavour.

Left (clockwise from the top): Hedgehog fungus, Horn of Plenty, chanterelles
Above left: Morels
Above right: Dried mushrooms
Right: Winter chanterelles

WILD MUSHROOMS AND OTHER FUNGI

Mushroom gathering, a seasonal event throughout Eastern Europe, Italy and France, is increasingly popular in Britain. The French are particularly enthusiastic: in autumn whole families drive to secret locations to comb the ground for prizes like shaggy ink caps or ceps. Wild mushrooms are sold in supermarkets.

OYSTER MUSHROOMS

These ear-shaped fungi grow on rotting wood. Cap, gills and stem are all the same colour, which can be greyish brown, pink or yellow. They are now widely cultivated, although they are generally thought of as wild. Delicious both in flavour and texture, they are softer than the button mushroom when cooked but seem more substantial, having more "bite" to them.

Buying and Storing

Fresh specimens are erect and lively looking with clear gills and smooth caps. They are often sold packed in plastic

boxes under clear film wrappings and will wilt and go soggy if left on the shelf for too long. Once purchased, remove them from the packaging and use as soon as possible.

Preparing

Oyster mushrooms rarely need trimming at all but if they are large, tear rather than cut them into pieces. In very large specimens the stems can be tough and should be discarded.

Cooking

Fry in butter until tender – they take less time than white mushrooms. Do not overcook oyster mushrooms as the flavour will be lost and the soft texture will turn more rubbery.

Above: Grey oyster mushrooms
Left: Pink and yellow oyster mushrooms

ENOKITAKI MUSHROOMS

This is another Japanese mushroom. The wild variety is orangey-brown with shiny caps but outside Japan, you will probably only be able to locate the cultivated variety, which are similarly fine, with pin-sized heads, but are pale coloured with snowy white caps. They have a delicate, sweet and almost fruity flavour. In Japanese cookery they are added to salads or used to garnish soups or hot dishes. Since they become tough if overcooked, add enokitaki mushrooms at the very last minute of cooking.

SHIITAKE MUSHROOMS

Shiitake mushrooms were once only available in oriental stores, but these Japanese fungi are now commonly found in supermarkets. They are among a variety of tree mushrooms (called *take* in Japan, the *shii* being the hardwood tree from which they are harvested). They have a meaty, slightly acid flavour and a distinct slippery texture. Unlike button mushrooms that can be flash-fried, shiitake need to be cooked through, although even this only takes 3–5 minutes. Add them to stir-fries for a delicious flavour and texture. Alternatively, fry them in oil until tender, sprinkle with sesame oil and then serve with a little soy sauce.

Above: Enokitaki mushrooms
Right: Shiitake mushrooms

MUSHROOM RECIPES

Nearly everyone has a favourite mushroom dish. Mushrooms have the ability to go with almost anything, which is why there is always such a range of dishes when it comes to these fungi. Cream of Mushroom Soup, Soufflé Omelette with Mushroom Sauce, Stuffed Mushrooms and Boeuf en Croûte with Mushroom Filling will appeal to traditional tastes but for those who fancy something different, try Gnocchi with Oyster Mushrooms or Tagliatelle Fungi.

CREAM OF MUSHROOM SOUP

A GOOD MUSHROOM SOUP MAKES THE MOST OF THE SUBTLE AND SOMETIMES RATHER ELUSIVE FLAVOUR OF MUSHROOMS. BUTTON MUSHROOMS ARE USED HERE FOR THEIR PALE COLOUR; CHESTNUT OR, BETTER STILL, FIELD MUSHROOMS GIVE A FULLER FLAVOUR BUT TURN THE SOUP BROWN.

SERVES FOUR

INGREDIENTS
275g/10oz/3¾ cups
  button mushrooms
15ml/1 tbsp sunflower oil
40g/1½oz/3 tbsp butter
1 small onion, finely chopped
15ml/1 tbsp plain flour
450ml/¾ pint/1¾ cups vegetable stock
450ml/¾ pint/1¾ cups milk
pinch of dried basil
30–45ml/2–3 tbsp single cream
salt and freshly ground black pepper
fresh basil leaves, to garnish

1 Separate the mushroom caps from the stalks. Finely slice the caps and finely chop the stalks.

2 Heat the oil and half the butter in a heavy-based saucepan and add the onion, mushroom stalks and half of the sliced mushroom caps. Fry for about 1–2 minutes, stirring frequently, and then cover and sweat over a gentle heat for 6–7 minutes, stirring occasionally.

3 Stir in the flour and cook for about 1 minute. Gradually add the stock and milk, to make a smooth thin sauce. Add the basil, and season with salt and pepper. Bring to the boil and then simmer, partly covered, for 15 minutes.

4 Cool slightly and then pour the soup into a food processor or blender and process until smooth. Melt the rest of the butter in a frying pan and fry the remaining mushrooms caps gently for 3–4 minutes until they are just tender.

5 Pour the soup into a clean saucepan and stir in the sliced mushrooms. Heat until very hot and adjust the seasoning. Add a little cream and serve sprinkled with fresh basil leaves.

SOUFFLÉ OMELETTE WITH MUSHROOM SAUCE

A SOUFFLÉ OMELETTE INVOLVES A LITTLE MORE PREPARATION THAN AN ORDINARY OMELETTE BUT THE RESULT IS LIGHT YET SATISFYINGLY FILLING.

SERVES ONE

INGREDIENTS
2 eggs, separated
15g/½oz/1 tbsp butter
sprig of parsley or coriander
For the mushroom sauce
15g/½oz/1 tbsp butter
75g/3oz/generous 1 cup button
  mushrooms, thinly sliced
15ml/1 tbsp plain flour
85–120ml/3–4fl oz/½ cup milk
5ml/1 tsp chopped fresh parsley
  (optional)
salt and freshly ground black pepper

1 To make the mushroom sauce, melt the butter in a saucepan or frying pan and fry the thinly sliced mushrooms for 4–5 minutes until tender.

2 Stir in the flour and then gradually add the milk, stirring all the time, to make a smooth sauce. Add the parsley, if using, and season with salt and pepper. Keep warm to one side.

3 Beat the egg yolks with 15ml/1 tbsp water and season with a little salt and pepper. Whisk the egg whites until stiff and then fold into the egg yolks using a metal spoon. Preheat the grill.

4 Melt the butter in a large frying pan and pour the egg mixture into the pan. Cook over a gentle heat for 2–4 minutes. Place the frying pan under the grill and cook for a further 3–4 minutes until the top is golden brown.

5 Slide the omelette on to a warmed serving plate, pour over the mushroom sauce and fold the omelette in half. Serve garnished with a sprig of parsley or coriander.

STUFFED MUSHROOMS

THIS IS A CLASSIC MUSHROOM DISH, STRONGLY FLAVOURED WITH GARLIC. USE FLAT MUSHROOMS OR FIELD MUSHROOMS THAT ARE SOMETIMES AVAILABLE FROM FARM SHOPS.

SERVES FOUR

INGREDIENTS
 450g/1lb large flat mushrooms
 butter, for greasing
 about 75ml/5 tbsp olive oil
 2 garlic cloves, minced or very
  finely chopped
 45ml/3 tbsp/¾-1 cup finely chopped
  fresh parsley
 40–50g/1½–2oz fresh white
  breadcrumbs
 salt and freshly ground black pepper
 sprig of flat leaf parsley, to garnish

1 Preheat the oven to 180°C/350°F/ Gas 4. Cut off the mushroom stalks and reserve on one side.

2 Arrange the mushroom caps in a buttered shallow dish, gill side upwards.

COOK'S TIP
The cooking time for the mushrooms depends on their size and thickness. If they are fairly thin, cook for slightly less time. They should be tender but not too soft when they are cooked. If a stronger garlic flavour is preferred, do not cook the garlic before combining it with the breadcrumb mixture.

3 Heat 15ml/1 tbsp of oil in a frying pan and fry the garlic briefly. Finely chop the mushroom stalks; mix with the parsley and breadcrumbs. Add the garlic, salt and pepper and 15ml/1tbsp of the oil. Pile a little mixture on each mushroom.

4 Add the remaining oil to the dish and cover the mushrooms with buttered greaseproof paper. Bake for about 15–20 minutes, removing the paper for the last 5 minutes to brown the tops. Garnish with a sprig of flat leaf parsley.

BOEUF EN CROÛTE WITH MUSHROOM FILLING

A DUXELLES FILLING OF FINELY-CHOPPED MUSHROOMS, SHALLOTS, GARLIC AND PARSLEY IS THE CLASSIC FILLING FOR BOEUF EN CROÛTE. THESE INDIVIDUAL VERSIONS ARE GOOD SERVED WITH BOILED OR STEAMED NEW POTATOES AND A GREEN VEGETABLE.

SERVES FOUR

INGREDIENTS
    4 fillet steaks, about
       115–150g/4–5oz each
    a little Dijon mustard
    25g/1oz/2 tbsp butter
    275g/10oz puff pastry
    25g/1oz/½ cup white breadcrumbs
    beaten egg, for glazing
    salt and freshly ground black pepper
    sprigs of parsley or chervil, to garnish
For the duxelles filling
    25g/1oz/2 tbsp butter
    4 shallots, finely chopped
    1–2 garlic cloves, crushed
    225–275g/8–10oz flat mushrooms,
       finely chopped
    15ml/1 tbsp finely chopped parsley

1 Preheat the oven to 220°C/425°F/ Gas 7. Rub a little mustard over each of the steaks and season with pepper. Melt the butter in a heavy-based frying pan and fry the steaks for about 1–2 minutes each side, so that they are browned on the outside but still red in the centre. Transfer to a plate to cool.

2 To make the filling, melt the butter and fry the shallots and garlic briefly. Stir in the finely chopped mushrooms.

3 Fry over a fairly high heat for about 3–4 minutes, stirring, until the juices run. Lower the heat and cook gently for 4–5 minutes until the mixture is dry. Add the parsley and seasoning and cool.

4 Cut the pastry into four and roll out each piece very thinly to a 18cm/7in square. Cut the corners from each square and spread a spoonful of the mushroom mixture in the centre. Top with a steak and sprinkle with a spoonful of fresh breadcrumbs.

5 Bring the sides of the pastry up to the centre and seal with water. Place seam side down on a baking sheet. Decorate with pastry trimmings and brush each with the beaten egg. Bake for about 20 minutes, until golden brown. Serve garnished with parsley or chervil.

GNOCCHI <u>WITH</u> OYSTER MUSHROOMS

GNOCCHI MAKE AN UNUSUAL AND PLEASANT ALTERNATIVE TO PASTA. THEY ARE BLAND ON THEIR OWN BUT BRING OUT THE FLAVOUR OF THE OYSTER MUSHROOMS IN THIS DISH WHILE THEIR SOFT TEXTURE CONTRASTS WITH THE FIRMNESS OF THE FUNGI.

SERVES FOUR

INGREDIENTS
  225g/8oz oyster mushrooms
  15ml/1 tbsp olive oil
  1 onion, finely chopped
  1 garlic clove, crushed
  4 plum tomatoes, peeled and chopped
  45–60ml/3–4 tbsp vegetable stock
    or water
  salt and freshly ground black pepper
  2 x 300g/11oz packet plain
    potato gnocchi
  a large knob of butter
  10ml/2 tsp chopped fresh parsley
  Parmesan cheese shavings,
    to garnish

1 Trim the mushrooms and tear into smaller pieces, if large. Heat the oil in a large frying pan; fry the onion and garlic over a low heat for about 4–5 minutes until softened but not browned.

2 Increase the heat, add the mushrooms to the pan and sauté for about 3–4 minutes, stirring constantly.

3 Stir in the chopped tomatoes, stock or water and seasoning. Cover and simmer for about 8 minutes until the tomatoes are very soft and reduced to a pulp. Stir occasionally.

4 Cook the gnocchi in a large pan of salted boiling water for 2–3 minutes (or according to the instructions on the packet) then drain well and toss with the butter. Place in a large warmed serving bowl and stir in the chopped parsley.

5 Pour the mushroom and tomato mixture over the top, stir briefly and sprinkle with the Parmesan cheese.

COOK'S TIP
If the mushrooms are very large, the stalks are likely to be tough, therefore they should be discarded. Always tear rather than cut oyster mushrooms.

SEAFOOD <u>AND</u> OYSTER MUSHROOM STARTER

THIS DISH IS REMARKABLY QUICK TO PREPARE. IT CAN BE MADE INTO A MORE SUBSTANTIAL DISH BY STIRRING 275-350G/10-12OZ COOKED PASTA SHELLS INTO THE SAUCE AT THE END.

SERVES FOUR

INGREDIENTS
  15ml/1 tbsp olive oil
  15g/½oz/1 tbsp butter
  1 garlic clove, crushed
  175g/6oz oyster mushrooms,
    halved or quartered
  115–175g/4–6oz peeled prawns
  115g/4oz cooked mussels, optional
  juice of ½ lemon
  15ml/1 tbsp medium dry sherry
  150ml/¼ pint/⅔ cup double cream
  salt and freshly ground black pepper

1 Heat the oil and butter in a frying pan and sauté the garlic for a few minutes, then add the mushrooms. Cook over a moderate heat for 4–5 minutes until soft, stirring from time to time.

2 Reduce the heat and stir in the prawns, mussels, if using, and lemon juice. Cook for 1 minute, stirring all the time. Stir in the sherry and cook for 1 minute.

3 Add the cream and cook gently until heated through but not boiling. Taste and adjust the seasoning and then spoon into warmed serving dishes. Serve at once with chunks of Italian bread.

WILD MUSHROOMS IN BRIOCHE

SERVES FOUR

INGREDIENTS
4 small brioches
olive oil, for glazing
20ml/4 tsp lemon juice
sprigs of parsley, to garnish
For the mushroom filling
25g/1oz/2 tbsp butter
2 shallots
1 garlic clove, crushed
175–225g/6–8oz assorted wild
   mushrooms, halved if large
45ml/3 tbsp white wine
45ml/3 tbsp double cream
5ml/1 tsp chopped fresh basil
5ml/1 tsp chopped fresh parsley
salt and freshly ground black pepper

1 Preheat the oven to 180°C/350°F/
Gas 4. Using a serrated or grapefruit
knife, cut a circle out of the top of each
brioche and reserve. Scoop out the
bread inside to make a small cavity.

2 Place the brioches and the tops on a
baking sheet and brush inside and out
with olive oil. Bake for 7–10 minutes
until golden and crisp. Squeeze 5ml/
1 tsp of lemon juice inside each brioche.

3 To make the filling, melt the butter in
a frying pan and fry the shallots and
garlic for 2–3 minutes until softened.

4 Add the mushrooms and cook gently
for about 4–5 minutes, stirring.

5 When the juices begin to run, reduce
the heat and continue cooking for about
3–4 minutes, stirring occasionally, until
the pan is fairly dry.

6 Stir in the wine. Cook for a few more
minutes and then stir in the cream, basil,
parsley and seasoning to taste.

7 Pile the mushroom mixture into the
brioche shells and replace the tops.
Return to the oven and reheat for about
5–6 minutes. Serve as a starter,
garnished sprigs of parsley.

WILD MUSHROOMS WITH PANCAKES

SERVES SIX

INGREDIENTS
225–275g/8–10oz assorted
   wild mushrooms
50g/2oz/¼ cup butter
1–2 garlic cloves
a splash of brandy (optional)
freshly ground black pepper
soured cream, to serve
For the pancakes
115g/4oz/1 cup self-raising flour
20g/¾oz/3 tbsp buckwheat flour
2.5ml/½ tsp baking powder
2 eggs
about 250ml/8fl oz/1 cup milk
a pinch of salt
oil, for frying

1 To make the pancakes, mix together
the flours, baking powder and salt in a
large bowl or food processor. Add the
eggs and milk and beat or process to
make a smooth batter, with about the
consistency of single cream.

2 Grease a large griddle or frying pan
with a little oil and when hot, pour small
amounts of batter (about 15–30ml/
1–2 tbsp per pancake) on to the griddle
or frying pan, spaced well apart.

3 Fry for a few minutes until bubbles
begin to appear on the surface and the
underside is golden, and then flip over.
Cook for about 1 minute until golden.
Keep warm, wrapped in a clean dish
towel. (Makes about 18–20 pancakes.)

4 If the mushrooms are large, cut them
in half. Melt the butter in a frying pan
and add the garlic and mushrooms. Fry
over a moderate heat for a few minutes
until the juices begin to run and then
increase the heat and cook, stirring
frequently, until nearly all the juices have
evaporated. Stir in the brandy, if using,
and season with a little black pepper.

5 Arrange the warm pancakes on a
serving plate and spoon over a little
soured cream. Top with the hot
mushrooms and serve immediately.

COOK'S TIP
This makes a delicious and elegant
starter for a dinner party. Alternatively,
make cocktail-size pancakes and serve
as part of a buffet supper.

INDEX

ACKNOWLEDGEMENTS

Photographs are by Don Last
William Lingwood, Patrick
McLeavey and Thomas
Odulate/© Anness Publishing
except for: p27 ml Harry Smith

Horticultural Photographic
Collection (HSHC); p69 t Clive
Simms; p95 tl HSHC; b/tr The
Garden Picture Library (GPL);
p96 br GPL; p98 br Clive Simms

(CS); p100m HSHC, tr A-Z
Botanical/Bjorn Svenson; p101
br GPL, tl Derek St. Romaine
(DSR); bl HSHC; p102 b HSHC;
p106 t DSR; p107 bl/br DSR;

p139 b CS; p111 b GPL; p172 l
Peter McHoy; p177 l HSHC, b
CS; p178t HSHC; p180 b GPL;
p183 t HSHC; p185 t CS; p190
t CS; and p196 t GPL.